# COOPERATIVE LEARNING IN THE SOCIAL STUDIES CLASSROOM

## SECOND EDITION

EDITED BY

**ROBERT J. STAHL**

**RONALD L. VanSICKLE**

and

**NANCY N. STAHL**

**NCSS**
**Bulletin 108**

W9-CPE-086

# National Council for the Social Studies

8555 Sixteenth Street • Suite 500 • Silver Spring, Maryland 20910

www.**socialstudies**.org

Editorial staff on this publication (Second Edition): Michael Simpson
Design/Production: Cowan Creative, www.cowancreative.com

Library of Congress Control Number: 2009929589
ISBN: 978-0-87986-102-5

# Table of Contents

What is cooperative learning? What is optimal cooperative learning? Why are social studies teachers encouraged to use cooperative learning? What are the differences between optimal cooperative learning and group activities and models that are not operating under the conditions of optimal cooperative learning? What are some of the assumptions that underlie the development and use of cooperative learning?

**From the beginning**, our intention has been to address questions such as these to assist both pre-service and in-service teachers. We have chosen not to provide a recipe book with step-by-step procedures that a teacher could follow starting tomorrow. Such procedural information is provided in detail elsewhere. In this updated second edition of *Cooperative Learning in the Social Studies Classroom*,[1] which includes a number of new articles, we want instead to provide a context for and an overview of cooperative learning that addresses major concerns and questions. The articles in this volume will be useful to both beginning and experienced teachers, as well as supervisors and parents who are interested in this group approach to teaching and learning in the social studies.

A further intention is to help social studies educators construct a sound conceptual foundation for cooperative learning while correcting or preventing misconceptions about it. We believe that without an adequate conceptual framework or philosophy of cooperative learning, teachers are unlikely to implement particular cooperative learning structures, models or activities to their optimal level of effectiveness. In addition, we want teachers to accept that doing cooperative learning well involves more than putting students in groups and having them do interesting things. We want to emphasize that in optimal cooperative learning, the learning is the focus and the cooperating is the means to ensure the learning. The chapters provide abundant details to assist in the construction of an adequate introductory conceptual framework for the use of cooperative learning as a viable alternative approach to teaching within the social studies classroom.

In the first chapter, definitions of key terms, underlying assumptions and important ideas concerning cooperative learning are stated as a foundation for this approach and for ideas and concepts that are introduced in the eleven chapters that follow. We address a sample of the many misconceptions about coopera-

tive learning that are rampant among educators at all levels today. In their stead, we provide clear fundamental guidelines for this alternative approach to instruction. We suggest that cooperative learning addresses the "social" and "study" requirements of social studies education and provides one vehicle whereby students can actually "get better together" at all grade levels. A list of the potential results of long-term use of effective cooperative learning group activities is provided. At the end of the first chapter, we invite classroom teachers at all levels to take steps toward using cooperative learning with their students.

The second chapter deals with the classroom environment and characteristics of classrooms with and without cooperative learning groups. Here, Robert Stahl takes a look at life in the classroom from the student's perspective. He presents two scenarios that contrast life with and without appropriate cooperative learning activities and groups. He introduces the concepts of the "academic loner" and the "academic teammate" or "academic partner," and describes the classroom experiences of these kinds of students. The chapter also describes the attributes of successful learners and outlines how cooperative learning groups can promote the success of students in acquiring knowledge and improving their skills.

The second section of this book provides a philosophical, theoretical and research basis for using cooperative learning. In chapter 3, David and Roger Johnson, two of the best-known and respected leaders in this field, identify a number of concepts that are important to constructing a sound philosophy of and rationale for implementing cooperative learning in social studies classrooms. Their ideas build on and support those offered in the first two chapters. They begin with a brief historical context for using groups in educational settings and move quickly into the philosophy and strategies of cooperative learning. This chapter addresses many teachers' concerns about whether cooperative learning can be a viable alternative strategy for them, and provides research findings that support the use of cooperative learning.

The two following chapters review the literature on the effects of cooperative learning in classroom settings. Ronald VanSickle presents a reader-friendly version of the research findings in the form of a hypothetical dialogue between an advocate of cooperative learning and a teacher seeking information about how effective this approach to teaching has been and can be. Those who are new to cooperative learning have reported this chapter to be very persuasive in helping them make the decision to work at learning enough about cooperative learning to give it an honest try in their classrooms. In chapter 5, Robert Slavin, Anne Chamberlain and Eric Hurley provide a review of classroom research related to specific cooperative learning approaches and to students' academic achievement, affective growth, and interpersonal and social interaction skills. These two complementary chapters synthesize the research and discuss its implications for social studies education. Slavin and his associates also make a solid case as to how cooperative learning, when implemented correctly over time, can balance the "social" and the "study" in social studies education.

Classroom teaching is the focus of the third section of this book. The positive responses that we received about the quality and value of three chapters focusing on the classroom in the earlier edition of this book led us to update them and include them again in the new edition (chapters 7, 9 and 11). New chapters by a team of middle school teachers (chapter 8) and one high school teacher (chapter 10) have been added. These complement the earlier chapters in ways that make our argument for the use of optimal cooperative learning even more persuasive.

At the start of the section, in Chapter 6, Robert J. Stahl and James Doyle Casteel point out that the use of jigsaw structures in the classroom is not necessarily in and of itself an effective form of cooperative learning. They describe the evolution of the Jigsaw concept, and identify the circumstances under which Jigsaws can achieve the desired academic outcomes. The chapter presents a taxonomy that distinguishes between different kinds of Jigsaw-like situations and Jigsaw group structures.

Robert Colomb, a former 2d grade teacher in Provo, Utah, describes his experiences using cooperative learning with students in grades 1 through 6 in Chapter 7. His insights, along with those of George Chilcoat and Nancy Stahl, describe the growth of one elementary-level teacher into a highly effective facilitator of cooperative learning groups.

In Chapter 8, four northwest Indiana middle school teachers collaborated with teacher educator Dwight "Doc" Holliday, now at Murray State University, Kentucky, to describe their cooperative learning classroom environments. Janet McKenna, at Donald E. Gavit Middle School; Joel Johnson, at Joseph L. Block Jr. High School; and Trudy Floyd and Victor Vazquez, both at Henry W. Eggers Middle School, have all been highly successful in their early efforts and are still growing to become effective users of cooperative learning theory and strategies.

Four middle school teachers, one assistant principal, and one university-level social studies methods instructor collaborate in Chapter 9 to describe the progress of four middle school teachers in their efforts to use cooperative learning in their respective classrooms. William McKendry, a strong early proponent of cooperative learning in his school, facilitated the growth of three of his colleagues, Dennis Dool, Michael Smith, and Myra Wolpert. All four grew rapidly in their knowledge and expertise in using the different cooperative group structures and cooperative learning in their classrooms. They helped as well as critiqued each other to refine and hone their conceptual, theoretical and practical knowledge and abilities in this area. Their efforts and the support provided by Assistant Principal Philip Selim are described here with the assistance of Eric Luce, a social studies teacher educator who spent many years working with, observing and interacting with these middle school educators in their school. Importantly, the authors have continuously expanded their use of these structures and of cooperative learning over the 12-plus years since they wrote their original chapter.

Quinton Priest describes his success with cooperative learning in chapter 10. As an experienced high school social studies teacher in Tucson, Arizona, he provides details on how he began using cooperative learning and how he implements the approach in his classroom. He wrote this chapter to familiarize other teachers with the process of getting started in using bits and pieces of cooperative group structures, in learning the philosophy and concepts behind optimal cooperative learning, and in implementing cooperative group activities in the classroom. He has successfully used several cooperative learning models for over a decade, and expands his use of cooperative learning every year.

Robert Mattingly, who wrote Chapter 11, has recently retired from classroom teaching. However, his chapter describes how he got into cooperative learning after many years of teaching and found it so effective that he continued to expand his use of cooperative learning and many of the cooperative group structures until he left the classroom. Mattingly provides details of his initial use of cooperative learning and the field tests he conducted of one structure—Jigsaw with expert groups—in his classroom. He shares with us some of the trials and tribulations of this approach to teaching, and ends with news of his successes—and the success of his students as well.

Classroom teachers, supervisors and administrators at all levels should read these chapters. They provide a unique perspective on the transition from using traditional teaching methods to the successful use of cooperative learning in typical school situations. Here, the teachers disclose their initial concerns, efforts, sources of frustrations, and the process by which they became skillful users of the cooperative learning theory, philosophy, and strategies. In many ways these chapters are the most powerful in this volume.

Chapter 12 provides, in dialogue form, an account of a group of teachers engaged in the transition of becoming cooperative learning teachers under the guidance of a staff development team from Stanford University. Elizabeth Cohen, Rachel Lotan, and Jennifer Whitcomb describe a number of concerns teachers have about using cooperative learning and cooperative groups as an alternative teaching strategy in their classrooms. An introduction to Cohen's complex instruction model is provided, along with an example of classroom activities that fit the model. This chapter illustrates how a staff development team may work collegially and cooperatively with in-service teachers, enabling them to become successful users of cooperative learning.

Chapters 11 and 12 provide key vocabulary and practical guidelines for placing students in heterogeneous groups, for computing improvement and bonus points, and for determining group rewards. These chapters can be used with nearly all cooperative learning models and will answer many questions teachers have about setting up groups, determining which teams to reward, and dealing with individual student test scores in a fair and systematic manner.

We hope that this volume will help the reader reflect upon the gains that students and social studies educators can make by rejecting many of the old myths surrounding the value of competitive and rugged individualism and replacing these with a cooperative perspective on learning. What can we gain by having students work cooperatively in small groups rather than spending much of their time doing their academic work alone? What evidence is available that social studies students achieve more by working together cooperatively than by working alone or by competing for a limited number of rewards? What instructional alternatives might enable more of our students to achieve the attitudinal social studies goals we set? What might a teacher gain by using cooperative learning groups as an alternative to conventional individualistic and competitive instructional strategies? These and countless more questions are answered in the pages that follow.

**Robert J. Stahl, Ronald L. VanSickle** and **Nancy N. Stahl**

**NOTE**

1. The original edition of this book was published in 1992 as NCSS Bulletin 87. See Robert J. Stahl and Ronald L. VanSickle, *Cooperative Learning in the Social Studies Classroom: An Introduction to Social Study* (Washington, D.C.: National Council for the Social Studies, 1994).

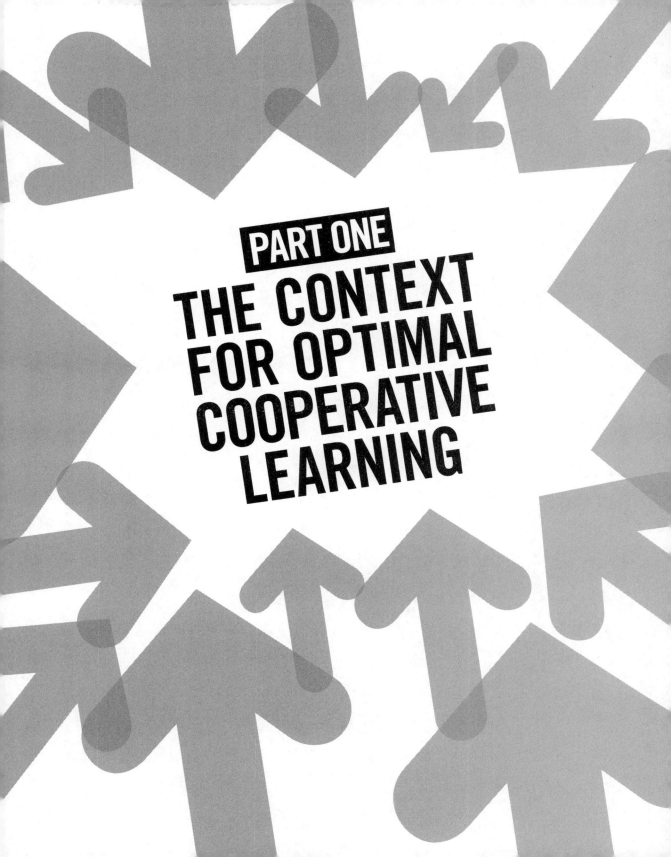

# PART ONE

# THE CONTEXT FOR OPTIMAL COOPERATIVE LEARNING

# CHAPTER 1

# Using Optimal Cooperative Learning for Effective *Social Study* in the Classroom

**Robert J. Stahl**, Arizona State University, Tempe, Arizona, and
**Ronald L. VanSickle**, The University of Georgia, Athens, Georgia

Nothing is so practical as a good theory.
KURT LEWIN

**One of the strongest illusions** for many educators and parents is that competition automatically brings out the best in everyone. We frequently hear expressions like "Only the strongest survive," "It's a dog-eat-dog world," "If you aren't the winner, then you're a loser," "Everybody loves a winner," and "Competition makes the world go around." Educators and parents influenced by these ideas are likely to elevate non-cooperative attitudes, environments and activities as they prepare students for the real, competitive world that presumably exists out there beyond the school yard and the school years. We tend to forget that the "real world" exists for students every moment they are outside school and inside their school as well.

A complementary illusion is that of the mythical rugged individual—i.e., the strong, self-sufficient, and fiercely-independent individual working and struggling *alone*, coping *alone* and achieving great things *alone* against great odds. Individuals such as Charles Lindbergh, Jane Addams, Martin Luther King, Jr., and George Washington are lauded for their personal accomplishments as though they had no colleagues or support groups who worked cooperatively to help them achieve their dreams and hopes. Focusing on what such individuals did as though they were alone during all their efforts is to overlook and misrepresent how these individuals worked with others to achieve their goals. As students find answers to questions such as "How was it possible for Charles Lindbergh to fly nonstop across the Atlantic?" and "What factors contributed to the success of Jane Addams's Hull House in Chicago?" they discover the network of cooperative supporters who contributed greatly and frequently to the successes associated with each individual.

Social studies educators should strive to enable their students to become educated and competent so that they will be successful in the world. Students should study individual and group ideas, actions, and artifacts in ways that will (a) facilitate their achievement of selected social studies knowledge, understanding and abilities, and (b) enable them to function well with others both inside and outside the social studies classroom. As professional educators our task is not to establish a mini "real world" in the classroom where students are left to sink or swim on their own as though the primary purpose of school is providing sink-or-swim survival situations. Rather, we need to focus our work in our classrooms so that whenever and wherever students "hit the water" in "real" world situations, they are sufficiently competent to be able to "swim" very well on their own in whatever situations they encounter. In fact, we want them to be very good at using their social studies knowledge and skills to adapt and adjust to ever-changing real world situations and still be successful. Of equal importance, we want them to be able to successfully interact and participate with others in the many social worlds they will also encounter.

We believe that social studies teachers can establish and provide instructional opportunities that result in nearly all students achieving the highest level of academic expectations we set for them. One potentially powerful approach to achieving these results is appropriate cooperative learning.

This chapter builds a conceptual framework for understanding cooperative learning as a powerful approach to teaching and learning in social studies, history, and social and behavioral science classrooms at all levels.

## Assumptions About Students and Teachers

To introduce the cooperative learning approach in social studies, we present 12 assumptions about students as learners and about commitments needed by social studies educators to achieve the maximum learning for their students.

*1. We assume that almost all students can achieve high levels of success in almost every set of knowledge, abilities, and perspectives that social studies educators expect them to learn.* We are optimistic about what nearly all students can learn within appropriate instructional environments. The question is not, "Are they able to?"; rather, it is, "Will the instructional factors selected and managed by teachers enable students to achieve what they have the potential to achieve?" Our view of learners values each student as an individual capable of achieving success in the classroom regardless of conditions outside that classroom. This view of learners accepts that under the optimal learning environments that each teacher and school are capable of providing, far more students can attain far greater academic achievement than is now the case. As they become more confident in their potential, students will be motivated to learn more about social studies topics, content, and abilities. This view reinforces the belief that every student should attain important social studies goals and abilities.

*2. We assume that most students initially enter social studies classrooms wanting to succeed academically and not merely to survive.* They want to leave school with new knowledge, abilities, and perspectives that will enable them to function well in the world as well as within the school and the social studies classroom. However, just because they want to be successful in the academic part of their social studies courses does not mean that they have the knowledge and skills to do so. Most realize from the start that they need a great deal of help to achieve the level of academic learning associated with A- and B-grade-level performance on nearly all tests and assignments.

*3. We assume that students want their studies to make sense and to mean something important from their own perspectives.* In order for this to happen, they must do more than listen to their teachers, read the text, and answer study questions. It also means that they should not spend their time in fun and games activities and in individual and group projects that focus a great deal on just doing things with *very little focus on mastering academic content and skills.* Students must take time and be guided towards assigning positive, useful meanings for what they study and to make personally important connections between what they study and do and what is needed in their present and future lives.

*4. We assume that academic success eventually leads students to engage actively in activities likely to build on and continue that success.* To achieve academic success, students need to do well in mastering, storing and using the prerequisite content for each ability they are expected to learn and master. Students who do well in particular areas of the social studies tend to be interested in other topics and data they perceive as related to these areas. Students who do well in the prerequisite knowledge and abilities are more likely to be successful and interested in complex and challenging related topics, knowledge bases, and abilities. Conversely, students who do not have the prerequisites or prior successes will rarely remain interested in related social studies topics. Social studies teachers must not assume that topics, activities, and teacher personality will automatically motivate students who lack the prerequisites to become successful, interested, and studious. Therefore, teachers who are concerned about the levels of their students' interest and achievement need to consider using strategies that facilitate student success. These teachers will find that as they use these strategies appropriately, their students will tend to improve their learning and subsequently their interest and involvement in social study.

*5. We assume that the social studies classroom should be an academic work place, where the primary task of students is to work hard to achieve targeted academic content, perspectives and abilities.* This does not mean that students have to be miserable, bored and passive, or that they should work in an environment that lacks excitement, enjoyment and active participation. It does mean that teachers are aware of the need of students to work hard in their study and during their on-task thinking and learning to achieve targeted goals in mastering content and skills. Even during the best cooperative learning activities, students work toward their own academic mastery and ensuring that all others on their team learn at a high level of achievement. Cooperative learning does not mean a break from the serious work of academic achievement.

*6. We assume students expect their teachers to do what is necessary to facilitate each student's successful attainment.* They hope that their teachers are committed to taking them from where they are to as high a level as they are able to achieve. They hope their teachers do not intend to teach only as much as is convenient for the entire class to cover. These expectations and hopes are consistent with an essential reason for providing social studies education—to prepare young people to be humane, civil, rational, participating citizens in a world that is increasingly interdependent, pluralistic, and changing.

*7. We assume that along with the academic focus of instruction, social studies teachers are seeking ways to improve the social dimensions of their classrooms.* These efforts include increasing and enhancing their students' interactions with one another and their abilities to collaborate with others as partners in learning. If this is to occur, then teachers need structured ways of having students work collaboratively in academic teams so that they can learn and practice using guidelines for interacting with others.

*8. We assume that social studies educators are willing to seek out, seriously consider, and, where appropriate, learn to use alternative instructional models to help students achieve maximum success.* Consequently, we assume that in situations where students are not mastering the academic content and skills, teachers will seek out instructional approaches that offer promise for changing these situations in their classrooms. Cooperative learning is one approach that, from theory through actual classroom practice, can work to help students achieve high levels of academic success.

*9. We assume that teachers whose students are achieving and cooperating at acceptable levels will continue to search for and use instructional strategies that may increase the positive results of their present strategies even further.* In other words, we assume that social studies educators have a continual desire to improve their teaching.

*10. We assume that cooperative group structures and cooperative learning are means to the end of high levels of academic achievement for nearly all students rather than ends in and of themselves.* Teachers should not want to use groups and cooperative learning simply for the sake of having groups and doing cooperative learning. The major advocates of cooperative learning emphasize that cooperative groups and group structures are strategies or methods for facilitating student learning. Cooperative learning is an instructional tool that enables academic achievement and should never be viewed as an "end" in itself.

*11. We assume that individual teachers within a school or department can implement cooperative group structures and cooperative learning on their own and alone.* This assumption is important for two reasons. One is that we know of many teachers who are successful users of cooperative learning who started out as the only teachers in their department or school to use this approach. It can be done. Secondly, we encourage teachers not to believe that until most or all of their colleagues in their department or school implement cooperative learning, they cannot do it themselves. Of course, even a single teacher who goes it alone can benefit if others in his or her department or school also later use cooperative learning.

*12. We assume that as more and more teachers in a school cooperate with and support one another in this instructional approach, they will benefit from a compounding and multiplying effect.* When groups of social studies teachers cooperate to help make cooperative learning work for all of them, then all teachers enhance their chances of ensuring optimal conditions for social studies in which students learn to cooperate and cooperate effectively to learn and achieve. As this happens, students' acomplishments in one class will enhance their involvement, study, interaction and achievement in other courses.

## *Social Study* in the Social Studies Classroom: A Unique Perspective

Teachers sometimes assume that, merely by putting students together in a group, they have done what is needed for most students to master the abilities needed to work cooperatively and productively with others. Teachers who want to use cooperative learning need to realize from the start that nearly all students need to learn the many abilities that are needed to work well within groups.

Effective social studies teaching also requires appropriate *social study.*

In this context, the word "social" reminds us that the words and language rules we use in the classroom are part and parcel of the culture in which we live. We think and speak using words, symbols, grammar, and meanings that are integral parts of the language that we share within our society. Although students construct and ultimately must make knowledge their own, they do so in one or more societies or subgroups that influence, share, and interact using language. In addition, students use, share, negotiate, and revise meanings according to the verbal and nonverbal language others use in their social world. Students also need feedback as to how adequate they are in using the language and symbols of their society.

"Social" also refers to the need to engage in worthwhile, goal-oriented tasks within supportive interpersonal environments. To be effective, these social tasks and environments need to occur relatively frequently, to include accurate feedback and to endure over extended periods of time. Within such environments, individuals must become active, contributing and integral parts of the social community that in turn benefits from their participation. To be effective within this social environment, students must learn and practice the knowledge, abilities and attitudes necessary to function effectively within the social groups and as part of the social communities within which they live. Individuals must have a sense of belonging to, participating in, and contributing to one or more groups as a viable, personally meaningful, social community.

To be social requires students to interact with many others in many situations and about many things. To do this well, students need to learn the concepts, abilities and guidelines for interacting. They need to learn to become more adequate listeners as well as talkers. They need to learn how and when to interact, to share, to give and take, to contribute, to step up, to encourage, to be supportive and to be quiet. Classrooms should be places where those who need it actually learn the skills needed to effectively interact with others.

According to these conceptions of "social," it is not enough to be in a classroom of students who may on occasion interact or do things together in small groups or as a class. Individuals in a class must come to sense that they constitute a meaningful social community in which certain actions and attitudes are acceptable and others are unacceptable. They must come to value what the community and the required social interactions mean and can do for them. If we generate such environments in the classroom, students will see themselves as more than individuals in a class, but rather as viable members of a close-knit community that happens to meet in a social studies classroom.

This view of "social" is consistent with the essence of effective citizenship within any community. If individuals are to participate and contribute, they must have a sense that the community is worthwhile and that their involvement will have positive personal and social consequences. They must come to believe that their voices can help to change their community and that their votes count to change and improve that community and each member of it. Individuals must develop a strong sense of personal power within their group and believe that the group will benefit from their contributions. Likewise, students must perceive and receive benefits from positive participation within their classroom community and in their many communities outside the classroom.

From our perspective, "social study" should become a primary component of social studies teaching. To make this happen, teachers must find ways to enable students to form viable social communities that work cooperatively and systematically as academic teams—sometimes as "academic gangs"—to master and acquire new discipline-based information and abilities. Members must view these groups as beneficial both for themselves and for the group. This is most likely to come about when each student becomes a highly successful learner and the achievement of all other group members is also very high. To be optimal, teachers need to structure classroom activities, rewards, and student roles so that students create a genuine cohesive community, establish an academic study and learning environment, and participate as effective members of this community as they focus on achieving targeted academic learning goals.

Teachers should never lose sight of the fact that their own focus for teaching has to be the academic achievement of their students. Cooperative group structures are merely one of the means by which social studies teachers can arrange for, promote, and reward social study in their classroom. These group structures are something the teacher turns to in order to structure student activities toward academic achievement. Only when teachers view these structures and the teams created as ways by which students are to cooperate to master the content and skills will their students eventually change their perceptions of the group tasks from "doing" and "getting done" into team activities where optimal academic achievement by all is the primary task of all teammates.

These models and structures, however, are rarely used appropriately unless the teacher has an adequate conceptual view of cooperation and cooperative learning.[1]

### Getting Better Together

Teachers should not make the mistake of considering all groups where students are working well together to be highly effective cooperative learning teams. There are far too many situations in which teachers use groups but students fail to get better academically and fail to get better together in and through the group. We cannot overstate the fact that effective cooperative learning is different from most group work and group activities that currently take place under the name of cooperative learning.

One way to envision participation in and benefits from cooperative learning groups is captured in the expression "Getting Better Together."[2] By working with one another in appropriate ways, students enhance each other's information bases, concepts and abilities as well as their own. By working together and facilitating each other's academic mastery, students can "get better" individually and "get better together" as a team focused on team success — a success that is achieved only when every member greatly increases his or her own academic achievement. Cooperative learning teams and team activities are a means by which students can get better together.

## Building a Conceptual Framework for Effective Cooperative Learning

The mere fact that students work cooperatively in small groups does not mean that they are cooperating to ensure their own academic mastery and retention, much less cooperating to maximize the academic achievement of all other members of their group.[3] Cooperative groups must be more than collections of students who sit together, complete essentially independent tasks, and fit their individual parts together so that they have a single product as proof of their cooperative effort. Students are expected to work in structured academic teams and not merely as groups.

However, in typical group activities in social studies classrooms, students primarily work, share and cooperate in order to get done—*not* primarily to maximize their own academic achievement, much less the academic achievement of all other group members. In typical group work, what and how much each student learns and retains from his or her participation is *incidental* to completing the job that has to be done.[4] This incidental learning tends to occur even when the focus of study, work, interaction and the final product includes academic content. This lack of on-task effort to maximize one's academic achievement is one reason why, after typical group tasks, most students most of the time (a) have little comprehension and recall of important academic constructs (e.g., information, concepts and procedures) and (b) advance very little in their academic abilities and achievement. During these activities, students tend to spend a great deal of time on superficial factors aimed at making a final report or presentation attractive to their teachers. They spend very little time ensuring that all members of their group adequately comprehended, mastered *and* retained the targeted academic content and abilities.

The extent to which individuals are engaged in successful cooperative learning is always determined by the quantity and quality of the content, understandings and abilities each team member *retains from* their cooperative work together. Consequently, the quality of each student's academic accomplishments should be measured by a score on a rigorous individual test taken alone and after the team has finished its cooperative efforts. This test is the primary criterion for determining how effective the cooperation-to-learn was during the group's activities.

Slavin has delineated "cooperative learning" as a distinct instructional approach only when a set of particular essential criteria or elements are present in the situation. For him, the presence of these elements along with the strong academic achievement requirement clearly are the two primary factors that separate cooperative learning team work from all other group work and group activities. Originally, Slavin claimed that the necessary elements were:

- ▶ Placing from four to six students in maximally-heterogeneous groups (i.e., groups balanced first on academic abilities, then on the basis of gender, ethnicity, race, etc.);
- ▶ Providing clear instructional objectives for what is to be learned;
- ▶ Focusing students on what is to be learned and then on them individually mastering it
- ▶ Providing a clear and attractive reward system for group achievement;
- ▶ Making students individually accountable and mutually responsible for each other's academic success; and
- ▶ Making students take an individual test, which reinforces the academic learning requirement and provides the only credible evidence of the extent of the academic achievement for each member of each team.[5]

For their part, David and Roger Johnson advocate at least five "essential elements" for cooperative learning.[6]

After reviewing the literature and talking with countless researchers and teachers concerning what seems to be crucial to making groups highly successful academic teams, Stahl proposed 38 elements that consistently seemed to be needed for teams to operate under optimal cooperative conditions that produce the highest level of academic learning for most teams and team members nearly all of the time.[7] (See Table 1 for a list of some of these essential elements.) For Stahl, these elements are interwoven, so that the absence or weakening of one has a multiplier effect of weakening more than one of the other essential elements, with each absence or weakening of an element directly reducing the quality of learning by one or more team members. Stahl also supports Spencer Kagan's claim that group structures and corresponding group activities following those structures are not in and of themselves cooperative learning groups or activities. For Stahl, *optimal cooperative learning* occurs only when all the conditions that are under the teacher's and learners' control exist or occur when and as needed and as appropriate so as to ensure maximum academic achievement by all group members. Given the number and requirements for many of these essential elements, Stahl claimed that although many group activities are

**Table 1:  A sample of the 38 essential elements of optimal cooperative learning as proposed by Robert J. Stahl.**

## OBJECTIVES

1. A set of clear, specific student academic outcome objectives that describe clearly and exactly what information and abilities students are to construct, rehearse, master and retain.
2. Students complete their academic study within maximally heterogeneous teams.
3. Students have a clear notion as to what particular academic content and abilities they are to learn and master in their teams —and what they must be able to do on their own after their group has stopped meeting.
4. Students feel assured that what they are assigned to learn in their groups will indeed be what will be on their after-group individual test.

## ORIENTATION OF STUDENTS

5. Students accept that their primary task as individuals and as team members is to maximize their own academic achievement and the achievement of all teammates.
6. Students accept the notion that the awards for academic success come to the team rather than to individuals independent of the team.
7. Students have a clear and complete set of directions or instructions as to the academic tasks they are to complete to optimize their academic achievement.
8. Students in each team believe they have an equal opportunity for academic success.

## GROUP BEHAVIOR

9. Students have a sense of and engage in behaviors consistent with positive and academically-productive interdependence.
10. Students must test one another and provide appropriate feedback and feedforward information regarding each other's academic progress.
11. Students engage in productive "face-to-face" interaction and appropriate "knee-to-knee" posture.
12. Students demonstrate positive social interaction roles, behaviors and attitudes.
13. Students demonstrate positive task-completion roles, behaviors and attitudes.
14. Students demonstrate positive group-maintenance roles, behaviors and attitudes.
15. Students have and must spend sufficient productive time learning.
16. There is an absence of structured competition within and among teams.

## ASSESSMENT

17. Each student is held individually responsible and accountable for his or her academic success by taking an individual academic test after the team has stopped meeting.
18. The awards and the award structure are linked directly and solely to academic achievement of all team members as determined by the individual academic tests.
19. Teams receive timely and adequate public recognition and awards for their academic achievement.

## DEBRIEFING

20. Students complete structured post-team "reflection" (or "debriefing") tasks concerning their within-team behaviors.
21. Students actually use the do-and-don't results of their debriefing tasks by employing the behaviors in future group activities.

labeled cooperative learning, most are closer to cooperative *doing* groups than cooperative *learning* groups, and far from being optimal cooperative learning teams.

After over two decades of advocating the need to implement the essential elements of cooperative learning first proposed by Slavin and the Johnsons, it is still common for teachers to believe that because students will learn something during these so-called "cooperative learning" group activities, then cooperative learning must have taken place.

Teachers are most likely to use cooperative learning strategies correctly once they build an adequate conceptual framework that provides the perspective needed to carry out the models on a moment-by-moment and day-by-day basis.[8] This framework should work to modify present misconceptions about cooperative learning groups and prevent future misconceptions from arising. Below are 20 very important ideas that should be permanent components of any conception of cooperative learning.

*1. The focus of optimal cooperative learning is and must always be on maximizing the academic achievement of all team members.* It is very easy to get caught up in the group structures, the group activities, and the cooperative activities directed at completing projects and presentations, while losing sight of the primary reason for cooperative learning. While cooperation is necessary for learning, it is not sufficient. Academic learning at a high level of achievement for all team members *is required* for the teacher to claim that cooperative learning took place in his or her classroom.

*2. Not all cooperative groups are instructionally effective.*[9] All cooperating groups are not equal; only those that meet the guidelines and standards for cooperative learning warrant this label. Later chapters will introduce a number of the elements necessary to ensure that cooperating groups become successful cooperative learning groups.

*3. Just because students are cooperating and talking about the topic and subject matter content does not mean that cooperative learning is occurring or successful.* In cooperative learning, students need to ensure maximum mastery of targeted content, understandings and skills for all teammates. While teachers must ensure that students learn to cooperate, they must also ensure that their students cooperate to learn and master the academic content and skills.

*4. Cooperative learning is an approach and set of conditions; it is not a particular group model, activity or structure.* According to the definition and the criteria for cooperative learning established over 25 years ago by Johnson and Johnson, the primary focus of cooperative learning and the cooperation within groups is to ensure that every member of every team first and foremost attains a high level of academic achievement as measured by an individual test students take a day or more after all group work has ended. To even approach optimal levels of cooperative learning, certain things need to happen before, during and after students meet in their groups and complete their tasks. In view of this, we cannot claim that a particular model for setting up and using groups, a particular group activity or a particular group structure automatically *is* a cooperative learning model, activity or structure. For instance, Jigsaw-with-expert-groups can become a cooperative learning Jigsaw-with-expert-groups, but it is not automatically a cooperative learning group, model, structure or strategy. The same is so for all models, activities or structures that are popularly referred to as cooperative learning models, activities or structures. To have students engaged in a cooperative learning activity, students must complete a group activity that has been infused with the essential elements of cooperative learning. Without this combination, cooperative group activities can never become cooperative learning team activities.[10]

*5. While students need to learn to cooperate and need experience improving their cooperative roles and skills, the primary purpose and goals of the cooperation must always remain those of ensuring that each group member masters the must-learn academic content, understandings and abilities.* In cooperative learning, students should cooperate primarily to maximize the academic achievement of each group member rather than cooperate merely to have more opportunities to get better at cooperating.

*6. Cooperative learning is not opposed to all competition.* Advocates of cooperative learning are not opposed to all competition; rather, they oppose inappropriate competition.[11] One cooperative group model, Teams-Games-Tournament (TGT), includes a competitive-like phase, the "games-within-tournament" phase. However, in TGT, teams and students are not in competition with one another, because every student could earn full points for his or her team without depriving all other players at the game table from earning the maximum number of points for his or her team.

Proponents of competition believe that cooperative groups in and of themselves do not guarantee quality, positive interaction, group success, and individual achievement. For them, only a competition with winners and losers can truly cause students to learn the most. They believe that competition automatically forces and motivates all students to do their very best to succeed. Such, however, is rarely the case. No research study to date has validated this claim. Nonetheless, many teachers claiming to be doing cooperative learning purposely structure their group situations to foster a high degree of competition. Stahl, however, asserted that no teacher should structure any cooperative learning situation or activity so that win-lose competition exists and is required. It is essential that all students and all teams have access to the highest level of team rewards, and no team should be denied access to a level of rewards when its team score meets or surpasses the minimum score for earning that level of reward.[12]

*7. While cooperative learning is not against all competition, the teacher should never build in competition during a cooperative learning team activity.* While using a particular cooperative group structure and having students complete their team activities, teachers should never create situations where students in teams or the teams themselves are competing against one another for the highest score, grade or prize. Rather, all students and teams must be able to earn the highest scores, grades and prizes available, and the attainment of a particular score, grade or prize by one student or team does not prevent another team from earning the same score, grade or prize. In effect, under the system of awarding Improvement Points to individuals and teams, it should be possible for every student to earn the top score on the individual test and every team to earn the Improvement Points needed to receive the highest category of reward or prize for academic achievement. In a cooperative learning classroom, a teacher should not highlight the way that the scores, grades and rewards are structured based on competition among individual students or teams. If teachers want competition, then they should do it outside the framework of cooperative learning.

*8. Cooperation is not a miraculous activity that works merely because one engages in or is expected to cooperate.* Teachers should not view cooperation as something in and of itself that will work miracles for all students. Most teachers can cite examples, for instance, of a basketball team that operated as five individuals on the court who just happened to wear the same color of uniform. Although these individuals played alongside one another, the extent of their productive cooperation in a particular game or season was minimal. For cooperative learning groups to be effective, students must cooperate continuously and productively in many positive ways.

*9. Cooperative learning should not replace all other models of teaching in social studies classrooms.* Cooperative learning is intended to be an alternative approach to structuring teaching and learning tasks. Consequently, teachers may continue to use instructional models and activities that effectively help students attain the many positive goals they set. Students need to learn how to succeed as individuals in activities such as exploring personally interesting topics or becoming proficient at desired skills. They also need to engage occasionally in competitive situations so that they learn to handle both the challenges of competition and the fun involved in pursuit and rivalry. Using the group structures and cooperative learning elements, social studies teachers should modify, not replace, their current teaching styles and methods.

*10. Cooperative learning and cooperative group structures and models are instructional options; they are not curriculum guides.* It is a gross misconception to view the cooperative group structures or cooperative learning as a curriculum. Cooperative learning and its models are guidelines for structuring instructional activities within classrooms—activities supposedly intended to facilitate students' achievement of the content and skills outlined in the curriculum. They cannot substitute for, improve, replace, or make up for poor curriculum decisions.[13] They are tools that teachers select and use to facilitate student progress toward achieving the cognitive, affective, and social outcomes set by the curriculum used. These models and cooperative learning are what teachers use *after* the curriculum decisions have been made.

*11. Teachers should never plan a "cooperative learning lesson" or "cooperative learning unit"; the planning should focus on the academic topic, content or skill students are to learn and master.* A teacher who plans to use an informal lecture or a video followed by discussion should not say, "I am planning an informal lecture lesson," or "I'm planning a video followed by a discussion unit." Teachers should talk about the topic or content that will be the focus of the lesson or unit, during which they will use a lecture or video and discussion as the instructional approach chosen. If the teacher is using cooperative learning and cooperative group structures or models, the teacher can plan a lesson or unit such as "The impact of the western movement on Native American cultures," and use Jigsaw-with-expert-groups as the instructional approach.

*12. Cooperative learning and cooperative group structures and models are independent of the outcomes or objectives selected.*[14] Teachers should never establish student outcome objectives after a particular cooperative group model is selected; rather, they select a particular cooperative group model after the learning objectives have been selected, with the group model selected being the means to facilitate students' attainment of those objectives.

*13. Cooperative learning and cooperative group structures and models are independent of the materials students are to use during the group tasks.*[15] Teachers may use many cooperative group structures in connection with textbooks, content-filled handouts, or other printed resources—nearly any resource aligned with the knowledge and abilities students are to learn. If a teacher uses a structure only in reference to a textbook, however, the teacher's decision—and not the structure—is solely responsible for this textbook dependency. If a teacher uses a particular group structure only to help students memorize and recall basic facts and low-level skills, this also reflects a decision the teacher has made. Under most conditions, every cooperative group structure, when used appropriately and with all the essential elements, can enable students to move beyond the text, memorization of basic facts, and learning lower-level skills. Depending on the course objectives and the decisions the teacher makes in developing a lesson or unit, each structure can be used to help students become proficient transferers of academic and social knowledge and abilities.

*14. Teachers who are confident that their students engaged in optimal cooperative learning are not afraid to have students take academically rigorous individual tests after the groups have ended their meetings.* Many teachers who claim to be using cooperative learning do not make students take individual tests on the content and skills supposedly learned during the group activities. This is especially true in cases where the focus of the group activities was completing a project or presentation together—as if the final product or presentation was evidence that all group members learned everything included in the product or presentation. Sometimes, teachers refuse to give individual tests because they sense that their students will not score well

on them. Some teachers even claim that cooperative learning is against tests and testing when students cooperate well in their groups. Nothing could be more inaccurate. Cooperative learning advocates from the very beginning have insisted that students be held individually responsible and accountable for their academic achievement and that teachers and students alike need solid, external evidence of the extent of the academic achievement of each student after the groups have stopped meeting.

*15. Cooperative group models provide a well-defined structure and carefully-sequenced guidelines for operating within a classroom; they are not in and of themselves cooperative learning.* One key for ensuring that cooperative learning models work is to envision each model as describing a particular way to structure the learning, the learning task, and the learners' roles.[16] Such structures provide steps, guidelines, and requirements that, when met, will allow students to achieve their maximum potential in alignment with clear outcomes. Teachers may use structures such as Jigsaw, Co-op-Co-op, and Teams-Games-Tournament repeatedly and across an extremely wide range of topics, content, grade levels, and outcomes.[16] These structures differ according to their cognitive processing, academic, affective, and interpersonal emphasis, length of time for completion, required teacher and student roles, usefulness for selected content, and degree of complexity. However, implementing any of these structures does not mean in and of itself that a teacher and his or her students are doing cooperative learning.

*16. Cooperative group structures and models do not guarantee students will learn to cooperate or cooperate to maximize each other's academic success.* Teachers should never assume that a particular group structure or activity will automatically enable students to learn how to cooperate, to cooperate successfully, or to cooperate in ways that enable almost every group member to learn all the content and skills expected. It is difficult for students to play their roles in a group in a way that makes their cooperative efforts optimal for maximizing the academic success of all members. Teachers need to teach these roles, assign them as needed, monitor the students' fulfillment of these roles, and provide critical and corrective feedback when and as needed to enable students to become experts at these roles while they become experts in the content and skills being studied.

*17. Optimal cooperative learning requires each student to be an effective teacher to all other members of his or her team.* Teachers tend to overlook the fact that during cooperative learning, each student is expected to be an effective teacher of at least part of the content and skills to all other group members. The students have not had courses in how to plan to teach, how to teach or how to monitor and assess student learning. Therefore, it will often be necessary to take some time before students begin the teaching phase of their work and describe a number of clear guidelines that students might follow in planning their "teaching," and in asking questions and doing other things to monitor the extent that their peers are learning the necessary content and skills. Students must learn ways to test or quiz one another, to provide corrective feedback, to diagnose problems their groupmates are having, to provide prescriptive feedback on how to improve their understandings and skills, and to provide encouragement and support. Teaching for others to learn is different from providing guidance to complete a project, such as a presentation, where it is possible for the presentation to go well but for most students involved still to have very little mastery of the content and skills represented in the presentation. In cooperative learning, all group members are both teachers and learners, and one of the important things all students need to learn early is how to teach so that all their peers achieve the high level of learning needed.

*18. Each team member needs to learn and then use one or more appropriate roles to guide his or her within-team behaviors.* Students must acquire, practice, and refine the variety of positive group behaviors necessary for them to work *as a team* so that they become skilled users of these abilities and accompanying attitudes. Table 2 lists some of these roles. We should not expect the majority of students to bring all the appropriate knowledge bases, abilities and attitudes about relevant roles to these teams or to develop them simply by being told to work as a group. In the early stages of using this approach, teachers need to take time before they form the groups, during the group interactions, and after the groups have finished to describe particular productive and dysfunctional group behaviors and attitudes. Mastering these roles is a major focus of the process of learning to cooperate. Proponents of cooperative learning emphasize the need to help students learn and use the roles that are necessary to contribute to their team's academic achievement efforts.

*19. Appropriate cooperative learning and accompanying cooperative group models and guidelines are neither simple nor easy to implement.*[17] For nearly three decades, Johnson and Johnson have insisted that learning to establish, facilitate, manage and monitor effective cooperative learning activities is hard work and that achieving optimal cooperative learning on a day-to-day basis in even one classroom is not simple, comfortable or easy. Although the concept of cooperation is simple and appealing, teachers should not assume that achieving the high levels of cooperation needed for maximizing academic learning will be easy. Students are used to cooperating to get a task or project finished: cooperative learning requires a totally different focus of their cooperative efforts. The various cooperative models and structures require the typical teacher to use a number of new behaviors that will take time to perfect. Old notions that run contrary to effective cooperative learning are likely to persist. Realistically, nearly every teacher who consciously works at implementing optimal cooperative learning effectively on a day-to-day basis will take at least two if not three years to master this approach so that it operates smoothly, efficiently and optimally in his or her classroom. A teacher should not expect to become an expert overnight or in the first semester, or believe that learning and mastering cooperative learning will be free of frustrations, anxiety and stress. However, once mastered, the rewards for students and teachers will have made all these things worth it, and will free teachers from some of these problems in the future.

*20. Cooperative learning can be effective when only one teacher in the school or department is using it.* Sometimes a teacher has the sense that if he or she is the only one using cooperative learning, his or her students will not gain much by its use. This teacher may try a few cooperative learning activities and then stop to wait for the day when every teacher in his or her department or school uses them. It is important not to make this mistake. Cooperative learning has been effective in achieving many of the valued goals of social studies education even when only one teacher in a school uses it. Social studies teachers should consider its use on the basis of the classroom evidence such as that described later in this volume. We encourage teachers to become the first cooperative learning teacher in their departments or schools. With the success that is likely to follow, colleagues will join this movement toward expanding the cooperative learning concept and group structures to other courses and into other departments.

In this part of the chapter, we have addressed fundamental conceptions of appropriate cooperative learning, in part to correct many popular misconceptions that need to be rejected. Educators need to include these ideas as a part of a large, comprehensive, conceptual framework for cooperative learning. Social studies educators may read these and other materials on cooperative

**Table 2: A sample of major roles that students may need to learn and will need to use in nearly all groups.**

1. **Clarification Seeker**: Asks for clarification of statements, opinions or reasoning made by other members of the group; asks how the group feels; asks for clarification of comments in terms of their factual adequacy, relevancy, or source. May even paraphrase a statement or question.

2. **Coach**: Checks to see how group members are doing, and where they need help; offers assistance and advice to help members develop, acquire, refine, perfect and successfully use the relevant information, strategies, and ideas being considered or those which are necessary if each member is to learn and then master the academic content and abilities.

3. **Connector**: States and clarifies relationships, associations, or connections among information, opinions, and ideas or suggests an integration of the information, opinions, and ideas of subgroups.

4. **Consensus-Decision Tester**: Checks to find out when and whether group members agree with each other; checks to see whether members are ready to decide or vote; sends up "trial balloons" to determine how close the members are and to determine how they want to proceed to make the final decision.

5. **Diagnostician**: Indicates the problems, deficiencies, handicaps, shortcomings, etc. in terms of the amount and quality of the academic content being studied or learned, evaluates how well each member has mastered the targeted content and abilities, and probes each member to identify deficiencies and then suggest improvements or corrections.

6. **Elaborator-Clarifier**: Elaborates ideas and contributions made by others; offers rationales for suggestions; tries to deduce how an idea or suggestion would work if adopted by the group.

7. **Energizer**: Presses the group and individual members to initiate action, to stay on task, to stay focused on the inquiry and learning, to stay focused to get the job done, and to keep everyone going to ensure that the required academic learning has been achieved.

8. **Evaluator-Critic**: Analyzes the group's task operations, data base, or accomplishments according to some set of standards; checks to see that consensus has been reached.

9. **Information Giver**: Provides details, explanations, generalizations, etc. that are important to the academic content and abilities to be learned; suggests possible sources of information; helps others to find new sources or to investigate sources already identified.

10. **Information Seeker**: Asks for information (i.e., factual and descriptive details rather than hearsay and opinions) relevant to the problem, situation or task; suggests the particular kinds of information that the members need to consider before making decisions.

11. **Initiator-Contributor**: Voluntarily introduces ideas and suggestions; voluntarily proposes alternative strategies, resources, perspectives, materials, solutions or options at various points along the group's efforts; voluntarily proposes new ideas or states old ones in a novel fashion.

12. **Opinion/Belief Monitor**: May request statements of beliefs or assumptions, or may restate or clarify beliefs or assumptions that have been uttered; states clearly what the group's attitude appears to be, should be, could, must, or may be or is; may challenge stated or unstated beliefs or assumptions one or more members appear to have.

13. **Orienter-Summarizer**: Summarizes what has taken place; points out departures from agreed upon goals; tries to bring the group back to the central issues; raises questions about the direction in which the group is heading.

14. **Procedure Caretaker**: Handles routine tasks such as seating arrangements, obtaining equipment, and handing out pertinent papers; invents or relies upon procedures to get tasks done; parliamentarian; makes sure that the stated procedures or guidelines for completing the activity and for helping each other master the academic content and abilities are followed in the order outlined.

15. **Recorder**: Keeps notes on the group's interactions, data base, and progress.

learning and believe that they are already engaged in cooperative learning in their school or classroom. The ultimate criteria for whether optimal cooperative learning is occurring are the long term results that are achieved by students. The following paragraphs will help teachers begin a systematic assessment of the results of their current group activities to determine the extent to which they are already practicing optimal cooperative learning.

## Results a Teacher Can Expect From Using Optimal Cooperative Learning

One way to determine whether group activities and assignments are consistent with optimal cooperative learning is by collecting systematic, objective data about the actual long-term effects of the group activities on the majority of students. For instance, when students are involved in cooperative group tasks over an extended period, nearly all

- Show remarkable and consistent improvement in their scores on academic tests
- Have longer periods of retention of academic content, understandings, concepts and abilities
- Have high levels of proficiency in critical reasoning abilities and strategies
- Reduce their disruptive behaviors and increase on-task behaviors
- Have many of the positive attitudes necessary for interacting and working effectively with others
- Feel positively about others in their groups
- Are more willing to share and interact positively within group settings
- Integrate their academic learning and social and intergroup relations
- Voluntarily increase their positive personal contacts with many other students both inside and outside the classroom
- Have strong feelings of group membership
- Work cooperatively in small group settings toward attaining a common goal
- Voluntarily improve relations with individuals of a different gender or of an ethnic, racial or socio-economic background other than their own
- Are willing to express and discuss their own ideas in public
- Improve their opinions about and relationships with handicapped and other special needs students

- View many of their peers in a more positive light than when only individualistic and competitive strategies are used
- Increase the number of voluntary friendships based on human qualities
- Have enhanced positive self-concept and self-esteem
- Are positively adjusted psychologically
- Have high levels of intrinsic motivation to learn
- Accept their peers as knowledgeable agents in learning, i.e., as learning resources
- Increase the amount of time they spend on-task, especially during well-structured group tasks where the focus is on academic achievement
- Have very positive attitudes toward teachers, principals, and other school personnel
- Have very positive attitudes toward learning, school, and the subject matter content.

These results occur only when learning teams function over an extended period of time and under conditions where the focus of the cooperation consistently achieves high levels of academic success for nearly every student in the class. If the group structure and activities being used are not making noticeable progress along many of these lines by the end of the first few weeks, then teachers should reassess the extent to which they are actually engaging students in optimal cooperative learning.

## An Invitation

Rather than a conclusion section, we bring this chapter to an end with an invitation to social studies educators. We invite you to study and reflect upon the information in the chapters of this book. We invite you to acquire a conception of optimal cooperative learning and to envision how you might use these structures, conceptions and guidelines in your classroom. We invite educators to arrange for face-to-face communication with colleagues in their department, district, conference session, or college classroom to review this information and develop this vision cooperatively. By taking such steps in their department, social studies educators will be working collaboratively and cooperatively to increase the effectiveness of cooperative learning groups in their classrooms. Finally, we invite social studies educators to ensure that their social studies classroom activities facilitate successful *social study* via optimal cooperative learning conditions using cooperative group structures. When these are done, done well and done often, the evidence suggests that when teachers "do it right," then students can and will "get significantly better together." 🖼

## NOTES

1. Additional information on this point is provided in Chapter Two of this volume.

2. The motto "Getting Better Together" originated with Jim Weyand, former principal of Bill Reed Junior High School in Loveland, Colorado. A most remarkable educator, Jim invented and used many of the concepts and principles later associated as essential elements of cooperative learning with his faculty and staff. Beginning in the early 1970s, he built and maintained cooperatively one of the most powerful, effective, and collegial instructional staffs one author, Robert Stahl, has personally encountered. Jim's genuine concern for students and student success evolved into a collegial faculty team whose members, by working as a staff development cooperative learning team, "got better together" to enable students over a number of years to achieve remarkably high levels of academic, affective, and social abilities. By the end of the second year, all faculty in his school volunteered to participate in the faculty team whose goal was to maximize every student's achievement in every content area. They accomplished this in such a way that eventually every student gained an average of 3.75 years of academic growth in every subject offered in the school over the 3 years the students attended Bill Reed Junior High School. What made this even more remarkable was that students were required to take six academic courses each semester. Jack Wilson, Don June and Howard Wenger, at the time, Principal and Assistant Principals, respectively, of Loveland High School, followed up on and collaborated with Jim Weyand and eventually were able to guide the Loveland High faculty to reach a level of cooperation, camaraderie and effectiveness that few educators will ever experience in their careers. At the height of their work, the progress of each student at Loveland High taking six academic courses per semester achieved the amount of growth as did students at Bill Reed. In part, this chapter honors Jim's contributions and the accomplishments of these administrators and those of their respective faculties for what they assisted their students to achieve. In these two schools, as administrators and faculty concentrated on collaboratively improving their curriculum and instruction, they did truly did "get better together," and the consequences of their efforts in their respective classrooms were that students excelled in their academic achievement, their critical thinking abilities, their self concepts and their abilities to interact in positive ways in and outside the school grounds.

3. Robert J. Stahl, "Essentials of Cooperative Learning: Key Concepts, Requirements, and Guidelines for Implementation," presentation at the annual meeting of the Arizona Council for the Social Studies, Mesa, Ariz., October 1990, and "The Essential Elements for Optimal Cooperative Learning," paper presented at the annual meeting of the American Educational Research Association, Seattle, Washington, April 2001.

4. Introductory descriptions of a number of cooperative learning models are available in the works referenced at the end of these chapters.

5. Robert E. Slavin, *Introduction to Cooperative Learning* (New York: Longman, 1983).

6. David W. Johnson, and Roger T. Johnson, *Learning Together and Alone: Cooperative, Competitive, and Individualistic Learning*. 3d ed. (Englewood Cliffs, N.J.: Prentice Hall, 1991), and "*Learning Together* in the Social Studies Classroom," edited by Robert J. Stahl, *Cooperative Learning in the Social Studies Classroom: A Handbook for Teachers* (Menlo Park, Calif.: Addison-Wesley, 1994). See also their chapter in this volume.

7. The listing, descriptions of and guidelines for these essential elements are beyond the scope of this chapter. Interested readers may wish to contact the author, Robert J. Stahl, for these details.

8. David W. Johnson, Roger T. Johnson, and Edythe J. Holubec, *Cooperation in the Classroom*. 3d ed. (Edina, Minn.: Interaction Book Company, 1990) and *The New Circles of Learning: Cooperation in the Classroom and School* (Alexandria, Va.: Association for Supervision and Curriculum Development, 1994).

9. Robert E. Slavin, *Cooperative Learning: Theory, Research, and Practice* (Englewood Cliffs, N.J.: Prentice–Hall, 1990).

10. Robert J. Stahl, "The Essential Elements for Optimal Cooperative Learning," *op. cit.*

11. David W. and Roger T. Johnson, *Learning Together and Alone: Cooperative, Competitive, and Individualistic Learning*, 3d ed. (Englewood Cliffs, N.J.: Prentice Hall, 1991).

12. Stahl, "Essentials of Cooperative Learning: Key Concepts, Requirements, and Guidelines for Implementation," *op. cit.*

13. *Ibid.*

14. *Ibid.*

15. *Ibid.*

16. Spencer Kagan, *Cooperative Learning Resources for Teachers* (San Juan Capistrano, Calif.: Resources for Teachers, 1989), and "The Structural Approach to Cooperative Learning," *Educational Leadership* 47 (December/January 1989-90):12-15.

17. David W. Johnson, Roger T. Johnson, Edythe J. Holubec, and Patricia Roy, *Circles of Learning: Cooperation in the Classroom* (Alexandria, Va.: Association for Supervision and Curriculum Development, 1984); David W. Johnson, Roger T. Johnson, and Edythe J. Holubec, *The New Circles of Learning: Cooperation in the Classroom and School* (Alexandria, Va.: Association for Supervision and Curriculum Development, 1994).

# CHAPTER 2

# "Academic Loners" Become Highly Successful "Academic Teammates"
## An Inside-the-Learner Perspective on Optimal Cooperative Learning

**Robert J. Stahl**, Arizona State University, Tempe, Arizona

**Students enter K-12 classrooms** expecting to complete the bulk of their academic learning alone and to receive grades based on their individual accomplishments. Not surprisingly, students in these classrooms typically complete activities as individuals, working almost exclusively alone as learners.

Sometimes, teachers assign students to complete tasks in groups. Unfortunately, in the majority of these groups, students spend most of their time and effort working independently of peers, even though they may sit side-by-side with them. In these groups, students copy each other's work, make sure each other knows the assignment, check their answers with those of their peers, or share information they find without checking to make sure anyone has learned it. As they interact, we might overhear statements such as: "This is the correct answer to this question," "You can copy my answers," and "This is where I found the answer to that question." Quite frequently, students divide the work just to get done. They focus and arrange their time and efforts to complete the task or project, rather than to comprehend and give academic meaning to the content and topics being considered. Each completes a separate part, and then they put the parts together into a final report or project. A and B+ grade students may spend some time helping their peers but are cognizant of the point where they will cut off this time and assistance when they see them endangering their own chances for a good grade. When they view helping others as threatening their personal success, they typically withdraw to complete their work alone or see themselves as forced to do most of the group's work by themselves. It is as though they say, "If helping you hurts my grade, then I'm outta here and you are on your own!" When they cannot completely sever their connection to those in their group, they seem to say, "If helping you hurts

my grade and you are not going to do your part, then I have no choice but to do my part and your part just so that my grade doesn't suffer. I don't like having to do your part, but because I have to, I'll do what needs to be done by myself." Unfortunately, such thoughts are quite frequent among high achieving students in most groups at every level of schooling, from elementary through graduate school.

Even after more than three decades of emphasis on co-operative learning and avoiding traditional group work, most teachers continue to focus group activities almost exclusively on students completing one or more tasks or projects rather than on mastering and retaining particular content and skills. This task-completion focus remains the main purpose of most group work and the single-minded goal of nearly every student. One student's comment, "Right or wrong, what does it matter? The most important thing is getting it done!" expresses this view well. Students sense that the purpose of most group assignments is to create an acceptable product regardless of what they learn or do not learn in the process. In these situations, teachers find far too few opportunities to provide the individualized attention certain students need. Within traditional groups, most of the time, most students place little emphasis on ensuring that they learn, much less master, what the group studies. Students are well aware that they are primarily accountable for completing their respective subtasks or the entire project rather than mastering the content and skills that their teachers might have associated with the tasks' or projects' academic goals. They typically spend far more time making a presentation or project look nice, interesting and appealing (if not entertaining), than they do in trying to comprehend and retain important content and abilities. At best, *they cooperate in groups primarily to do and to get done,* NOT *to learn.* Consequently, they rarely master targeted academic content and skills, and even more rarely do they make sure all other members of their group attain this same high level of mastery.

Within social studies classrooms, the vast majority of students are "academic loners," if not "academic strangers" to one another, in the midst of other students acting essentially the same way. Although some may be social peers to one another, few students are perceived, much less perceive themselves, as being "academic partners," "academic teammates" or "academic colleagues" of their classmates. Even fewer students believe their individual academic achievement and high level of academic test scores are directly dependent on the assistance they receive from one or more classmates. On another note, few students are perceived as bona fide academic resources to their classmates. Indeed, students depend on nearly everything except their classmates as resources to help them maximize their academic learning. Many students devalue the knowledge and support of classmates because of the personal risks they associate with being wrong in front of them. This risk of being wrong in public is one major reason why so many students never volunteer to answer questions or ask questions when their teacher invites them. Furthermore, without the information, abilities and practice on how to work and cooperate with others to ensure the academic mastery of all group members, the chances are great that the efforts of most students placed in groups will not attain the group or individual success teachers expect.

The social setting of learning activities and the interpersonal processes involved within cooperative environments play powerful roles in student academic and social activities. For one thing, the learning activities are social in that the very words and language rules used are part and parcel of the culture(s) in which students live. As Bruner recognized,[1] most learning in most settings occurs as a communal activity, as a sharing of the culture. For Bruner, students must construct and make knowledge their own. In most instances, this knowledge-building is accomplished within a community of influential others who share their environment. In life inside and outside the classroom, students must make sense of, construct personal versions of and assign meanings to the information they encounter. These processes occur with or without a direct dialogue about the academic content or personal feelings among students or between students and the teacher. Students cannot escape using the language tools of their society and classroom although they infrequently get to interact directly with anyone but the teacher. The ideal for each classroom is that there exists one tight-knit interpersonal and academic community consisting of the teacher and all students. There should not be 30 small communities, each consisting of just one student and the teacher. Furthermore, in such strong, all-encompassing classroom communities, each student has a chance to share, negotiate, and revise understandings and meanings in light of specific feedback from the teacher and all classmates.

In all small communities, each member assesses the competence of all other members. This goes on in every classroom as well. Like it or not, in all school settings, students make inferences about the types, amount and quality of the academic abilities each peer has and what each seems capable of achieving under the existing circumstances. They also make inferences about the types of relationships and interactions they will and could have with every other student in the same classroom. Consequently, many students infer that although their classmates may be called upon to help them complete projects or to learn, they themselves can do little to help their peers master the content and abilities considered during these projects. Given such perceptions, teachers should not be surprised that students become quite good at carrying out the outward appearances of helping each other learn while spending their time and effort merely to cooperate to get the work or project done to meet their teachers' expectations. Students realize that as far as their teacher is concerned, getting students simply to work together in a civil manner and do a "good" project is equivalent to attaining learning and retaining mastery of the content and skills. Students are quite aware of the fact that they can do these things well and still learn very little of the content and skills their teacher believes they are learning.

In contrast, when optimal cooperative learning is implemented, many of the characteristics described above change drastically. Within optimal cooperative learning settings, teachers do many things to change the existing academic and social dimensions of their classrooms. They significantly alter the factors that weaken, threaten and interfere with the quality of the academic, social and cultural life of students. Teachers make and enforce these changes in order to maximize the academic achievement of every student. To describe what often is the case for students and what can become the situation for nearly every student, the next two sections introduce the concepts of the "academic loner" and the "academic teammate." These descriptions take a first person point of view in the hopes of helping teachers to place themselves first as an individual student in a classroom without groups or with traditional group activities and then one where optimal cooperative learning is implemented.

## What It Is Like to Be an "Academic Loner?"
## An Inside-the-Learner Scenario

The following scenario illustrates a student's perspective on what it means to be an "academic loner" or an "academic stranger" to one's peers.

### Me, the Student, as an "Academic Loner"

In my social studies classroom, I learn mostly by working by myself to complete assignments. Nearly all my efforts to master the need-to-learn content and abilities expected are done alone. I engage in most tasks independently of what all other students in my class are doing or achieving. In non-competitive instances, I know that what I do, how well I do it and what I learn are unrelated to the accomplishments of others. My success, or lack of success, has no bearing on the rewards and grades others receive.[2] The rewards and grades I receive are my own based solely on what I have achieved.

At times, working as an individual is a positive experience with worthwhile academic and personal benefits. In these situations I have the chance to learn about things in which I am personally interested. Having to focus on and master subject matter content and skills by myself is not necessarily bad; especially if I like the topic. Most of the time, however, I have to work to learn content and abilities that I'm not interested in. Even my teacher likes some topics a great deal and has little interest in other topics we are supposed to study. Perhaps there are ways that I can study social studies content and topics that will make the studying and learning easier—and maybe even more interesting while helping me to improve my achievement as measured by the chapter and unit tests.

Nearly all of the classroom routines are set up for me to work most of the time alone next to classmates who are also working alone. Therefore, I rely heavily upon my teacher and the textbook or the Internet to provide most of the information I am expected to learn. My assignments usually require completing certain projects such as reading the chapter, finding answers to questions, completing worksheets, or solving problems that I am suppose to do by myself.

Almost always I am informed as to what I am to do rather than what I am to learn. For instance, I am directed to complete a worksheet on the information in a chapter, draw Pilgrims or Indians on the class mural before Thanksgiving, or write a short essay on my reaction to some past or current event. I might be told to read the chapter and write answers to the 10 to 15 questions at the end of the chapter. However I know I can find and write answers to all these questions and won't remember a single answer the next day. What my teacher doesn't realize is that most of my classmates are like me. In fact, most teachers mistakenly call what we do in these activities "learning." But it *isn't* learning—it's just doing! We do assignments either alone or in groups just to do the assignment, and at the end of the period or the next day we can't remember very much about what we studied. There are lots of times when it seems my teacher isn't even sure what I am to learn, but my teacher always seems to know what I am supposed to be doing. What I really needed to learn in order to focus my learning efforts and to be highly successful is usually not clear until I am handed a test.

Even when it is clear what I have to learn, I find I am not always sure that what I come up with as the correct answer is actually the answer the teacher will accept. My teacher doesn't have the time or desire to check every student who is working alone in order to find out if our answers are right or wrong. The same is true for situations when I am trying to comprehend what I am reading, to understand what I am studying or process information while analyzing, comparing and forming concepts. In many cases, the only feedback I get as to whether I am right or wrong is *after* I take a test. By then it is too late!

I frequently see myself as being in a "sink or swim" situation with no one to help me "swim," much less greatly improve my "swimming." When my teacher urges me to try harder or spend more time, I feel like I'm dog-paddling in the middle of an ocean, realizing that time and effort alone will never get me to even the closest shore. In these situations I either get real nervous and unsure of myself or I feel helpless and see my situation as hopeless. To avoid feelings of frustration, failure or despair, it is often easier for me just to give up or not even try. Why bother making an effort day after day when I know I can't succeed by effort alone?

When I am done with my assignments, I usually think I understand the material or topic even though I know that later I find out all or a portion of my ideas, information or skills are inaccurate, inappropriate or incomplete. Like all people, if my personal versions of what I study make sense to me, then I continue to treat my versions of the content and skills as being correct until I decide I have to revise them. When I work alone, I get no feedback so I don't know whether my versions of what I am studying are or are not correct, appropriate or complete. As with my classmates, I depend entirely upon my teacher to tell me when and where I need help and to supply positive feedback. Once again, most of the time this feedback, if it comes at all, comes after I take my test. Then it is too late because the teacher has already started a new chapter or topic, and all I know from my returned test is what parts of my comprehension, understanding and skills for the last chapter were correct and incorrect. We never go back so that I can unlearn and correct the wrong stuff and merge it with what I had right. In other words, taking a test isn't a chance for the teacher to find out where we need help and then to help us. What taking a test really means is that neither my classmates nor I will get the help we need to learn what we should have learned.

Unfortunately, my teacher, like I, usually discovers we need help when our test is graded and at a time when the entire class is moving on to new topics or content. We don't expect the teacher to help us go over what we didn't learn. However, as we go from chapter to chapter getting not-so-good test scores, we realize we must not be very good at this thing called 'social studies' and can't learn much of it. As this happens, it gets harder and harder for us to find anything in social studies, or history, or geography, or economics interesting, relevant, worth learning or important. Eventually, when students sense that they are too far behind, that effort and time spent learning will not enable them to catch up, and that they will not get the help they need, they stop paying attention, spending time, and exerting effort to learn what is expected. As one student said, "If I know I'm going to fail no matter how hard I try, why bother trying?"

Sadly, my teacher views students who are behind and who need a lot of help as being "slow learners" or "special needs" students, or as students who don't have a high enough aptitude to learn what is covered in class. Such students are none of these. These students are "slow" and do things associated with special needs and low aptitude learners because they are so far behind in the prerequisites they need. As a result they either have too much to learn to catch up, won't attempt to catch up, or, more frequently, aren't able to catch up without a lot of very focused help. If my teacher or someone else, such as one or more of my classmates, doesn't help these students catch up, then they will get further and further behind. What a shame this happens: the bigger shame is that it continues to happen when it could be prevented.

## Competition Means That for Me to "Win," A Classmate Has to "Lose"

For me, competition exists when I find myself striving to achieve something that is available in such limited quantities that not everyone can attain it regardless of how well they do. For instance, in a basketball tournament, only one team can become champion. All teams compete against each other to achieve something (first place) that from the start everyone knows only one team can achieve. Thus, for one team to become champion,

another team has to lose, no matter how well its members played, how much effort they put into it, and how close they came to matching the score of the winner. In the classroom, when the rewards are limited to only a few, competition exists although my teacher may not think it does. For me and most of my peers in a competitive classroom, no matter how hard we work or how much we learn, when the teacher will give out only a few As and Bs, there is no hope for most of us that we will earn one of those grades.

Like most teachers, my teacher believes competition is good for everyone. My teacher believes competition will motivate everyone, will bring out the best in everyone, and help everyone become better students and learners. My teacher creates a competitive environment by limiting the number of rewards, such as "A" grades, that will be given out for a particular test or at the end of the course. For each student in my class who receives an "A," at least one other student—a classmate—is automatically prevented from earning an "A." Like in a basketball tournament, once one team becomes the champion, then all other teams are automatically excluded from being the champion for that tournament. That is the nature of competition; having anyone win requires that someone else has to be excluded from the winner's prize. In my classroom, the competitive situation exists only for those students who strive to achieve the few high rewards available. Those who choose to compete realize from the start that not all of them will be allowed to make "A" grades.

Many of my classmates, however, choose from the start not to compete for high grades. They are not motivated by competition. Rather they are turned off by it, because they know that no one, especially our teacher, will help them get the help they need in order to earn an "A." They also have learned that in these competitive situations, our teacher tends to spend a lot of time and effort helping the better students in the class so they will earn their "As." Because low-achieving students aren't my teacher's primary concern, many of us are cynical about those few times when our teacher does spend time with us.

Even whole-class question-and-answer sessions are often competitive.[3] We compete for the teacher's attention and praise as individuals operating independently of all others in the class. When the teacher selects me and I answer correctly, all others lose the chance to answer and be praised. In order for others to be praised, the first student selected must answer incorrectly or incompletely—that is, in these situations, my chances for more attention and praise depend directly on the failure of my classmates. Most of my teachers are not aware that certain whole-class discussion behaviors generate competition. Many of these behaviors discourage our participation and, hence, our achievement. One obvious sign of this effect is that fewer and fewer of my classmates vie to answer questions as the school year progresses. Unfortunately, traditional classroom learning environments are rarely structured to enable most of us to become active and successful participants.[4]

Teachers who begin the year opposing the notion of competition may resort to it out of frustration or desperation as many of their students continue to score low on tests, fall behind, and become increasingly apathetic. The teacher may add friendly competition for limited rewards to entice us to participate and exert the effort necessary to succeed on particular tasks. We sometimes even play our own versions of "Jeopardy!," "Family Feud," or "Twenty Questions," as a means to have fun and change our classroom routine. These are sneaky ways the teacher tries to bring fun into a classroom that we already know can only end in winners and losers—and guess who has the most fun? Students leave these contests or games being perceived as "winners" or "losers"—or "smart" or "dumb"—by their classmates. The excitement of the contest passes quickly, but once the winners are revealed, everyone continues to live with the knowledge of who the "winners" and "losers" were.

Consequently, many such competitive activities lead us to resist involvement, the achievement of high levels of academic learning, and the hope of success in future activities. As the ranking of students' abilities becomes public and clear, these competitive activities widen the existing differences among my classmates' academic knowledge and abilities, which in turn widens the negative perceptions of others on the basis of their gender, race, or ethnicity. In effect, by sorting students into "winners" and "losers," competition perpetuates conditions in which nearly all students lose out in terms of what they could potentially achieve. I find it interesting that teachers believe that these competitive situations will always improve my self concept. Actually these situations make it quite clear to most of us that we are too far behind and have no chance of being highly successful without a great deal of help. Hence, we are helpless, and the situation, should it remain the same, is hopeless for us. The results of the competition make it even more unlikely that my classmates will make an effort to help me or I them.

In all these activities it is no wonder that we continue to see ourselves as academic strangers to one another and in many instances even as threats to each other's academic growth and success. Indeed, many of us who make the effort are merely trying to survive academically in this very alone and often competitive environment, where the focus is not really so much on our mastering the content and skills but the teacher covering the topics and chapters and giving us things to do. Heck, I might even want to learn more about social studies topics and content if my teacher could find meaningful ways to help me study the content and actually learn a lot of it and the skills I need to go along with this content learning.

## My Work Alone in Groups Rather Than as an "Academic Partner"

Sometimes my teacher decides to change things by putting me in groups and making us complete assignments in these groups. Unfortunately, these groups are rarely more than just collections of students like me who sit together, complete essentially independent tasks, and fit our individual parts together so we have a single product as proof of our cooperative effort. In most instances, our interactions focus on: who is to do what, when is it due, when is it finished, and how do we put the parts together? In these instances, my classmates and I primarily work independently of one another in what are referred to as "groups." We almost never work as genuine academic partners or academic teammates. Instead, I work near other members of my group instead of with them as part of a team of learners. In such situations, the frequency, quantity, and quality of our interactions are low and the achievement for all is much lower than it should be considering the time we supposedly spend learning. We rarely participate in extended, focused and face-to-face academic dialogues. Even more rare are our efforts to really teach each other or to rigorously test one another to find out whether our groupmates have learned all that was expected.

When we work in these groups, a number of roles emerge that reinforce the notion that we are to work in our groups primarily to finish an assignment. The *Divvy-uppers* ensure that the assignment is divided into parts with each person assigned to work alone on a part. The *Lookouts* position themselves to survey the room to let us know when the teacher is approaching and when certain limited resources, such as atlases, dictionaries and the Internet, are available. More often than not there are the *Slough-offers*, who are those who deliberately don't do what is required because they believe someone else will take over their part to get the work done. Others, the *Moaners and Groaners*, spend their time complaining about doing one or more of the tasks or making any effort to help a groupmate get the work done well and on time. Much of the time, these individuals express their attitudes and beliefs in non-verbal ways or at times when the teacher is too far away to hear. And I can't forget the *Negotiators*, who spend time and efforts negotiating with groupmates by offering to do certain things while trying to get out of doing something else. These students even spend time trying to bargain with our teacher in hopes of cutting down some of the work, lowering the standards for the assignment, extending the amount of time given us, or allowing us to narrow the amount of content or abilities we were originally suppose to master.

Opposite these are the *Get-it-doners*. These students try to make sure at least some of us stay on task to get the assignment done. These students may even do the work of others just to get a project finished. The *Put-it-togetherers* emerge as we need to assemble the different parts, make them fit, and make up the transitions, introduction, and ending. The *Make-it-look-gooders* do the polishing off work. Their major concern is to do what seems necessary to make the final project, report or presentation look good for the teacher. The *Intimidators* or *Bulliers* are those who send verbal and nonverbal messages that one or more group members better get their work done right and on time or else there will be not so pleasant consequences for them. Some classmates who are trying to at least pass are easily threatened by these intimidators. There may even emerge one or more *Bail-outers*. These students will work along with the others at the beginning, but will essentially drop out of the group and go it alone if they sense that staying with the group's effort will be bad for their grades or rewards. In some emergency cases, these students reverse their role and become *Do-it-myselfers* who will do nearly the entire assignment themselves and put everyone's name on it just to prevent adverse consequences. While these roles frequently are carried out in the vast majority of group activities, these roles are ignored or consciously overlooked by many teachers when it looks on the surface like we are cooperating and our final product or presentation is acceptable to them.

In most instances, we spend no time making sure that another group member has—much less all members have—learned the content and abilities as well as they could and should. I sometimes learn from my groupmates. They may learn a few things from me. But, most of what we do learn is unrelated to the content we are studying. I can say that for most of us, the academic learning that results from nearly all group work is mainly a surprising byproduct rather than the major intended outcome of our group effort. At the same time we do not seem to learn much about how a group is supposed to work. Each group operates according to the personalities of the people involved rather than according to guidelines about ways we need to think and act as a team and within a team. Even when the teacher asks us to come up with a "team name" and "team logo," we play the teacher's game and come up with these things. Yet we know from the start that we don't see ourselves as a learning team and will spend little time

ensuring the learning. We realize that in almost every case, the teacher is concerned that we get along well enough to get the work, project or presentation done.

I find that even in the midst of my classmates in the groups my teacher assigns, I still do most of the work alone. Only infrequently do I interact with peers in ways to promote and check my academic learning. Furthermore, even after being in several groups that my teacher lauds as being successful, the perception persists among my classmates that we are strangers to one another in all areas associated with maximizing each other's achievement. At best I am a partner to the doing and the finishing. I am only incidentally a partner in the sparse academic learning that my groupmates achieve.

We cooperate to do and to get done, not to maximize and ensure our academic learning. We engage in behaviors that my teacher accepts as being cooperative and collaborative. It seems my teacher believes that as long as we seem to be civil, work together in peaceful ways and get all or most of our work done, that we are working as cooperative learning groups and my teacher is using cooperative learning. I am amused when my teacher tells us and other teachers that we are doing cooperative learning in my classroom. If we were doing cooperative learning correctly, why aren't my scores and the scores of all my classmates a great deal higher than they are?

███████████

Of course, the above scenario does not hold for every student in every group in every class. Its purpose is to illustrate a perspective that is rarely considered as teachers make decisions about individual and group assignments. Part of this scenario was abstracted from the literature on cooperative learning, especially as it has been contrasted with individualistic, competitive and typical groups and group work.[5] The remaining part reflects the authors' experiences in observing and talking with all too many students as they shared what it was like for them in typical classroom situations and in situations where teachers were using groups in traditional ways while insisting their groups were doing cooperative learning.

Cooperative learning advocates reject the notion that students remain "academic loners' and "academic strangers" to one another. They stress the absolute necessity for each student to play a vital role in the academic success of other students. Cooperative learning groups lead to group success that can be accomplished only by the personal academic achievement of each group member.

## What It Is Like to Be an "Academic Teammate": An Inside-the-Learner Scenario

This section describes the perspective of students in social studies classrooms using appropriate cooperative learning structures and guidelines. The hypothetical student's perspective contrasts sharply with the previous scenario of student life in many noncooperative classroom settings.

### Students as Cooperative Learning Team Members
*No Longer "Academic Loners" or "Academic Strangers" to One Another*

In my social studies classroom, we often work in groups and have group tasks to complete. However, these groups are not like most of the groups I have worked in before; they are different in a number of ways. When my teacher places us in groups to learn social studies content and abilities, I have noticed that a number of features occur each time we form groups. First, my teacher tells us that we are on teams and that we should view each other as teammates who are directly responsible for each others' learning.

One thing I noticed about these teams is that my teacher makes it very clear that the primary purpose of our team is to make sure we master the particular content and skills for the unit. We are to make sure everyone else on our team masters these as well. Every day we are reminded that our primary mission is to master the content and skills, not just to complete an assignment such as answering the questions on a study guide or at the end of a chapter. We are also informed that we should not view ourselves as successful until every team member has mastered the content and skills. It is clear that we are on and in our teams to learn and master rather than merely to do and complete things.

My teacher expects all the members of each team to be real teammates to every one else, just like my coach expects me to be a teammate to everyone on my basketball team. We are expected to work together, to help each other, to interact with one another, to teach as well as learn from one another and to be concerned about every teammate's progress in terms of learning all that is expected. We are informed that we are not to work alone and learn alone, off to ourselves and independently of our teammates. My teacher works hard to set up everything we do or have so that we really do believe and feel as though we are teammates to one another. We are told to view ourselves as partners rather than strangers to each other's learning. We are told that we are successful when every team member scores very well on the test we will take after our team has stopped meeting. After a while,

we began to meet these expectations and to reap the rewards of our work at learning.

One thing I noticed from the start is that individually and as a team, we are informed from the start exactly what content and skills we are to learn. My teacher, sometimes with the help of us students, sets *clear, specific individual and team academic outcome goals* for all members of every team to achieve.[6] From the start, each team and each team member has a clear notion of exactly what is to be learned and what evidence beyond the team activities is required to verify that we have mastered and retained the targeted content and abilities. Unlike most situations where a group might be assigned to complete a project or worksheet, my teacher's team assignments require that we learn the information and abilities that the assignment stresses. We believe that our teams are our way of making sure we learn, not something that we are in just to get a project done. I learned early that having a good-looking group report was not sufficient; all of us had to learn what was in the report. None of us was accustomed to such clear and specific details about what we must learn.

I see myself as *being on a team with real teammates* rather than being in a group with no real reason to view myself other than as someone to help complete a project. Therefore, like all good teammates, I do my best to improve my own knowledge and skills, improve on my ways of interacting and working with my teammates, and make sure that each of them masters all the knowledge and skills we are suppose to learn. We also know that besides our individual test scores, the teacher will award an extra prize to every team that shows high levels of academic learning. However, these prizes or awards only go to teams, not individuals. So even if I make a perfect score, if other members of my team don't score well on the individual test, then even my perfect score will not get me that prize or award. It took a while for us to begin to think in terms of being a real "team" in the classroom where the focus was on academic achievement, but once we began thinking this way, it changed a lot of things we said and did during our team meetings to enable us all to help each other as partners in our learning.

In most instances, each group and team is as *maximally heterogeneous as is possible*, starting with a mixture of academic abilities, and then there is a balance of students according to gender, ethnicity, race, and socioeconomic background.[7] I am not only on the same team with high-, medium- and low-achieving students. I find that I am challenged to help them learn all the content and skills just like they have to meet the challenge of helping me to learn all that the teacher expects. We all find that everyone can contribute in some way to each other's academic success, and that our teammates can contribute to our own personal success as well. Man, this *is* different!

One bonus to this kind of heterogeneous mixture is that it ensures that I come in close contact with and actively interact with everyone in the class, including students other than those of my own academic abilities, gender, race and ethnic background. When these groups function as well as they should as teams and when we achieve as well as we are achieving, I find myself revising in positive directions a number of my perceptions of my peers, including who they are as human beings, what they can achieve and what they are able to contribute to my success.

I sense that every student in my class and on my team has an *equal opportunity for achieving a maximum level of academic success*.[8] This is important because in the past when we were put into groups, it was clear to all of us students that some groups had advantages over the rest of us because of who the teacher put in those groups. Now all the teams seem to be about as equal academically as the teacher can make it. This helps all of us feel like our own team really has a chance to score high on the test and to earn the rewards. Thus my teacher establishes conditions that allow each student to be as successful as every other student on the team and in the class as a whole.

I am reminded by the teacher and frequently by my teammates that the primary purpose of working in groups is for everyone to learn everything that we are suppose to learn. In other words, *our primary goals are to master what we are to learn and to help all our teammates master it as well*. Hence, we don't just get in our groups to do things; we get in teams so we can learn things so well that we will do very well on our individual tests. When we do well on our tests, we can earn all kinds of nifty prizes or rewards.

In every situation, from the very start of when our teams meet, there are *clear directions for the specific tasks we are to complete* and the order in which we are to do it. These directions enable us to get on task quickly and to stay on task because we aren't spending our time trying to figure out what we have to do. Interestingly, we find that the directions are a way to focus our primary activities on what we are to learn and how we should go about teaching one another.

I find that not only is my team responsible for completing the learning tasks as a team but *each of us is held individually accountable for the quantity and quality of our academic achievement*.[9] Not only is each team responsible for learning the targeted content and abilities, the teacher also tests and assesses each of us independently to determine the extent of our personal achievement. I have to do more than complete the work in a team,

I have to learn to the best of my ability and help each teammate learn it to the same high level of mastery. We can no longer hide behind the team project without learning all the content and abilities ourselves. After my team finishes its meetings, I have to take an individual test with no outside help. I get a grade for my personal achievement on this and only this test.

It is not surprising that all the items on each test are aligned directly with the learning goals the teacher set at the beginning of the unit or lesson. In addition, these test items are aligned directly to the major content and skills the teacher had us study and learn in our teams. It did not take us long to realize that when we paid attention to the learning goals and focused our study on the content and skills stressed in the activities our team had to complete, we would do quite well on the individual tests. Even I began to trust that if I learned what the teacher said I needed to learn and if I learned the content and skills we were directed to learn in the team tasks, my test scores would rise quite a bit. As I became more successful on these tests, I found that I had the content knowledge and skills that enabled me to be more interested in what we were studying in class.

I also liked that the teacher set up *a clear reward structure* and provided *worthwhile team awards*.[10] When all the individual test scores for a team are high enough, the teacher rewards all members of that team on the basis of each member's score on his or her individual test. Sometimes the reward is a certificate or our names printed in the class newspaper. This highlights the various teams' progress like I might find on a sports page of the newspaper. I had never received a certificate before for how much I learned about anything, so I still cherish my certificates and the other things we can earn. We know, however, that each team member must meet the teacher's high expectations in order for all of us to get the highest level of reward. We also realize that the teacher wants all of us to learn the material well, so every team can earn the highest reward.

There is no doubt that a very serious *"sink or swim-together" attitude* prevails among all the members of each team. To us, "swimming" means that we did well enough in our learning to enable all of us to earn the reward as a team. To "sink" means that one or more of us did not learn enough and did not help everyone else learn enough, and so all of us lost out in earning an award for achievement. I see it like being on a relay team in a track meet: either the entire team works together to run a fast enough time to earn a ribbon, or the team doesn't run fast enough and thereby no one on the team earns a ribbon. Like on a relay team, we all know that either all of us on the same team learn at a high enough level to earn a team reward, or no one on the team earns any reward, no matter how well he or she did. In other words, if we don't do enough to help each other learn at a high enough level, then we all fail to earn the team rewards, which none of us can earn by ourselves, or we all "swim" together and make sure we all learn, and thereby earn the rewards as a team, as no individual, alone, can earn those awards.

In order to achieve our learning goals, the structure of the teamwork is such that a *division of required individual tasks* is necessary. My teacher provides clear guidelines to ensure that we all have separate tasks to complete successfully as an integral part of the final team goal. When necessary, my teacher takes time from classroom activities to help each of us with comprehending and refining our individual tasks. From the start it is not a guessing game for us. Besides, the earlier I know exactly what I need to do to help the team succeed, the sooner I can get to work and achieve what is necessary.

Teams are successful only when there is *positive interdependence* among their members.[11] My teammates and I quickly realized that we need *to* help as well as need *the* help of others. Every one of us eventually accepts the responsibility for our own learning and achievement and for the learning and achievement of all team members. We share resources, materials and information. We try to make up for what our teammates lack or need, and they do the same for us. This interdependence is necessary for us to function as a team and for us to ensure that all of us master the content and abilities. It is vital for us to attain our team's learning goals collectively. The team guidelines ensure as much as possible that each of us is dependent upon all other members in order for all of us to achieve our team and individual goals.

An extensive amount of *face-to-face interaction* is necessary for us to work and succeed as a team.[12] Each time our team meets, I engage in direct and continuing face-to-face dialogues with my teammates as we share and consider the content, our ideas and abilities and check our own learning. We arrange our chairs and desks so that this face-to-face dialogue can occur. Much of the time we are nearly *knee-to-knee* as we huddle together *using our 12-inch voices* to talk to one another. This interaction works to ensure that all team members learn the required information and abilities, complete the shared assignment, and achieve the academic goals. This close proximity to one another while having focused academic discussions makes me believe that all of us are partners in rather than strangers to this venture.

As we work together in these structured ways, we learn how to be civil and practice civility.[13] We acquire, refine, and use perspectives and behaviors that will enable each of us to be effec-

tive members of the social community and culture of the group. My teacher points out that we should use these same abilities and attitudes in our everyday life, including situations outside of school. In order to establish and maintain a civil environment for our team interactions and work, we communicate as clearly as possible; resolve disagreements through compromise, persuasion, and negotiation; share knowledge, abilities, and self; and facilitate completion of team subtasks. Instead of dreading coming to class each day, I find that the class is socially attractive, encouraging, and powerful.

From the beginning, my teacher has described and made us practice, refine and use the many *roles associated with effective group processes* that are necessary for our teams to function well. These roles are also important in other groups in which I participate outside of class. Like each team member, I am expected to carry out various roles. These roles include but are not limited to those of *Recorder, Encourager, Checker, Leader,* and *Reader.* Eventually I will have to master attitudes and behaviors associated with all these roles. I am learning how to carry out these roles in addition to learning my social studies content and skills. My teacher tells us that these roles and those associated with being civil contribute to the social study part of citizenship and social studies education.

I have been especially pleased with my team assignments because my teacher allows sufficient time for learning what each of us needs to learn. In most cases, my teacher allows each student and each team *enough time to learn* the required content, understandings and abilities. When we do not have enough time to learn, the academic and other benefits of our social study using cooperative learning groups are limited.[14] Since my teacher began using cooperative learning with well-structured team activities, we get started faster on our assignments and stay on them for extended periods of time. As a result, we have more time to complete our team work. More importantly, we have more time to learn and to help our teammates learn. The end result is that more of us learn more than when less time was allowed for team work. To make sure that we are indeed "on task," my teacher frequently walks from team to team monitoring what we are doing and learning.

Once the teams complete their work and we take our individual tests, my teacher takes time to announce publicly the teams who have high levels of achievement. Then my teacher *distributes the rewards in a public ceremony* only to those teams who attained or surpassed the standards established for earning rewards. This is an exciting time for us, especially because the number of teams whose members succeed is so high. Because each teammate needs all the other teammates to be successful on the test for any member of a team to earn a reward, the fact that so many teams earn rewards means for me that a lot of us are really learning a great deal. I know I am. Everyone knows that the only reason why they earned a personal reward is because of what the entire team achieved.

When we are finished with our team work and the rewards are distributed, my teacher takes the time to guide us to *reflect on our interpersonal and group-processing efforts*.[15] As an individual and as a team member, I am asked to stop and assess my own and my teammates' behaviors, interactions, and contributions to the academic success of the whole team. I am then asked to decide how I might improve my interpersonal and group-processing abilities to increase the effectiveness of my group as a learning team. Of course all of us are expected to use the best behaviors and attitudes the next time we are assigned to learning teams.

As I think about it, being a member of a team whose members really focus on learning and academic achievement was at first a totally new experience for me and all my classmates. In the past we got in groups just to do things, not really to learn much, if anything. Over a period of two or three weeks in these new groups, my teammates and I began to feel like we really belonged on a team and with one another. We came to rely heavily on one another to make sure we learned what we were suppose to learn. We even found ourselves spending more time with one another outside of class time and making time outside of class to complete our work and to help each other master the material. When we do things in this new kind of group, I no longer feel alone and isolated from my peers in my efforts to master the content and abilities. In addition, I feel very much a partner in my teammates' efforts to succeed, and they feel as though I am their partner as well. What makes all these things really great is that every one of my classmates is learning more than we ever learned. We are scoring better on our tests even though the new tests test us on more difficult material than the old tests.

I had a thought the other day that is really powerful in my way of thinking. The environment of our classroom teams and the effects of what we do and achieve in them makes it seem like I am a member of an "academic gang." All my teammates feel a strong sense of belonging to the team and with one another. We feel dedicated to one another as individuals and as teammates, to helping each other improve if not excel, and to learning what we need to learn so that the entire team is successful and gets recognized for our academic accomplishments as a team. We find the time and ways to help each other master the content, understandings and abilities each of us needs to learn. We

prod, encourage, support and challenge one another to excel. We don't let our teammates give up, slack off, or avoid doing what is needed to achieve the level of mastery each is capable of reaching. We interact with each other inside and outside the classroom. We feel that each other's successes are our individual successes. What is quite remarkable is that, as I have greatly improved my academic learning, I have a much higher concept of myself as a learner, a person and an individual capable of dealing effectively in interpersonal relations and situations. Do I like the effects of cooperative learning when done well and often? Absolutely!

As with the first scenario, this description does not hold for every student in every cooperative learning team or situation. It is proposed to represent the sharp contrast between typical group activities and optimal cooperative learning situations. We have found that when teachers use optimal cooperative learning conditions appropriately over an extended period of time, a perspective like the above becomes prevalent among students. Ultimately, working in cooperative learning groups produces many positive results because these groups enable students to gain access to and complete many of the internal processing tasks they need to complete to be highly successful. As depicted here, teachers should realize how using optimal cooperative learning will transform students from being "academic loners" and "academic strangers" to one another into "academic teammates."

The next section introduces three critical elements for individual learner achievement that appropriate cooperative learning groups provide.

### What Each Student Needs in Order to Be a Highly Successful Learner: An Inside-the-Learner Perspective

Social studies educators need an adequate conception of students' needs from an inside-the-learner perspective to complement their notions of what they need to provide outside the learner in the form of cooperative learning guidelines and team goals.

### The Student as Learner

Students are dynamic, always-active constructors and users of information and processes. Like all adults, they are continually generating, inventing, revising, organizing, applying, testing, and assessing their personal versions of the world, themselves, and their experiences. The results of these inventing, sense-making, and meaning-making activities are labeled "constructs," which are known by many other names, such as information, concepts, generalizations, conceptions, worldviews, perspectives, and infoschemata.[16] Students ultimately decide individually which events, materials, and data they will attend to and how each "infobit" will be made meaningful and be related to other info-bits.[17] Students invent meanings and make sense of what they encounter by using previously-invented and -stored constructs (e.g., information, concepts, ideas) to think about, assess, act upon and manipulate newly-encountered information. The sets of constructs they have stored and then retrieve constitute their activated "prior knowledge" at a particular moment.

Each student also decides, almost always nonconsciously, how permanently stored information and schema will be used to make sense of and assign meaning to newly encountered material and data. The student even decides whether something is a problem or is worthy of further attention. All individuals assign personal meaning to the external information and events they encounter and perceive to exist as well as to all information and conceptions they generate internally. This meaning and this meaning alone influences personal judgments. The meanings, perceptions, conceptions, and results of sense-making decisions may be either stored permanently in the brain or forgotten, sometimes within seconds.

This view of students is consistent with that of neurocognitive researchers who tell us that no individual's brain operates as a sponge that absorbs external information and holds it permanently in the brain. Rather, the neuro-cognitive system operates more like a sieve, dropping information out at a far faster rate than it ever stores information permanently. Stahl claims that no matter how hard they try, all individuals probably store no more than 5% of the constructs and infobits they create during a particular experience, such as during the reading of any chapter in this book or during any class period or class activity.[18] Furthermore, teachers should not assume that information outside learners can be directly transferred into their brains as if the neural system were a video recorder. Essentially, from the moment a student encounters an external event, situation or information, a series of high-speed mostly nonconscious decisions that assign personal meaning to what is encountered is begun. The result is a version of what the student thinks occurred or thinks the material says and means from his or her own point of view. This meaning may be, and often is, different in intent, content, and form from that of the source, such as a teacher or textbook. In these instances, unless students assess and change the meanings initially assigned to the information, they will consider their original versions of an event or content as accurate and complete. Students, like their teachers, use their invented versions as a base to make sense of other events and information they encounter within and outside the classroom. In far too many instances students construct misconceptions or inadequate versions of what they encounter in social studies classes as they strive to achieve the targeted understandings and abilities. Unfortunately, most students do not receive the personal help they need to revise their inadequate versions, so they proceed as though their inadequate versions are accurate, complete and viable.

If students are to master targeted social studies content and abilities, they must eventually construct, store and use sets of clear, complete, adequate and organized constructs (e.g., information, concepts) that are directly aligned with each goal. These constructs serve as the prerequisites for guiding decisions and actions consistent with targeted academic goals. In addition, students should be able to use their correct constructed versions when and as needed to activate academic, social, and affective abilities. Processing cannot replace the prerequisite constructs; and many valued academic processes such as inquiring, analyzing and comparing are not possible without the application of appropriate constructs. Another way of viewing what each student needs to be a successful learner is through a model of learning in school settings that emphasizes what the student needs rather than what the teacher wants to provide or have students do.

## A Model of School Learning

In educational settings, learning may be viewed as acquiring new constructs or new abilities to use these constructs such that the new construct or ability is accessible to the person 23 or more hours *beyond* the class period in which either the constructs (e.g., information) or the ability was first encountered or used.[19] Learning involves a series of internal construct-processing events that each person must complete to transfer any new construct or ability into permanent storage. Essentially, learning involves making one or more changes both in the existing constructs students have stored permanently and in the ability to use these constructs at some future time. Given this definition, the teacher and student alike cannot confirm what has been learned until approximately 23 or more hours after a class period has ended.

Therefore, the mere fact that students are active, having fun, cooperating and appear to be learning something new does not mean that what they are thinking about or doing during that class period has been or will be learned. Ample evidence from numerous research studies and from teachers' classroom experiences verify that students frequently forget much of what they appear to have learned quite well on a previous day.

In addition, social studies educators should not assume that the processing associated with learning guarantees that what is learned, as determined by the learner or some external standard, is correct, complete, appropriate, or relevant to a task, an expected ability, or a future need. LeSourd, for instance, revealed that students can show evidence of learning one thing during a class period, and within two or three days have conceptions of a topic or subject that are quite different, sometimes almost opposite, to what they said or wrote on the first day when the learning was supposed to have happened.[20] Even the individual learner cannot guarantee that certain information, conceptions, or abilities will be stored permanently. Furthermore, no learner can guarantee that the constructs he or she stores for the long term will be accurate or will be retrieved when needed.

Three major variables that determine the extent of learning success can be expressed in the following way:

$$\text{Degree of Success} = f \left[ \left( \frac{\text{relevant infobits possessed and able to be used at the moment}}{\text{relevant infobits required}} \right) \left( \frac{\text{appropriate internal processing events completed up to that moment}}{\text{appropriate internal processing events needed to be completed}} \right) \left( \frac{\text{actual productive time already spent learning}}{\text{actual productive time needed to be spent learning}} \right) \right]$$

Note that the terminology in this equation uses "infobits" rather than constructs because information is something readily familiar to teachers at all grade levels and subject areas, and is used here for convenience. A more psychologically-minded version of this model featuring the concept of "constructs" rather than infobits and described within the context of a constructivist perspective is available from the author.

As the equation suggests, the three critical variables necessary for successful learning are, in abbreviated form, (a) appropriate and sufficient infobits, (b) appropriate and sufficient internal processing tasks completed and possible to complete, and (c) sufficient productive time spent learning that same ability to a particular level of mastery.[21] The information one needs depends upon the particular ability to be learned and the level of success one wishes to achieve. For instance, to be competent inquirers, students will need a set of procedures that are very different from those needed to be skilled at applying a concept to distinguish between examples and nonexamples. Processing tasks refer to what the learner needs to be able to do internally in order to manipulate, transform, assign meaning to, apply and use information required for the particular ability being

used or learned. Processing tasks include but are not limited to paraphrasing, organizing, analyzing, comprehending, interpreting, forming associations, drawing conclusions and applying information. Thus it is not sufficient just to have enough of the needed constructs or content. Each student must be able to retrieve and use each construct when and as required for each particular ability. The time-spent element refers to the actual number of minutes, hours, days, weeks, and months each student must spend trying to achieve the desired level of success.

All three variables are interrelated and interdependent; none is the most important in its own right. For instance, to place high value on having students process infobits without having them acquire and process each infobit directly aligned with the targeted ability, or without having students spend sufficient time to complete the required processing, will not enable them to master the targeted ability at a high level of proficiency or retain that ability over weeks, months or years. Social studies teachers, therefore, will want to provide students opportunities to attain 100 percent of what each student needs of each of these three variables for every ability to be learned.

Returning to the above formula, the degree of success for every ability can range from 0 to 100 percent, with 100 percent representing the highest level of achievement that is acceptable at a particular moment. The higher the expected level of achievement, the more of each of these three variables will be required. The three variables within the parentheses reflect ratios, not fractions. The bottom section for each is always 100 percent of what is needed for a particular level of success. The top section of each ratio may range from 0 to 100 percent. To be 100 percent successful, the top of each variable ratio must always be 100 percent. To the extent that any one or more of these variables is below 100 percent of what is needed, the learner will be less successful than if all three were completely fulfilled. Desire and effort cannot replace what is needed in each of these three critical variables.

For any ability, an overabundance in one variable can never compensate for less than 100 percent of what the learner needs in one or both other variables. For instance, giving students more time without them constructing all the information they need will not make up for the lack of must-learn information, no matter how long a period of time they take trying to learn. In other words, time and effort are not sufficient to ensure quality learning. Similarly, having students encounter information they must learn without the opportunities to process this information in appropriate ways will not lead to the learning teachers may expect. The requirements for the bottom section of each ratio will vary from one ability to another and will likely vary from one student to another. At the beginning of instruction, students in a single classroom will likely vary in the extent to which they approach 100 percent for each of the three variables. Bloom's review of classroom research on the prerequisites for academic success found essentially the same thing as described in this model,[22] but he never created a model to reflect what he found. In one sense, this Information-Constructivist Model of School Learning is a model that he might have invented had he made an effort to do so.

## Implications of This Model for Social Studies Education

Social studies instruction will be effective to the extent that it provides students access to the appropriate constructs, processing, and time they need in order to be successful. Invariably, students will differ in the quantity and quality of what they have and what they need to be successful in regard to each of the three critical variables. In addition to the academic content and abilities to be learned, learners also need descriptive and supportive feedback on the extent to which they are actually acquiring the infobits and abilities required for the achievement level expected. To the extent that such feedback is not provided or allowed, the instructional environment will always be less than optimally effective no matter how good the model, the method, or the teacher appears to be. Conversely, no teaching model will be optimally effective if its implementation limits students' fulfillment of the three variable areas required for high levels of achievement for any ability for any student at any time.

## Optimal Cooperative Learning Provides Students Access to What They Need to Be Successful

Cooperative group structures or models provide students with many opportunities to gain access to the information they need, to complete the processing they need to complete, and to spend extended on-task time learning in direct alignment with the social studies goals selected. When these structures are complemented by the essential elements of cooperative learning described in Chapter 1, then the conditions for optimal cooperating for learning and cooperative learning are present.

Groups function as academic teams to maximize the learning and achievement of all team members. By building a community of learners, on-task cooperative teams serve to (a) increase the relevant information that would otherwise be available to a single person, (b) provide and support alternative versions and perspectives of what they are studying, (c) help students complete appropriate internal information processing, (d) increase the use of self-regulatory abilities to stay focused, (e) monitor students' thinking and actions such that correction and reinforcement will be more immediate, frequent, and constructive, and (f) verify students' ideas and abilities within moments after being expressed. When students work as and in academically-focused teams to facilitate each other's achieving mastery, each student still needs sufficient engaged time to master the content and processing abilities aligned with each targeted ability. The second scenario presented earlier illustrates how cooperative learning teams tend to provide more students with improved access to what they need to learn effectively. 🖾

## NOTES

1. Jerome Bruner, *Actual Minds, Possible Worlds* (Cambridge, Mass.: Harvard University Press, 1986)

2. David W. Johnson and Roger T. Johnson, "Cooperative Learning Methods: A Meta-analysis," *Journal of Research in Education* 12(1, 2002): 5-14; David W. Johnson, Roger T. Johnson, Edythe J. Holubec, and Patricia Roy, *Circles of Learning: Cooperation in the Classroom* (Alexandria, Va.: Association for Supervision and Curriculum Development, 1984); David W. Johnson, Roger T. Johnson, and Edythe J. Holubec, *Circles of Learning*, 3rd ed. (Edina, Minn.: Interaction Book Company, 1990).

3. Spencer Kagan, "The Structural Approach to Cooperative Learning," *Educational Leadership* 47 (December/January 1989-90): 12-15.

4. Kagan, *ibid.* and in *Cooperative Learning* (San Juan Capistrano, Calif.: Kagan Publishing, 1994).

5. Johnson, Johnson and Holubec, *op. cit.*

6. Johnson, Johnson, Holubec and Roy, *op. cit.;* Robert E. Slavin, *Using Student Team Learning*, 4th ed. (Baltimore: Center for Research on Elementary and Middle Schools, Johns Hopkins University, 1994), *Cooperative Learning: Theory, Research, and Practice* (Englewood Cliffs, N.J.: Prentice-Hall, 1990), and "Synthesis of Research on Cooperative Learning," *Educational Leadership* 48 (February 1991): 71-82.

7. Kagan, *op. cit.;* Johnson, Johnson, Kolubec and Roy, *op. cit.;* Slavin, *Using Student Team Learning, op. cit., Cooperative Learning, op. cit.,* and "Synthesis of Research," *op. cit.*

8. Slavin, *Using Student Learning, op. cit.,* and Robert J. Stahl, "The Essential Elements for Optimal Cooperative Learning," paper presented at the annual meeting of the American Educational Research Association, Seattle, April 2001.

9. Johnson, Johnson, Holubec and Roy, *op. cit.;* Robert E. Slavin, "When and Why Does Cooperative Learning Increase Achievement?", as well as *Cooperative Learning, op. cit.* and *Using Student Team Learning, op. cit.*

10. Johnson, Johnson and Holubec, *op. cit.;* Robert E. Slavin, "When and Why Does Cooperative Learning Increase Achievement?", and *Cooperative Learning, op. cit.* and *Using Student Team Learning, op. cit.*

11. David W. Johnson and Roger T. Johnson, *Learning Together and Alone: Cooperative, Competitive and Individualistic Learning,* 2nd ed. (Englewood Cliffs, N.J.: Prentice Hall, 1987).

12. *Ibid.*

13. J. Doyle Casteel, interview with author, University of Florida, Gainesville, July 1990.

14. Johnson, Johnson and Holubec, *op. cit.;* see also John B. Carroll, "The Carroll Model: A 25-Year Retrospective and Prospective View," *Educational Researcher* 18 (January/February 1989): 26-31; Frank N. Dempster, "The Spacing Effect: A Case Study in the Failure to Apply the Results of Psychological Research," *American Psychologist* 43 (1988): 627-34, and "Synthesis of Research on Reviews and Tests," *Educational Leadership* 44, no. 7 (April 1991): 71-76; Robert J. Stahl, "Time Alone Does Not Mastery Make: Extending Carroll's Model of School Learning in Light of an Information Processing Perspective," paper presented at the annual meeting of the American Educational Research Association, San Francisco, California, April 1989, and "Meeting the Challenges of Making a Difference in the Classroom: Students' Academic Success is the Difference that Counts," *Social Education* 59, no. 1 (January 1995): 47-53.

15. Johnson and Johnson, *Learning Together, op. cit.;* Robert J. Stahl, "The Essential Elements for Optimal Cooperative Learning," paper presented at the annual meeting of the American Educational Research Association, Seattle, April 2001.

16. Infoschemata (singular, infoschema) is a term used to label the organized clusters of interrelated information learners construct, store, and use as their "prior knowledge."

17. Infobit (plural, infobits) is a term coined by the author in 1983 to denote any piece or bit of information or data.

18. Remarks during a Symposium on the Information-Constructivist Perspective sponsored by the Constructivist Theory, Research and Practice Special Interest Group at the annual meeting of the American Educational Research Association, San Diego, Calif., April 2004.

19. Stahl's refinements of this model in 1999, 2003 and 2004 to make it more compatible with the research in cognitive science and his own evolving constructivist theory replaced "information" with "constructs" within this model. However, for our purposes here, "information" is used, as it represents a factor that teachers can easily identify with as they view what students need and what teachers may help provide within typical classroom situations. The complete model has six variables, but only three are featured here due to space. For those desiring more details, please contact the author. See Robert J. Stahl, "Time Alone Does Not Mastery Make...", *op. cit.,* "Meeting the Challenges...", *op. cit.,* and "The Information-Constructivist (IC) Perspective: An Exclusively Psychological Constructivist Theory with a Sample of Implications for Curriculum and Instruction," paper presented at the annual meeting of the American Educational Research Association, San Diego, Calif., April 2004.

20. Sandra LeSourd, "Perspective Consciousness: A Practical Framework and Implications for Social Studies Education," *The International Journal of Social Education,* 16, 2(Fall/Winter 2001).

21. See Robert J. Stahl, "Time Alone Does Not Mastery Make...", *op. cit.,* "Meeting the Challenges...", *op. cit.,* and "The Information-Constructivist (IC) Perspective...", *op. cit.* See also Bloom, *Human Characteristics, op. cit.;* John B. Carroll, "The Carroll Model: A 25-Year Retrospective and Prospective View," *Educational Researcher* 18 (January/February 1989): 26-31; and Frank N. Dempster, "The Spacing Effect: A Case Study in the Failure to Apply the Results of Psychological Research," *American Psychologist* 43 (1988): 627-34, and "Synthesis of Research on Reviews and Tests," *Educational Leadership* 44, no. 7 (April 1991): 71-76 for a similar claim pertaining only to the time variable.

22. Bloom, *Human Characteristics, op. cit.*

# PART TWO
# CONCEPTUAL FRAMEWORK, PHILOSOPHY AND RESEARCH

# CHAPTER 3

# Implementing Cooperative Learning in Social Studies Classrooms
## A Conceptual Framework and Alternative Approaches

**David W. Johnson** and **Roger T. Johnson**, University of Minnesota, Minneapolis, Minnesota

Two are better than one, because they have a good reward for toil. For if they fall, one will lift up his fellow; but woe to him who is alone when he falls and has not another to lift him up... And though a man might prevail against one who is alone, two will withstand him. A threefold cord is not quickly broken.

ECCLESIASTICS 4:9-12

**Cooperative learning is an old idea**, or as some social studies teachers might say, "cooperative learning has a long history." The Talmud clearly states that in order to learn you must have a learning partner. In the first century, Quintillion argued that students could benefit from teaching one another. The Roman philosopher Seneca advocated cooperative learning through such statements as, *qui docet discet* (when you teach, you learn twice). Johann Amos Comenius, in the seventeenth century, believed that students would benefit from both teaching and being taught by other students. In the late 1700s, Joseph Lancaster and Andrew Bell made extensive use of cooperative learning groups in England, and the idea was brought to the United States when a Lancastrian school was opened in New York City in 1806. Within the Common School Movement in the United States in the early 1800s there was a strong emphasis on cooperative learning. In the last three decades of the nineteenth century, Colonel Francis Parker brought to his advocacy of cooperative learning enthusiasm, idealism, practicality, and an intense devotion to freedom, democracy, and individuality in the public schools. His fame and success rested on his power to create a classroom atmosphere that was truly cooperative and democratic. Parker's advocacy of cooperation among students dominated U.S. education through the turn of the century.

Following Parker, John Dewey promoted the use of cooperative learning groups as part of his famous project method

in instruction. In the late 1930s, however, schools began to emphasize interpersonal competition. In the late 1960s, individualistic learning began to be used extensively. After fifty years of exploring competitive and individualistic learning, and after numerous research studies demonstrating the efficacy of cooperative learning, schools in the United States are returning to cooperative learning.

### Enabling Definitions
*Cooperation* is defined as working together to accomplish shared goals. Within cooperative activities in the social studies classroom, individual students seek outcomes that are beneficial to themselves and beneficial to all other group members.

*Cooperative learning* is defined as instructionally using small groups so that students work together to maximize their own and each other's learning.[1] Within cooperative learning groups, students are given two responsibilities: to learn the assigned material and to make sure that all other members of their group do likewise. In cooperative learning situations, students perceive that they can reach their learning goals only if the other students in their learning group also achieve the goals. Students discuss the social studies material with each other, help each other to understand it, assist each other in using the information and abilities appropriately, and encourage each other to work hard.

Cooperative learning groups may be used to teach specific content (formal cooperative learning groups), to ensure active cognitive processing of information during a lecture (informal cooperative learning groups), and to provide long-term support and assistance for academic progress (cooperative base groups) in the classroom.[2] Any assignment in any curriculum for a student of any age can be done cooperatively.

## The Effectiveness of Cooperative Learning

Teachers can use cooperative learning with confidence at every grade level, in every subject area, and with any task. Research participants have varied as to economic class, age, sex, nationality, and cultural background. A wide variety of research tasks, ways of structuring cooperation, and measures of the dependent variables have been used. Many research workers with markedly varying orientations working in various settings, countries, and decades have conducted the research. The research findings on appropriately-implemented cooperative learning groups are both valid and generalizable to a degree rarely found in the educational literature.

We know a lot about cooperative learning and we have known it for some time. Since 1898, more than 550 experimental and 100 correlational research studies have been conducted on cooperative, competitive, and individualistic efforts. We know more about cooperative learning than we do about lecturing, age grouping, departmentalization, inquiry teaching, critical thinking, starting reading at age six, or the fifty-minute period. We know more about cooperative learning than about almost any other aspect of education.

We know that productive cooperation is a generic human endeavor that affects many instructional outcomes simultaneously. Research over the past century focused on such diverse outcomes as achievement, higher-level reasoning, retention, achievement motivation, intrinsic motivation, transfer of learning, interpersonal attraction, social support, friendships, prejudice, valuing differences, social support, self-esteem, social competencies, psychological health, and moral reasoning. These numerous outcomes may be subsumed within three broad categories: effort to achieve, positive interpersonal relationships, and psychological health (see Figure 1).[3]

Working cooperatively with peers, and valuing cooperation, results in greater psychological health and higher self-esteem than does competing with peers or working independently.[4] Personal ego-strength, self-confidence, independence, and autonomy are all promoted by being involved in cooperative efforts with caring people, who are committed to each other's success and

## Figure 1: Outcomes of Cooperation

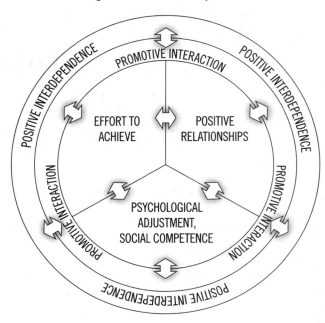

Reprinted with permission from: David T. Johnson and Roger T. Johnson, *Cooperation and Competition: Theory and Research.* Edina, MN: Interaction Book Company, 1989.

well being, and who respect each other as separate and unique individuals. The more individuals work productively as well as cooperatively with others, the more they see themselves as worthwhile and as having value.

The powerful effects of productive cooperation on such diverse outcomes make it important that educators understand the different approaches to implementing cooperative learning. Knowing that cooperative learning can significantly increase a wide variety of instructional outcomes (compared with competitive and individualistic learning) when properly implemented does not mean, however, that all operationalizations of cooperative learning will be effective or that all operationalizations will be equally effective. An examination of the different approaches to cooperative learning needs to be conducted.

## Classifying the Cooperative Learning Methods

One of the strengths of cooperative learning is the diversity of methods for implementing it in schools. Each of numerous modern methods has its strengths and weaknesses. Methods of cooperative learning have been and may be classified by:

*Researcher-developer:* Cooperative learning methods that are defined by individuals who developed a specific approach to cooperative learning and directly involved themselves in both researching and implementing the approach.

*Essential elements:* Cooperative learning methods that are defined by the hypothesized essential elements that must be contained in a cooperative procedure in order for it to work.

*Implementation assumptions:* Cooperative learning methods that are defined by the assumptions made about teacher training and the implementation of cooperative learning.

## A. Researcher-Developer

The primary, most common, method is that of the researcher-developer. Numerous teachers invent new ways of using cooperative learning daily. Many researchers have contributed to our understanding of the power and dynamics of cooperative learning. It is the researcher-developers, however, who developed cooperative learning procedures, conducted programs of research and evaluation to assess the method's effectiveness, and then involved themselves in teacher-training programs. These research-developers are commonly credited as the creators of modern-day cooperative learning.

The largest number of cooperative procedures have been created and researched by the Johns Hopkins Center for Social Organization of Schools. Their methods began with David DeVries and Keith Edwards' *Teams-Games-Tournament* (TGT) and continued with Robert Slavin's *Student-Teams-Achievement Divisions* (STAD) and *Team-Assisted Instruction* (TAI) and with Robert Stevens's *Cooperative-Integrated-Reading-and-Composition* (CIRC). The authors of this chapter have developed two cooperative learning procedures, known as *Learning Together* and *Academic Structured Controversy*. Working primarily in Israel, the Sharans developed *Group Investigation*. Aronson and his colleagues formalized the Jigsaw procedure, Stahl and his colleagues[5] the *Group Decision Making Episodes* model, Steinbrink and associates[6] and Cohen developed her *Complex Instruction* approach.[7] Spencer Kagan summarized the largest number of cooperative procedures in his book, *Cooperative Structures Methods*, but although he has conducted research on cooperative learning he has conducted no specific research on his cooperative structures. Elizabeth Cohen has conducted research on expectation-states theory as a way of organizing cooperative learning and has researched complex instruction, but unfortunately not in a way from which effect-sizes could be computed.

## B. Essential Elements: What Makes Cooperation Work?

A second way to classify the cooperative learning procedures is by the posited essential elements. Simply placing students in groups and telling them to work together does not in and of itself result in cooperative efforts. There are many ways in which group efforts may go wrong. Seating students together can result in competition at close quarters or individualistic efforts with talking. Teachers need to master the essential elements of cooperation for at least three reasons. First, teachers need to understand the essential elements that make cooperation work in order to implement cooperative learning effectively. Second, teachers need to tailor cooperative learning to their unique instructional needs, circumstances, curricula, subject areas, and students. Third, teachers need to diagnose the problems some students may have in working together and intervene to increase the effectiveness of the student learning groups.

Four of the researcher-developers have posited that certain conditions are necessary in order for cooperative learning to work. The differences in theoretical and practical orientations among the researcher-developers are highlighted by these posited conditions. The authors, with the help of their colleagues and students, have conducted a long-term program of research to identify the basic elements of cooperative learning.[8] Robert Slavin conducted a review of research to validate his two elements.[9] Stahl expanded the original list of essential elements to a much larger number.[10] Kagan and Cohen have not conducted research to validate their basic elements. From the Johnsons' theorizing, the basic elements of effective cooperative efforts are positive interdependence, face-to-face promotive interaction, individual and group accountability, appropriate use of social skills, and group processing.

Social studies teachers with real expertise in using cooperative learning structure five essential elements into their instructional activities. Well-structured and poorly-structured cooperative learning lessons in social studies classrooms at all levels can be distinguished on the basis of these elements. These essential elements, furthermore, should be carefully structured within all levels of cooperative efforts. Five essential elements are described below:[11]

1. *Positive interdependence.* The heart of cooperative learning is positive interdependence. Students must believe that they sink or swim together. Within every cooperative lesson, positive goal interdependence must be established through mutual learning goals. Teachers must structure the group and the group task so that all students learn the assigned material

and make sure that their groupmates learn the assigned material. Positive interdependence can be strengthened in three ways: (a) providing joint rewards (e.g., if all members of a group score 90 percent correct or better on the test, each receives five bonus points); (b) dividing resources equally among all members; and (c) assigning complementary roles to each member (e.g., reader, checker, encourager, and elaborator).

2. *Face-to-face promotive interaction.* Once teachers establish positive interdependence, they must ensure that students interact to help each other accomplish the task and promote each other's success. Students are expected to discuss what they are learning, explain to each other how to solve the assigned problems or complete the assignments, and provide each other with assistance, support, and encouragement. Silent students are uninvolved students who are not contributing to their groupmates' or their own learning. Promoting each other's success results in both higher achievement and in getting to know each other on both a personal and a professional level.

3. *Individual accountability.* The purpose of cooperative learning groups is to make each student stronger in his or her own right. Students learn together so that they can subsequently perform better as individuals. To ensure that each member is strengthened, teachers hold students individually accountable for doing their share of the work. The teacher assesses each student's performance and returns the results to the group and the individual. It is 'important that the group knows who needs more assistance, support, and encouragement in completing the assignment. It is also important that group members know they cannot hitchhike on the work of others.

4. *Social skills.* Contributing to the success of a cooperative effort requires interpersonal and small-group skills. Placing socially unskilled individuals in a group and telling them to cooperate does not guarantee that they will be able to do so effectively. Students must be taught social skills for high-quality collaboration and then motivated to use these skills. They also must be taught leadership, decision making, trust building, communication, and conflict-management skills just as purposefully and precisely as academic skills.

5. *Group processing.* Teachers need to ensure that members of each cooperative learning group discuss how well they are achieving their goals and maintaining effective working relationships. Groups need to describe which member's actions are helpful and which are unhelpful, and make decisions about which behaviors to continue or change. Appropriate processing enables learning groups to focus on group maintenance, facilitates the learning of social skills, ensures that members receive feedback on their participation, and reminds students to practice collaborative skills consistently. Five keys to successful processing are (a) allowing sufficient time for processing to take place, (b) making processing specific rather than vague, (c) maintaining student involvement in processing, (d) reminding students to use their social skills while they process, and (e) ensuring the teacher has communicated clear expectations about the purpose of processing.

Social studies educators need to learn to implement the essential elements of cooperation for at least two reasons. First, they need to tailor cooperative learning to their unique instructional needs, circumstances, curricula, subject areas, and students. Second, they need to diagnose any problems students have in working together and intervene to increase the effectiveness of the student learning groups. Simply placing students in groups and telling them to work together does not in and of itself result in cooperative efforts or positive effects on students. Group efforts may go wrong for many reasons. Seating students together but working primarily alone can result in competition at close quarters or give way to individualistic efforts with talking added. Teachers must understand the essential elements of cooperation if they are to implement cooperative learning successfully. Teachers need enough training and practice on the essential elements of cooperation to become educational engineers who can take their existing lessons, curricula, and courses and structure them cooperatively.

Conceptual understanding and skillful use of cooperative learning are two sides of the same teaching expertise coin. Theory is the cutting edge of practice. Through the attainment of conceptual understanding of how to teach, true teaching genius can emerge and be expressed. The complexity and promise of conceptually understanding cooperative learning make adherence to the guidelines for implementing cooperative learning essential. In short, unless social studies teachers follow the guidelines and criteria, they should not expect to obtain the multitude of positive results cooperative-learning strategies can achieve. Once social studies teachers understand and learn the essential elements of cooperative learning, they can fine-tune and adapt it to their specific circumstances, needs, and students.

## C. Implementation Assumptions

A third way of classifying cooperative learning procedures is according to the assumptions made about the nature of teaching and how best to train teachers. Teachers may be trained to be technicians who implement very specific procedures (a direct approach) or engineers who design their own cooperative lessons (a conceptual approach).

a) *Direct Applications*. A direct application is a prepackaged strategy, script, structure, lesson, or curriculum that is used in a lock-step, prescribed manner. Teachers are trained to conduct a specific cooperative learning lesson, how to use a specific cooperative learning curriculum, or how to use a specific cooperative learning strategy. These direct applications are basically atheoretical. The goal of the direct approaches is to train teachers to use lock-step (step 1, step 2, step 3), prescribed procedures and curriculum materials that have been successfully used in another classroom (i.e., idiographic knowledge). Teachers are told what the specific lesson, script/strategy, or curriculum is, it is demonstrated or modeled, and then the teacher practices the procedure. Such training assumes that the same strategy, curriculum, or lesson is equally effective in all schools because all classrooms and students are basically the same, that teachers need to know only the steps involved in using cooperative learning, and that, given enough practice, they will become skillful technicians.

Direct cooperative learning methods tend to be atheoretical and developed from practical experience. The research conducted on the methods is typically aimed at demonstrating the effectiveness of the procedure or curriculum. The strengths of the direct methods are that they are easy to teach and implement. A weakness is that they do not enable teachers to be flexible in their implementations and to adapt cooperative learning to new problems. Direct methods tend to be static in that once formulated they remain fixed. Cooperative scripts/structures have been developed by Kagan among others.[12] More complex cooperative strategies were developed by Aronson and his associates,[13] Stahl and his associates,[14] the Sharans[15] and others. Cooperative lessons have been developed by practitioners such as Burns.[16] Cooperative curriculums have been developed by Slavin and others.[17]

Direct approaches have value within the context of long-term implementation of a training program emphasizing conceptual understanding of the essential elements of well-structured cooperative lessons. Without the conceptual context, direct approaches are, in the long run, inadequate at best and counterproductive at worst. Simply presenting a theoretical framework, on the other hand, is also inadequate. An effective training program requires a combination of a conceptual understanding of the essential elements of cooperative learning, concrete examples of lessons and strategies, opportunities for practice with feedback, and implementation over an extended period of time in the teacher's own classroom.

b) *Conceptual Applications*. A conceptual application is an expert system of how to implement cooperative learning that is used to create a unique adaptation to an educator's specific circumstances, students, and needs. Conceptual applications are based on theory that is validated by research and operationalized into practical procedures through the elements identified as essential to cooperative efforts. The conceptual frameworks are developed from theory and the research conducted on them is aimed at validating theory as well as the procedure. Conceptual methods tend to be dynamic in that they are changed and modified on the basis of new research and refinements of the theory. Conceptual applications assume that each teacher faces a complex and unique combination of circumstances, students, and needs and, therefore, cooperative learning needs to be adapted and refined to uniquely fit each teacher's situations. Teachers are taught both a conceptual understanding of cooperative learning (its nature and essential components) and the skills to use that understanding to uniquely tailor cooperative learning lessons, strategies, and curriculum units for their specific students and circumstances. The conceptual approach requires social studies teachers to learn both a conceptual understanding of cooperative learning (its nature and essential components) and the skills to use that understanding to plan and teach cooperative learning lessons, strategies, and curriculum units uniquely tailored to their specific students and circumstances. In addition, by understanding and skillfully implementing the essential elements, teachers are able to think creatively about cooperative learning and to produce any number of strategies and lessons.

The goal of the conceptual approach is for teachers to take any activity, lesson, unit, or curriculum and transform it into a cooperative learning experience automatically, at a routine-use level (where they can automatically structure a lesson cooperatively without preplanning or conscious thought). In essence, teachers are taught an expert system of how to implement cooperative learning that they use to create unique adaptations. Teacher expertise is reflected in the ability to:

▶ take any lesson in any subject area and structure it cooperatively.

- practice using cooperative learning strategies and essential elements until they are at a routine and integrated level of use and implement cooperative learning at least 60 percent of the time in their classrooms.
- describe precisely what they are doing and why they are doing it in order to (a) communicate to others the nature of cooperative learning and (b) teach them how to implement cooperative learning in their classrooms and settings.
- apply the principles of cooperation to other settings, such as collegial relationships and faculty meetings.

The most highly conceptual approaches to cooperative learning have been developed by Elizabeth Cohen and the authors of this chapter.[18] Cohen bases her conceptual principles on expectation-states theory while we base our conceptual principles on the theory of cooperation and competition Morton Deutsch built from Kurt Lewin's field theory. The strengths of the conceptual approach include that once integrated into a teacher's practices, it becomes part of the teacher's professional identity and is maintained throughout the teacher's career. Weaknesses include that conceptual methods are difficult to learn and initially apply.

The conceptual approach is used in all technological arts and crafts. An engineer designing a bridge, for example, applies validated theory to the unique problems imposed by the need for a bridge of a certain length, to carry specific loads, from a bank of one unique geological character to a bank of another unique geological character, in an area with specific winds, temperatures, and susceptibility to earthquakes. Teachers engage in the same process by (a) learning a conceptualization of essential components of cooperative learning and (b) applying that conceptual model to their unique teaching situations, circumstances, students, and instructional needs. The conceptual approach to implementing cooperative learning is based on theory that is validated by research and made operational through the elements identified as essential to cooperative efforts.

## Contrasting Direct and Conceptual Approaches

We might place approaches to implementing cooperative learning within social studies classrooms on a continuum with conceptual applications at one end and direct applications at the other. Conceptual applications are based on an interaction among theory, research, and practice. Teachers are taught a general conceptual model of cooperative learning that they use to tailor cooperative learning specifically to their circumstances, students, and needs. In essence, teachers are taught an expert system of how

to implement cooperative learning to create a unique adaptation. Direct applications are packaged lessons, curricula, and strategies that teachers use in a prescribed manner. The direct approach may be divided into three subcategories: strategy, curriculum package, and lesson approaches.

Essentially, the conceptual approach requires social studies teachers to be engineers who adapt cooperative learning to their specific circumstances, students, and needs. Direct approaches train teachers to be technicians who use the cooperative learning curriculum or strategy without understanding how it works. As engineers, teachers can solve implementation problems and adapt cooperative learning to their specific circumstances, students, and needs. As technicians they cannot. The development of expertise in using cooperative learning depends on understanding cooperation conceptually. The conceptual approach promotes a personal commitment by teachers to cooperative learning as they adapt it to their situations. The direct approach does not.

When social studies teachers gain expertise in cooperative learning through conceptual understanding, they become independent of outside experts and can generate new lessons and strategies as the need arises. They can also transfer their use of cooperative learning to improve cooperative collegial relationships, staff meetings, relationships with parents, and committees. They become important figures in the staff development process as they train their colleagues to use cooperative learning.

### Implementing the Johnson and Johnson Cooperative Learning Methods: A Brief Overview With Guidelines
#### A. Implementing the Learning Together Method
The authors created three interrelated procedures for using cooperative learning. Cooperative learning groups may be used to teach specific content (formal cooperative learning groups), to ensure active cognitive processing of information during a lecture or demonstration (informal cooperative learning groups), and to provide long-term support and assistance for academic progress (cooperative base groups). Any assignment in any curriculum for any age student can be done cooperatively.[19]

1. *Formal Cooperative Learning.* Formal cooperative learning consists of students working together, for one class period to several weeks, to achieve shared learning goals and jointly complete specific tasks and assignments (such as decision making or problem solving, completing a curriculum unit, writing a report, conducting a survey or experiment, or reading a chapter or reference book, learning vocabulary, or answering questions at the end of the chapter).[20] Any course requirement or assignment

may be reformulated to be cooperative. In formal cooperative learning groups, teachers:

- ▶ Make a number of preinstructional decisions. A teacher has to decide on the objectives (academic and social skills) for the lesson, size of groups, the method of assigning students to groups, the roles students will be assigned, the materials needed to conduct the lesson, and the way the room will be arranged.
- ▶ Explain the task and the positive interdependence. A teacher clearly defines the assignment, teaches the required concepts and strategies, specifies the positive interdependence and individual accountability, gives the criteria for success, and explains the targeted social skills students are to engage in.
- ▶ Monitor students' learning and intervene within the groups to provide task assistance or to increase students' interpersonal and group skills. A teacher systematically observes and collects data on each group as it works. When it is needed, the teacher intervenes to assist students in completing the task accurately and in working together effectively.
- ▶ Assess students' learning and help them process how well their groups functioned. Students' learning is carefully assessed and their performances are evaluated. Members of the learning groups then process how effectively they have been working together.

Teachers create formal cooperative learning groups to complete specific tasks and assignments such as learning material from a textbook, writing reports or themes, investigating and explaining historical events, and reading and interpreting documents, graphs, books, or news articles. Using this type of cooperative group, the teacher introduces the lesson, assigns students to groups of two to five members, gives students the materials they need to complete the assignment, and assigns roles to individual students. The teacher then explains the task, teaches any concepts or procedures the students need to know to complete the assignment, and structures the cooperation among students. Students work on the assignment until all group members successfully understand the material and complete the group's task. While the students work together, the teacher moves from group to group systematically monitoring their interaction. The teacher intervenes when students do not understand the academic task or when problems arise from working together. After the groups complete the assignment, the teacher evaluates the academic success of each student and has the groups discuss

how well they functioned as a team. In working cooperatively, students realize they have a stake in each other's success; they become mutually responsible for each other's learning.

*2. Informal Cooperative Learning Groups.* Informal cooperative learning consists of having students work together to achieve a joint learning goal in temporary, ad-hoc groups that last from a few minutes to one class period.[21] During a lecture, demonstration, or film, informal cooperative learning can be used to (a) focus student attention on the material to be learned, (b) set a mood conducive to learning, (c) help set expectations as to what will be covered in a class session, (d) ensure that students cognitively process the material being taught, and (e) provide closure to an instructional session. During direct teaching the instructional challenge for the teacher is to ensure that students do the intellectual work of organizing material, explaining it, summarizing it, and integrating it into existing conceptual structures.

Informal cooperative learning groups are often organized so that students engage in three-to-five minute focused discussions before and after a lecture and two-to-three minute turn-to-your-partner discussions interspersed throughout a lecture. The teacher's roles are:

- ▶ *Focused Discussion 1*: Plan a lecture around a series of questions that the lecture answers. Prepare the questions on an overhead transparency or write them on the board so students can see them. Students will discuss the questions in pairs. The discussion task is aimed at promoting advance organizing of what the students know about the topic to be presented and creates an expectation set and a learning mood conductive to learning.
- ▶ *Turn-To-Your-Partner Discussions*: Divide the lecture into 10 to 15 minute segments. Plan a short discussion task to be given to pairs of students after each segment. The task needs to be short enough so that students can complete it within three or four minutes. Its purpose is to ensure that students are actively thinking about the material being presented. It is important that students are randomly called on to share their answers after each discussion task. Such individual accountability ensures that the pairs take the tasks seriously and check each other to ensure that both are prepared to answer. Each discussion task should have four components: formulate an answer to the question being asked, share your answer with your partner, listen carefully to his or her answer, and create a new answer that is superior to each member's initial formulation through the

processes of association, building on each other's thoughts, and synthesizing. Students will need to gain some experience with this procedure to become skilled in doing it within a short period of time.

▶ *Focused Discussion 2*: Give students an ending discussion task to provide closure to the lecture. Usually students are given five or six minutes to summarize and discuss the material covered in the lecture. The discussion should result in students integrating what they have just learned into existing conceptual frameworks. The task may also point students toward what the homework will cover or what will be presented in the next class session. Until students become familiar and experienced with the procedure, process it regularly to help them increase their skill and speed in completing short discussion tasks.

3. *Base Groups.* Base groups are long-term, heterogeneous cooperative learning groups with stable membership. The primary responsibility of members is to provide each other with the support, encouragement, and assistance they need to make academic progress. The base group verifies that each member is completing the assignments and progressing satisfactorily through the academic program. Base groups may be given the task of letting absent group members know what went on in the class when they miss a session and bring them up to date. The use of base groups tends to improve attendance, personalize the work required and the school experience, and improve the quality and quantity of learning. The base group provides permanent and caring peer relationships in which students are committed to and support each other's educational success. Base groups last for at least a semester or year and preferably for several years. The larger the class and the more complex the subject matter, the more important it is to have base groups. Receiving social support and being held accountable for appropriate behavior by peers who care about you and have a long-term commitment to your success and well-being is an important aspect of growing up and progressing through school.

4. *Integrated Use Of All Three Goal Structures.* When used in combination, these formal, informal, and base cooperative learning groups provide an overall structure to classroom life. A typical class session may begin with a base group meeting followed by a short lecture utilizing informal cooperative learning followed by a formal cooperative lesson followed by a summary lecture with informal cooperative learning followed by a closing base group meeting.[22]

### B. Implementing the Academic Controversy Method

In addition to these three types of cooperative learning, we have operationalized a procedure for creating intellectual conflict. Controversy exists when one individual's ideas, information, conclusions, theories, and opinions are incompatible with those of another, and the two seek to reach an agreement.[23] Being confronted with opposing points of view creates uncertainty or conceptual conflict, which creates a reconceptualization and an information search, which results in a more refined and thoughtful conclusion along with a variety of other important outcomes, such as the use of higher-level reasoning strategies and the long-term retention of what is learned. The teacher structures academic controversy by requiring students to (a) organize what is known into a position, (b) advocate that position to someone who is advocating the opposing position, (c) attempt to refute the opposing position while rebutting the attacks on one's own position, (d) reverse perspectives so that the issue may be seen from both points of view simultaneously, and (e) create a synthesis to which all sides can agree.

### C. Implementing Other Aspects Of Cooperative Learning

In addition to the general procedures to use cooperative learning, we have developed procedures for teaching social skills,[24] instituting a conflict resolution and peer mediation program based on teaching all students how to engage in problem-solving negotiations and mediate conflicts,[25] assessing and evaluating student learning,[26] structuring positive interdependence,[27] and managing the school environment and dealing with discipline problems.[28]

### Gaining Expertise in Using Cooperative Learning

In order for social studies teachers to implement cooperative learning at a routine-use level (where they can automatically structure a lesson cooperatively without preplanning or conscious thought), they need to gain experience in a step-by-step manner. They need progressively to refine their competencies by

▶ *Planning and teaching* a cooperative lesson;

▶ *Assessing* the strengths and weaknesses of the lesson;

▶ *Reflecting* on how to improve their teaching in the next lesson (thus clarifying the teacher's conceptual understanding);

▶ *Planning and teaching* a second cooperative lesson with the modifications suggested by the feedback received about the first; and

▶ *Assessing* the strengths and weaknesses of the second lesson, reflecting on how to improve their teaching on the next lesson, and teaching the third lesson. This process should be repeated continually until the person retires from teaching.

Social studies teachers must engage in cooperative learning for some time before they begin to gain expertise. This usually requires support, encouragement, and assistance from colleagues. Transfer and maintenance, therefore, depend largely on teachers organizing themselves into cooperative teams and collegial support groups that focus on helping all members progressively improve their competence in using cooperative learning.

## Summary and Conclusions

As described here, appropriate cooperative learning is a complex instructional procedure that requires conceptual knowledge as well as the skills of using specific lessons, curricula, and strategies. If cooperative learning is going to be institutionalized within a social studies department, school or district, teachers must become experts in the conceptual system of understanding how to structure cooperative lessons and how to solve the problems of adapting cooperative learning to their specific circumstances, students, and needs. Simply presenting or reading about this theoretical framework and the practical guidelines is not enough. There are no quick solutions or shortcuts to becoming an effective cooperative learning social studies educator.

Finally, gaining expertise in cooperative learning ultimately requires years of effort. Such long-term training and implementation programs require a support system. Collegial support groups at the building level and cooperative learning within the classroom go together. Each enhances the effectiveness of the other. 🔊

## NOTES

1. David W. Johnson, Roger T. Johnson, and Edythe J. Holubec, *Circles of Learning*, 3rd ed. (Edina, Minn.: Interaction Book Company, 1990), and *The New Circles of Learning: Cooperation in the Classroom and School* (Alexandria, VA: Association for Supervision and Curriculum Development, 1994).

2. *Ibid.*

3. David W. Johnson and Roger T. Johnson, *Cooperation and Competition: Theory and Research* (Edina, Minn.: Interaction Book Company, 1989).

4. *Ibid.*

5. Robert J. Stahl, Pamela Hronek, Amendia Shoemake-Netto, and Nancy Comstock Webster-Miller, *Doorways to the Past: Decision Making Episodes for the Study of History and the Humanities* (Tucson, Ariz.: Zephyr Press, 1995); J. Doyle Casteel and Robert J. Stahl. *Doorways to Decision Making: A Handbook for Teaching Decision Making Strategies* (Waco, Tex.: Prufrock Press, 1997); Robert J. Stahl and Nancy N. Stahl, *Society and Science: Decision Making Episodes for Exploring Society, Science and Technology* (Menlo Park, Calif.: Addison-Wesley Innovative Press, 1995).

6. Jones, R. M., and Steinbrink, J. E. "Concept Learning Strategies: Using Cooperative Groups in Science and Social Studies," *Southwest Journal of Educational Research into Practice*, 2, (1988): 43-49; John E. Steinbrink, and Robert J. Stahl, "Jigsaw III = Jigsaw II + Cooperative Test Review: Applications to the Social Studies Classroom," in *Cooperative Learning in Social Studies: A Handbook for Teachers*, edited by Robert J. Stahl (Menlo Park, Calif.: Addison-Wesley, 1994): 133-153.

7. Elizabeth G. Cohen, *Designing Groupwork: Strategies for Heterogeneous Classrooms* (New York: Teachers College Press, 1986) and *Designing Groupwork: Strategies for Heterogeneous Classrooms*, 2nd edition (New York: Teachers College Press, 1994).

8. David W. Johnson and Roger T. Johnson, *Cooperation and Competition: Theory and Research*, op. cit., and "Cooperative Learning Methods: A Meta-analysis," *Journal of Research in Education*, 12, no. 1 ( 2002): 5-14.

9. Robert E. Slavin, *Using Student Team Learning* (Baltimore: Center for Research on Elementary and Middle Schools, Johns Hopkins University, 1986). See also Chapter 5 of the current volume.

10. Robert J. Stahl, "The Essential Elements for Optimal Cooperative Learning," paper presented at the annual meeting of the American Educational Research Association, Seattle, Washington, April 2001. See also Chapter 1 in this volume.

11. Stahl (*ibid.*) proposed a much larger number of essential elements that can be generated from the research and theoretical literature as well as from comments from numerous teachers who pointed to the same specific factors that seemed to them to consistently enhance or prevent students from achieving high levels of academic knowledge, concepts and abilities that were originally targeted for them to learn, achieve and retain beyond the end of a unit or term.

12. Spencer Kagan, *Cooperative Learning* (San Juan Capistrano, Calif.: Kagan Publishing, 1994).

13. Elliott Aronson, Nancy T. Blaney, Cookie Stephan, Jev Sikes, and Matthew Snapp, *The Jigsaw Classroom* (Beverly Hills, Calif.: Sage, 1978).

14. See Steinbrink and Stahl, *op. cit.* and Stahl, Hronek *et al., op. cit.*

15. Shlomo Sharan and Yael Sharan, *Small-Group Teaching* (Englewood Cliffs, N.J.: Educational Technology Publications, 1976).

16. Marilyn Burns, "Groups of Four: Solving the Management Problem," *Learning* (September 1981): 46-51.

17. Slavin, *Using Student Team Learning, op. cit.*

18. See Cohen, *Designing Groupwork*, op. cit.; David W. Johnson, *Social Psychology of Education* (New York: Holt, Rinehart, and Winston, 1970); David W. Johnson, Roger T. Johnson, and Edythe Holubec, *Cooperation in the Classroom*, 7th edition (Edina, Minn.: Interaction Book Company, 1998) and *Advanced Cooperative Learning*, 3rd edition (Edina, MN: Interaction Book Company, 1998).

19. See two chapters by Johnson and Johnson, "Learning Together in the Social Studies Classroom," and "The Pro-Con Cooperative Group Strategy: Structuring Academic Controversy Within the Social Studies Classroom," in *Cooperative Learning in Social Studies: A Handbook for Teachers*, edited by Robert J. Stahl (Menlo Park, Calif.: Addison Wesley. 1994); see also Johnson, Johnson and Holubec, *Advanced Cooperative Learning, op. cit.*

20. Johnson, Johnson and Holubec, *Advanced Cooperative Learning, op. cit.*

21. *Ibid.*

22. The integrated use of cooperative, competitive, and individualistic learning is described in depth in David W. Johnson and Roger T. Johnson, *Learning Together and Alone: Cooperative, Competitive, and Individualistic Learning*, 3rd edition (Englewood Cliffs, NJ: Prentice Hall, 1975/1999)

and Johnson, Johnson, and Holubec, *Advanced Cooperative Learning, op. cit.*

23. See Johnson and Johnson, "The Pro-Con Cooperative Group Strategy: Structuring Academic Controversy Within the Social Studies Classroom," *op. cit.* and *Creative Controversy: Intellectual Challenge in the Classroom* (Edina, Minn.: Interaction Book Company, 1995).

24. See David W. Johnson, *Reaching Out: Interpersonal Effectiveness and Self-Actualization,* 7th edition (Needham Heights, Mass.: Allyn & Bacon, 2000); David W. Johnson and Frank P. Johnson, *Joining Together: Group Theory and Group Skills,* 7th edition (Boston: Allyn & Bacon, 2000) and David W. Johnson and Roger T. Johnson, *Learning Together and Alone: Cooperative, Competitive, and Individualistic Learning,* 3rd edition (Englewood Cliffs, NJ: Prentice Hall, 1975/1999).

25. David W. Johnson and Roger T. Johnson, *Teaching Students to be Peacemakers,* 3rd edition (Edina, Minn.: Interaction Book Company, 1995).

26. David W. Johnson and Roger T. Johnson, *Meaningful and Manageable Assessment Through Cooperative Learning* (Edina, Minn.: Interaction Book Company, 1996).

27. David W. Johnson and Roger T. Johnson, *Positive Interdependence: The Heart of Cooperative Learning* (Edina, Minn.: Interaction Book Company, 1992) and the videotape *Positive Interdependence: The Heart of Cooperative Learning* (Edina, Minn.: Interaction Book Company, 1992).

28. Johnson and Johnson, *Learning Together and Alone, op. cit.*

# CHAPTER 4

# The Evidence from Classroom Research
## Cooperative Learning, When Properly Implemented, Is Highly Effective

**Ronald L. VanSickle**, The University of Georgia, Athens, Georgia

**The hoopla over cooperative learning** is not all hype with no substance. Hundreds of educational research and evaluation projects over the past three decades have documented that co-operative learning is a research and development success story. The findings of these studies show the instructional effectiveness of cooperative learning with students in classrooms at all grade levels and nearly every subject area. These research and evaluation efforts also have contributed to the refinement of cooperative-learning theory, requirements and models.[1] Further-more, inquiry into cooperative learning has clarified the essential conditions under which educators can reasonably expect their students to engage in productive, cooperative work in settings outside particular cooperative learning models. Consequently, social studies teachers have a considerable information base on which to decide (a) whether to use cooperative learning and particular cooperative group models, (b) which group models to try, and (c) how to properly implement cooperative learning and the cooperative group model(s) they select.

This chapter presents research findings on using coopera-tive groups and cooperative learning written in the form of a conversation between a teacher and a cooperative learning advocate. The author uses this format and style to translate the language of research writing into an informal style that focuses on issues that are important to social studies teachers.

**Teacher**: If I use small-group cooperative learning models to teach my students, can I expect my students to learn more historical and social scientific knowledge than they do with conventional whole-class and individual seatwork instructional procedures?

**Advocate**: In general, the answer is yes. Many research projects have been conducted to study the effects of coopera-tive learning models and activities on academic achievement in middle school and high school classrooms. The findings of most studies support the claim that appropriate cooperation usually produces higher levels of student achievement than competi-tive and individualistic instructional activities. The academic effectiveness of cooperative learning varies, however, with the specific group models selected and how well the teacher and students implement the group models.

**T**: If I try cooperative learning, I want to use the best group model. In terms of students' academic achievement, which cooperative learning group model is the most effective?

**A:** Data are available for comparing several cooperative learning group models. However, please be cautious. Selecting the "best" group model requires more criteria than just a comparison of each group model's overall achievement effects. Nevertheless, having information about the academic achievement results of a particular group model is valuable.

Slavin investigated the effects of the various cooperative learning group models on students' achievement by reviewing sixty-eight school-based experiments that compared cooperative learning with other methods.[2] He examined reported research findings on the following group models: Student Teams Achieve-ment Divisions (STAD), Teams-Games-Tournament (TGT), Team-Assisted Instruction (TAI), Cooperative Integrated Reading and Composition (CIRC), Learning Together, Jigsaw, and Group Investigation. He also reviewed a handful of studies focused on other, lesser-known group models. Taken together, the cooperative learning group models produced superior academic achievement in 72 percent of the experiments; only 12 percent showed superior effects for the noncooperative comparison instruction.[3]

Slavin's examination also allows a comparison of the ef-fectiveness of the cooperative learning group models reviewed in the sixty-eight experiments. Student Teams Achievement Divisions demonstrated superior achievement effects in 86 percent of the studies (18 of 21). Teams-Games-Tournament demonstrated superior effects in 75 percent of the studies (9 of 12). Team-Assisted Instruction and Cooperative Integrated Reading and Composition each showed superior effects in 100 percent of the studies (i.e., Team-Assisted Instruction in 5 of 5, and Cooperative Integrated Reading and Composition in 7 of 7). Learning Together demonstrated superior results in 56 percent of its studies (5 of 9). Jigsaw achieved superiority in only 25 percent of the studies (2 of 8). Group Investigation produced superior effects in 60 percent of the studies (3 of 5).

**T:** It looks like the research says Team-Assisted Instruction and Cooperative Integrated Reading and Composition are the best cooperative learning group models, followed by Student Teams Achievement Divisions. Do you agree?

**A:** The research evidence does not tell us which group models are the "best." Research reports are a source of information we must interpret in light of our educational goals and the realities of the environment in which we teach. Some of the group models were developed to teach specific types of subject matter. For instance, Team-Assisted Instruction was designed to teach mathematics, and Cooperative Integrated Reading and Composition was designed for particular areas of language arts instruction. Meanwhile, Student Teams Achievement Divisions and Teams-Games-Tournament appear to work best with objectives that focus on the recall, comprehension, and application of specific content and skills. Group Investigation, on the other hand, was designed for higher-cognitive learning but in many studies the students only focused on and were tested on recall and comprehension level abilities. Academic achievement is an important learning outcome, but affective goals such as interpersonal relationships are also important.

**T:** I am usually suspicious of research. New group models, for example, can show excellent results because students' motivational levels are high due to novelty and the special attention students receive in an experiment. Were these experiments conducted in laboratories or in schools under more or less real-life conditions that I might find in my own classroom?

**A:** Slavin reported that he selected the sixty-eight studies out of a considerably larger set of cooperative learning research reports. The sixty-eight studies satisfied the following conditions. First, they lasted over at least twenty hours of instructional time (i.e., four weeks of classes). This long time period reduced the likelihood of attributing the results to novelty or motivation because of special attention. Second, students in the cooperative learning classes and in the comparison treatment classes studied the same material to achieve the same objectives; none used placebo treatments. Third, the studies provided evidence that students in both the cooperative and comparison classes were strikingly similar at the beginning of the study. This standard was met through either random assignment of students to classes or pretests that showed the groups to be similar. Finally, achievement tests assessed the same objectives in both instructional treatments. Nearly all the studies were conducted in schools, some of which were in settings and under conditions that were a far cry from that found in most new suburban schools.

**T:** This research sounds good, but I have another question. People talk about statistical significance, but I am more concerned about practical significance. The difference between two groups of students could be statistically significant but the difference could be so small that it has no practical value. If I am going to try cooperative learning, I want to be sure I am aiming for an achievement effect that will justify the time and energy I must put into a new teaching approach. What evidence is there about the sizes of achievement effects?

**A:** Fortunately, evidence is available about magnitudes of effect. The concept of effect size will help us think about this question. In order to compare different studies using different tests, students, subject matter, and materials, it is helpful to examine how the distribution of student achievement scores in various instructional conditions differs. A number of effect size statistics exist. The one that Slavin and others like myself use tells us how much students' test score distributions differ according to standard deviation units.[4]

Slavin applied this effect size concept to the achievement results of fifty-one studies that provided enough data to compute effect sizes. Overall, the effect size was .21 standard deviation in favor of the cooperative learning group models. Another way of stating the meaning of this statistic is that 58 percent of the students who participated in a cooperative learning treatment scored above the mean score of students in the noncooperative treatment classes.

Of course, the effect sizes varied with the group model. In the Student Teams Achievement Divisions studies, 61 percent of the experimental students scored above the comparison students. In the Teams-Games-Tournament studies, 65 percent of the experimental students scored above the mean of the comparison students. The following are the percentages of cooperative learning students who scored above the mean of the comparison noncooperating students for the other group models: Team-Assisted Instruction/Cooperative Integrated Reading and

Composition, 58 percent above the mean; Learning Together, 50 percent; Jigsaw, 52 percent; and Group Investigation, 55 percent. Much variation in effect sizes existed among studies of the same group model; for example, Teams-Games-Tournament effect sizes varied from a low of 48 percent above the comparison group mean to 98 percent above.

If no difference existed between cooperative and noncooperative instruction, we would expect 50 percent of the cooperative learning students to be above the Mean of the students in the noncooperative classes and vice versa. How large an effect must exist to be practical and to be worthy of attention by classroom teachers? The answer to that question depends on the return you expect for the time and energy you invest in learning to implement a new instructional approach. Given two classes of students having similar characteristics and studying the same subject with the same materials, how would you feel if a new instructional approach used in one class caused 58 percent of that group to score above the mean of the other group? If that sounds good, then the new instructional approach would be worthwhile if the time and energy required to implement it were reasonable. The size of effect you require will influence which cooperative learning group models appeal to you.

**T:** Student Teams Achievement Divisions and Teams-Games-Tournament still look good because more than 60 percent of the cooperative-learning students scored above the mean of the comparison group students. Learning Together and Jigsaw show no superior achievement effect or only a tiny positive effect. If traditional teaching group models are just as good, why would anyone bother with them?

**A:** One reason for considering them is that a number of desirable attitudinal, interpersonal, or behavioral outcomes might accrue that students do not achieve through more conventional instruction. The lack of a practical, superior achievement effect, however, is puzzling. Mattingly and VanSickle were particularly curious about Jigsaw's apparent failure to produce student achievement superior to noncooperative instruction. They examined the Jigsaw experiments and discovered that nearly all used a form of Jigsaw that included neither rewards to groups nor individual accountability of students within groups.[5]

Group rewards and individual accountability are major characteristics of Student Teams Achievement Divisions, Teams-Games-Tournament, Team-Assisted Instruction, and Cooperative Integrated Reading and Composition. Slavin developed a form of Jigsaw, Jigsaw II, which implemented these conditions.[6] In Jigsaw II, each team of students receives a group reward determined by summing points each student earns as a result of individual achievement test scores. Mattingly and VanSickle conducted an experiment using Jigsaw II and observed a difference in favor of Jigsaw II with an effect size of .81 standard deviation; 79 percent of the Jigsaw II students scored above the mean of students who received the noncooperative group instruction. Group rewards and individual accountability strengthened Jigsaw's academic effect dramatically.[7]

Slavin reported that two of the Learning Together studies showed statistically significant positive results.[8] Both of those studies, unlike the studies Slavin reviewed, implemented Learning Together with individual accountability. Unfortunately, the two positive effect studies did not report data needed to compute effect sizes.

The absence of group rewards and individual accountability seems to solve the mystery regarding why Learning Together and Jigsaw did not show substantially stronger achievement effects in the studies reported by Slavin. Further analysis of Jigsaw and Learning Together supports Slavin's claim that cooperative learning group models need both to provide group rewards and to hold individual students accountable for individual learning. Students' motivation to work toward academic goals in their learning teams is likely to be greater when their rewards are a function of their team performance and when their individual contributions to the team's performance are obvious to their teammates. More research is needed, but it appears that if Learning Together and Jigsaw are modified to meet these two criteria, then they are likely to produce the superior academic effects of Student Teams Achievement Divisions, Teams-Games-Tournament, Team-Assisted Instruction, and Cooperative Integrated Reading and Composition.

**T:** I understand how the structure of cooperative learning groups can be important. The lack of group rewards and individual accountability also explains why many small-group activities I have tried have resulted in one or two students doing most of the work. One of the reasons less capable students might learn more in a cooperative learning class is that the more competent students help them to learn the material. Does that mean cooperative learning group models should be used only in heterogeneous ability classes? Are these models academically valuable in homogeneous ability classes? In low-ability classes?

**A:** We have little research on the effects of cooperative learning group models in homogeneously grouped, low-ability classes. Allen and VanSickle used Student Teams Achievement Divisions and compared a low-ability 9th grade class with a class using whole-class and individual seatwork activities.[9] The mean IQ in each class was 75. The Student Teams Achievement Divisions students outscored the comparison students by 11.7 percent for an effect size of .94 standard deviation; 83 percent of the cooperative learning students scored above the mean of the comparison class. In light of the more general findings, Allen and VanSickle's study suggests that the motivational effect of the cooperative organization was strong enough to increase the learning effectiveness of the students in their study even in the absence of more capable students.

**T:** Do cooperative learning group models work better with some types of students than others?

**A:** A few studies address the question of interaction between cooperative instructional treatments and student characteristics. According to Slavin, Student Teams Achievement Divisions and Teams-Games-Tournament work equally well in rural, suburban, and urban settings.[10] Although both African-American and European-American students tend to perform at higher levels with cooperative instruction when compared to noncooperative instruction, African-American students tend to demonstrate a greater difference in favor of cooperative learning.[11] In terms of high, average, and low achievers, those who benefit most from cooperative learning vary from study to study.[12] One study reported that students who preferred to cooperate achieved higher scores through cooperative learning than students who preferred to compete.[13] The reverse was true in competitively structured instruction. Given the few studies addressing student-treatment interactions, we must interpret these findings cautiously.

**T:** So far most of what you have said focuses on students' academic progress or achievement. What are your reasons for paying so much attention to academic test scores?

**A:** Remember that what distinguishes cooperative learning from typical group work and just having groups that cooperate is that the major purpose of cooperative learning is for every member of every group to achieve the highest level of academic learning that is possible for him or her to achieve. In other words, the primary focus of all cooperative learning activities and groups is to maximize the academic learning of all group members. The reason why this is so is that in true cooperative learning, the focus of every group member is on the learning and the achieving, and the cooperating and the group are only means to maximize the quality of the learning. You put students in groups and have them work in and as cooperative groups to increase their academic learning. You do not have them work together and cooperate with one another just for the sake of having them cooperate.

Consequently, if cooperative learning is indeed occurring and is effective, students should learn at a very high level and should score high on tests to measure their academic achievement. Because academic achievement is so vital to the purpose and success of cooperative learning efforts, it stands to reason that if students are not achieving academically, then something is amiss in the implementation effort or in the conditions within which the students and groups are working. Remember earlier I pointed out that when Slavin found that student scores following standard jigsaw activities were no higher and sometimes lower than scores of students in nonjigsaw classrooms, he concluded that things were missing in the jigsaw classrooms that were inconsistent with ensuring students actually were spending their time and cooperative efforts to maximize their learning or academic achievement. When he added some of these missing elements, his new Jigsaw II model was found to consistently produce the high levels of academic achievement he expected. Like Slavin, you should expect first and foremost much higher levels of academic achievement than you are getting from nongroup activities. Promise that if you put students in groups primarily to have them cooperate or to complete assignments in groups where they might learn something, don't call these cooperative learning groups and what you are doing as cooperative learning. True cooperative learning is much, much more and results in actual high levels of academic achievement, not just some learning.

**T:** I've heard the cooperative learning is not good for high achieving students, especially gifted students. In fact several teachers told me that cooperative learning holds these students back because they have to waste their time serving as personal teachers or tutors to slow students. Is this true?

**A:** Well, when cooperative learning is not implemented properly and the teacher doesn't emphasize academic achievement, this can happen. But then, any method or model of teaching that is improperly implemented without an academic focus will result in little learning by almost every student, including high achievers and gifted students. Now to address your concerns directly, in the words of Bob Slavin, one of the major theorists and researchers in this area, there is "absolutely no support for this claim." In fact, "high achievers gain from cooperative learning relative to high achievers in traditional classes just as much as do low and average achievers."[14]

**T:** In addition to academic achievement, what kinds of affective outcomes do cooperative learning group models produce?[15]

**A:** Students in cooperative learning settings tend to develop more positive relationships with students of both similar and dissimilar ethnic backgrounds.[16] In fact, a major motivation for developing Student Teams Achievement Divisions and Teams-Games-Tournament was to improve race relations in desegregated schools. The benefits are generalizable, however, beyond African-American and European-American students in U.S. schools. Jigsaw II, for example, generated more cross-ethnic friendships among native Anglo-Canadian students, West Indian immigrants, and European immigrants.[17] In Israel, Group Investigation and Student Teams Achievement Divisions seemed to boost more positive cross-ethnic attitudes between Jewish students of Middle Eastern and European backgrounds.[18]

In mainstreamed classrooms, academically-handicapped students are frequently rejected by their nonhandicapped peers. Cooperative learning group models usually can help improve student relationships in this context as well. Madden and Slavin observed that nonhandicapped students in Student Teams Achievement Divisions classes rejected academically handicapped students less often than in comparison classes.[19] More positively, Team-Assisted Instruction produced more friendships as well as fewer rejections in another study.[20] Other cooperative learning group models (e.g., Learning Together) tend to create more positive relationships in class, but not out of class according to Ballard *et al.* and to a series of studies by Johnson and Johnson and their colleagues.[21] Studies by Slavin and Janke indicate that emotionally-disturbed students' on-task behavior and peer interaction are better during and following experiences with Student Teams Achievement Divisions than with conventional teaching and learning group models.[22]

Other studies have been conducted to investigate the effects of cooperative learning group models on other affective and behavioral outcomes including students' self esteem, locus of control, time on task, classroom behavior, and enjoyment of class. Some research data reveal that cooperative learning group models promote positive attitudes and classroom behavior. The research results, however, are mixed, and clear conclusions are difficult to draw at this time.

**T:** You have made it clear that that students and teachers benefit the most from using cooperative learning and cooperative group activities when things are properly implemented. What do you mean by "properly implemented?"

**A:** I'm glad you brought this matter up, because one of the important things you need to know about making cooperative learning work in your classroom is that it involves a lot of work and attention to detail. Cooperative learning is not just having groups and having students do group work. Cooperative learning can occur within groups and group settings, but it often does not occur. You, the teacher, must do a lot of things to make sure that it does occur in all of your groups nearly all of the time your groups are meeting in your classroom.

Remember that earlier I mentioned that Bob Slavin invented and advocates his Jigsaw II model because of his analysis of the research.[23] He concluded that unless a jigsaw group structure and activities were complemented by a number of very critical essential elements for cooperative learning, that little cooperation, little learning, and therefore far too little cooperative learning were occurring to warrant referring to most jigsaw groups and activities as instances of "cooperative learning." He concluded that what elevated a jigsaw to a bona fide cooperative learning group model and activity was the addition of many essential elements of cooperative learning. Since 1983, Slavin and nearly all the strongest proponents and experts in cooperative learning have advocated the inclusion of a number of elements that are necessary for groups to work as effective cooperative learning academic teams.

Stahl furthered Slavin's point by asserting that cooperative learning does not occur within or because of the group's structure or activities, but occurs when the essential elements for cooperative learning are present or occur in conjunction with a particular group structure.[24] In other words, to him, Jigsaw, Teams-Games-Tournament, and Group Investigation are not in and of themselves cooperative learning models, but are group models or structures that can become cooperative learning models only with the fulfillment of the essential elements that actually are the critical ingredients for cooperative learning to "happen" in classrooms. He asserted that the conditions for optimal cooperative learning are enhanced with the implementation or occurrence of each additional essential element of cooperative learning. Interestingly, very few of the group structures or models in and of themselves require any of these essential elements, and even in these instances they require only one or two of the more than thirty essential elements. That this is so is the major reason why Stahl has called on cooperative learning theorists, researchers, model builders and teachers alike to clearly separate the cooperative group structure and activity from the essential elements of cooperative learning.

So proper implementation is not limited to just putting students in groups, and getting them to work and do things together, and produce a product or complete an assignment together. Proper implementation means doing all these things as well as making sure all the essential elements of cooperative learning are also fulfilled within your classroom.

**T:** It is clear that cooperative learning group models provide opportunities for teachers to improve students' academic achievement and interpersonal relationships. What special benefits are there for social studies teachers who use cooperative learning group models appropriately?

**A:** Social studies teachers want both to teach their students to be active, effective citizens and to promote democratic values. Properly implemented cooperative learning and cooperative group models can do much to assist them to achieve these two goals along with their goals associated with their students' academic achievement. Teachers who want to promote democratic citizenship should establish classrooms characterized by at least the following five values:

EQUAL OPPORTUNITY: Each student has an equal opportunity to learn.

INDIVIDUAL WELFARE: The welfare of each individual is maximized.

MERITOCRACY: The system of rewards and penalties is responsive to and reflective of the quality of individual performance and achievement.

PERSONAL RESPONSIBILITY: Each individual is held responsible for his or her effect on the welfare of others.

SOCIAL RESPONSIBILITY: Knowledge, skills, and attitudes are taught that promote the welfare of each individual, the class as a group, and the larger society in such a way that they in turn are likely to enhance each individual's welfare.[25]

Group rewards and individual accountability in cooperative learning promote both personal and social responsibility. The positive academic achievement effects of cooperative learning promote equal opportunity and individual welfare. The positive interpersonal relationships generated in cooperative learning classrooms promote individual welfare and personal responsibility. The opportunities to demonstrate competence, make contributions to team success, and be recognized for those contributions support individual welfare, meritocracy, and social responsibility. In these ways, cooperative learning can support the broad goals of both social and social studies education.

Finally, numerous classroom experiments show that cooperative learning group models that provide group goals and rewards and hold students individually accountable for their learning are likely to produce higher academic achievement than noncooperative instruction. Research reveals that cooperative learning often produces more positive student interpersonal attitudes and interactions and might foster other positive attitudes as well. Also, cooperative learning and its effects are consistent with the goals and values of teaching social studies. Altogether, a great deal of evidence supports using cooperative learning group models in social studies classes. 🔳

## NOTES

1.  For our purposes, the various cooperative group formats, structures, and activities are referred to here as group models rather than "group models, techniques or methods." Kagan prefers the label "group structures" rather than models. See Spencer Kagan. *Cooperative Learning Resources for Teachers* (San Juan Capistrano, Calif.: Resources for Teachers, 1989) and *Cooperative Learning* (Boston: Charlesbridge, 1995), as well as Jeanne M. Stone and Spencer Kagan. "Social Studies and the Structural Approach to Cooperative Learning," in *Cooperative Learning in Social Studies: A Handbook for Teachers*, edited by Robert J. Stahl (Menlo Park, Calif.: Addison-Wesley, 1994): 78-97.

2.  Robert E. Slavin, *Cooperative Learning: Theory, Research, and Practice*, 2nd edition (Boston: Allyn & Bacon. 1995).

3.  Slavin and Johnson and Johnson updated their reviews of the research in the area of group work and cooperative learning. See Slavin (*ibid.*) and David W. Johnson and Roger T. Johnson, "Cooperative Learning Methods: A Meta-analysis," *Journal of Research in Education*, 12, no. 1 (2002): 5-14. The results of these studies and the authors' conclusions from their analysis are consistent with Slavin's 1990 findings. In some instances, data from the more recent reviews of the literature are included here. See also the chapters in this volume by Slavin and Robert M.Mattingly.

4.  See Benjamin S. Bloom, *Human Characteristics and School Learning* (New York: McGraw-Hill. 1977) and Jacob Cohen, *Statistical Power Analysis for the Behavioral Sciences*, revised edition (New York: Academic Press, 1977).

5.  Robert M. Mattingly and Ronald L. VanSickle, "Cooperative Learning and Achievement in Social Studies: Jigsaw II," *Social Education 55* (October 1991): 392-95.

6.  See Robert E. Slavin, *Cooperative Learning* (New York: Longman, 1983) and *Cooperative Learning: Theory, Research, and Practice*, 2nd edition (Boston: Allyn & Bacon. 1995). See also Ronald L. VanSickle, "Jigsaw II: Cooperative Learning with 'Expert Group' Specialization" in *Cooperative Learning in Social Studies: A Handbook for Teachers*, edited by Robert J. Stahl (Menlo Park, Calif.: Addison-Wesley, 1994): 98-132.

7.  Slavin was instrumental in pointing out particular essential elements that were needed to elevate and distinguish cooperative learning efforts from other types of group efforts and work. His conclusions and his stress on the vital role of these essential elements are expanded in answers to other questions posed in this chapter.

8.  Robert E. Slavin, *Cooperative Learning: Theory, Research, and Practice*, 2nd edition (Boston: Allyn & Bacon. 1995). The studies were those by Barbara Humphreys, Roger T. Johnson, and David W. Johnson. "Effects of Cooperative, Competitive, and Individualistic Learning on Students'

Achievement in Science Class," *Journal of Research in Science Teaching* 19 (May 1982): 351-56 and Stuart Yager, David W. Johnson, and Roger T. Johnson. "Oral Discussion, Group-to-Individual Transfer, and Achievement in Cooperative Learning Groups," *Journal of Educational Psychology* 77 (February 1985): 60-66.

9. William H. Allen and Ronald L. VanSickle. "Learning Teams and Low Achievers." *Social Education* 48 (January 1984): 60-64.

10. Robert E. Slavin, "Synthesis of Research on Cooperative Learning," *Educational Leadership* 38 (May 1981): 655-60, and *Cooperative Learning: Theory, Research, and Practice*, 2nd edition (Boston: Allyn & Bacon. 1995).

11. G. William Lucker, David Rosenfield, Jev Sikes, and Elliot Aronson, "Performance in the Interdependent Classroom: A Field Study," *American Educational Research Journal* 13 (Spring 1976): 115-23; Robert E. Slavin, "A Student Team Approach to Teaching Adolescents with Special Emotional and Behavioral Needs," *Psychology in the Schools* 14 (Fall 1977): 77-84; and Robert E. Slavin and Eileen Oickle, "Effects of Cooperative Learning Teams on Student Achievement and Race Relations: Treatment by Race Interactions," *Sociology of Education* 54 (July 1981): 174-80.

12. Robert E. Slavin, "Synthesis of Research on Cooperative Learning." *Educational Leadership* 38 (May 1981): 655-60.

13. R. Wheeler, "Predisposition toward Cooperation and Competition: Cooperative and Competitive Classroom Effects," paper presented at the annual meeting of the American Psychological Association, San Francisco, California, August 1977.

14. Robert E. Slavin, "Cooperative Learning in Middle and Secondary Schools," *The Clearing House*, 69, no. 4 (March-April, 1996): 200-204; "Are Cooperative Learning and Untracking Harmful to the Gifted?" *Educational Leadership*, 48, no. 6 (1991): 68-71; and *Cooperative Learning: Theory, Research, and Practice*, 2nd edition (Boston: Allyn & Bacon. 1995).

15. See the list of many of these affective outcomes in Chapter 1 as well as in the chapters by David and Roger Johnson and Robert Slavin and his colleagues in this volume.

16. See Slavin, *Cooperative Learning: Theory, Research, and Practice*, 2nd edition, *op. cit.*

17. Suzanne Ziegler, "The Effectiveness of Cooperative Learning Teams for Increasing Cross-Ethnic Friendship: Additional Evidence," *Human Organization* 40 (Fall 1981): 264-68.

18. Shlomo Sharan, Peter Kussell, Rachel Hertz-Lazarowitz, Y. Bejarano, S. Raviv, and Yael Sharan, *Cooperative Learning in the Classroom: Research in Desegregated Schools* (Hillsdale, N.J.: Lawrence Erlbaum Associates, 1984).

19. Nancy A. Madden and Robert E. Slavin, "Cooperative Learning and Social Acceptance of Mainstreamed Academically Handicapped Students," paper presented at the annual meeting of the American Psychological Association, Montreal, Quebec, August 1983.

20. Robert E. Slavin, "Team Assisted Individualization; Cooperative Learning and Individualized Instruction in the Mainstreamed Classroom," *Remedial and Special Education* 5 (November/December 1984): 33-42.

21. See Maurine Ballard, Louise Corman, Jay Gottlieb, and Martin J. Kaufman, "Improving the Social Status of Mainstreamed Retarded Children," *Journal of Educational Psychology* 69 (October 1977): 605-11, and Slavin, *Cooperative Learning: Theory, Research, and Practice, op. cit.*, for the studies by Johnson and Johnson.

22. Robert E. Slavin, "A Student Team Approach to Teaching Adolescents with Special Emotional and Behavioral Needs," *Psychology in the Schools* 14 (Fall 1977): 77-84; R. Janke, "The Teams-Games-Tournament (TGT) Method and the Behavioral Adjustment and Academic Achievement of Emotionally Impaired Adolescents," paper presented at the annual meeting of the American Educational Research Association, Toronto, Ontario, April 1978.

23. Robert E. Slavin, *Cooperative Learning* (New York: Longman, 1983).

24. Robert J. Stahl, "The Essential Elements of Optimal Cooperative Learning," paper presented at the annual meeting of the American Educational Research Association, Seattle, Wash., April 2001.

25. Ronald L. VanSickle, "Practicing What We Teach: Promoting Democratic Experiences in the Classroom," in *Democratic Education in Schools and Classrooms*, edited by Mary A. Hepburn (Washington, D.C.: National Council for the Social Studies, Bulletin no. 70, 1983).

# CHAPTER 5

# Cooperative Learning is a Powerful Way to Balance the *Social* and the *Studies*

**Robert E. Slavin**, The Johns Hopkins University, Baltimore, Maryland and
**Anne M. Chamberlain**, **Eric A. Hurley**, Success For All Foundation, Baltimore, Maryland

**Walk through any educational environment**, from preschool to postsecondary, and you are bound to see examples of cooperative learning in action. Cooperative learning is applied in a wide range of settings, with all age groups, in diverse disciplines. A national survey of US teachers conducted in 1993 found that 79% of elementary teachers and 62% of middle school teachers reported making some sustained use of cooperative learning.[1] In social studies, the use of cooperation for collaborative inquiry and to learn predates John Dewey's Project Method of the 1920s. In present-day social studies classrooms, cooperation for achieving academic learning should appear frequently and in a wide variety of forms.

The popularity of cooperative learning methods in social studies classrooms is due, at least in part, to their effects on the social development of students. In addition to strengthening and expanding students' comprehension of formal curriculum objectives, they impact affective outcomes inherent to social studies outcomes beyond curriculum mastery. These effects include empathy toward other peoples, including people in other cultures and eras, ideas supportive of active citizenship, and critical thinking.

Although cooperative learning is a powerful tool with which to accomplish academic, social and affective goals, it takes more than simply allowing children to work together in groups—an activity to which the cooperative learning label is often misguidedly affixed. More than 30 years of experimental research in schools indicates that outcomes, particularly academic achievement outcomes, are affected by how teachers structure and implement cooperative learning methods. One should think about effective use of cooperative learning in social studies as being attentive to both the *social* and the *studies*. This chapter begins with a review of those cooperative learning methods that have been most researched. Following this is a discussion of the elements

of those methods proven to impact achievement and social goals, with an emphasis on strategies that have been applied in the social studies and history, and that have been researched in comparison with traditionally taught groups.

## Cooperative Learning Models

Teachers have access to any number of cooperative learning methods, many of which are specific and come with training, manuals, or how-to materials, and many less formal variations. The most frequently researched methods used in the social studies are described below.

### A. Student Teams-Achievement Divisions (STAD)

In four-member heterogeneous learning teams, mixed by performance level, gender and ethnicity, students work together to make sure that each team member has learned a lesson presented by the teacher.[2] The typical cycle of Student Teams-Achievement Divisions activities takes three to five class periods. The cycle of activities that constitutes Student Teams-Achievement Divisions begins with a teacher presentation and then involves a period of group study, in which students work to make sure that they and their teammates have mastered the content. The lesson concludes with quizzes on the academic content and skills stressed in that lesson. Students take the quizzes individually, without helping one another and without access to notes, text or other sources of information. Quizzes are scored, and each student is awarded "improvement points" based on having met or exceeded his or her previous "base score." Team scores represent the sum or average of the individual members' improvement points. Teams earn certificates or other awards by meeting preestablished criteria for academic achievement.[3]

Student Teams-Achievement Divisions has been used in second grade through college classrooms in a wide range of subjects, including social studies. It is best suited for teaching toward well-defined academic objectives that stress content and skills for which there will be a single right answer. In the social studies, Student Teams-Achievement Divisions could be used as a strategy to teach such content and skills as map facts or skills in geography; details of events in history; economic and government principles; names and functions of parts of the brain and nervous system in psychology; or vocabulary, definitions or basic facts in any content area.

## B. Teams-Games-Tournament (TGT)

The initial steps of Teams-Games-Tournament (TGT) resemble Student Teams-Achievement Divisions.[4] However, the quiz component is replaced by weekly "tournaments" made up of a set of academic games. Through this series of games that together constitute a "tournament," students on the same academic ability level answer questions in a competitive-like environment with members of other teams in order to gain points for their own teams' score. What is important here is that when the rules are followed for scoring and earning points for one's Home Team, there is no "real" competition among the players at each game table or teams within the classroom.

## C. Jigsaw

In Jigsaw,[5] student teams of six work on academic material that has been divided into sections by the teacher. Each team member is responsible for a particular section. For example, if the material assigned were an historical event, one team member might be assigned a section on social context, one might be responsible for timeline, another might be responsible for long-term effects, and the other teammates might each be assigned a section on key participants. Each student reads his or her assigned section, after which the class reconfigures into "expert groups." Expert groups consist of the students responsible for a particular section in their respective teams. After expert groups discuss their sections, students return to their original teams, to teach that section to their teammates. This strategy encourages teammates to support each other's work. It is only by listening carefully to each other that team members can learn about the other sections, and understand how their piece fits into a larger puzzle.

There have been many modifications of Jigsaw, several of which are described by Spencer Kagan.[6] Jigsaw II is a modification made to Jigsaw by Slavin.[7] In this method, students work in four to five-member teams, as in Teams-Games-Tournament and Student Teams-Achievement Divisions. All students begin by reading a common narrative such as a story, textbook chap-

ter, or biography, before being assigned subtopics on which to become experts. Students reconfigure into expert groups based on common subtopics. Having discussed the subtopics and become "experts" in their particular part of what needs to be learned, students return to their original teams to share what they have learned with teammates. It is expected that each "expert" will teach his or her part well enough that all his or her teammates become experts as well. Finally, students take individual quizzes. Improvement on quiz scores results in points, which are brought back to the team to determine a team score, as in Student Teams-Achievement Divisions. Certificates or other rewards are distributed to high-achieving teams based on predetermined criteria.

Steinbrink and Stahl modified Slavin's Jigsaw II by adding a structured, cooperative test-review group activity to form a new model, Jigsaw III.[8] In Jigsaw III, students who complete a number of smaller or shorter units using Jigsaw II reassemble in their home teams the day before their major test over several units for the expressed purposes of reviewing what they have learned and preparing themselves and their teammates for the major test. This model has been successfully used in social studies, science, and language arts classes in a number of states.

## D. Learning Together

A team-generated work product, as opposed to individual products, is one of the distinguishing factors of the Learning Together model, developed by David and Roger Johnson at the University of Minnesota.[9] In Learning Together, students in maximally-heterogeneous, four- or five-member groups work on a single assignment sheet, which can earn them praise and rewards. There is an emphasis on team-building activities prior to group work, as well as regular within-group dialogue to determine how well the students are functioning together. (also see the chapter by Johnson and Johnson in this volume.)

## F. Structured Academic Controversy

In this model developed by Johnson and Johnson, students in groups of four are divided into pairs with each pair first responsible for finding details for either the "pro" or "con" position on a particular issue, dilemma or question.[10] After researching, assembling and then mastering their respective positions, each pair then teaches its position to its opposing position pair so that all four members of each group become experts on both positions. Finally, students in each group try to reach a compromise or new position based on all the data they have collected.

## G. Group Investigation

A general classroom organization plan, Group Investigation requires students to work in small groups and to use cooperative inquiry, group discussion, and cooperative planning and projects. This method, originally developed by Herbert Thelen, was refined by Shlomo Sharan at the University of Tel Aviv.[11] A unit topic is studied by the entire class, and students in groups of two to six select and study subtopics from this unit. The groups then divide their subtopics into individual tasks, and work collectively towards a group report. These reports are presented or displayed for the benefit of the rest of the class. Kagan developed Co-op Co-op, a variation of Group Investigation.[12]

## Research on Cooperative Learning

Among alternative methods to traditional instruction, cooperative learning is perhaps the method most extensively researched. A 1995 review by Slavin summarized the results of 99 studies that have rigorously evaluated the effects of cooperative learning. Sixty-seven compared achievement among students taught in regular elementary or secondary schools using cooperative learning, with students in traditionally taught control groups (with random assignment to cooperative or control conditions, or with controls matched on pretest achievement and other factors). All of these studies used measures of objectives pursued by both cooperative and control classes, and followed students over a period of at least four weeks. Although only a few of these studies involved social studies, other studies have clear implications for the teaching of social studies.

## A. Academic Achievement

Thirty-nine of the 67 studies on cooperative learning and student achievement (58 percent) found that achievement is significantly greater for students in cooperative learning classes, compared to control classes. No differences were found in 27 of the studies (40 percent). In the one remaining study, a control group outperformed the cooperative learning group.

The method of cooperative learning that is used has a considerable impact on the effectiveness of cooperative learning. For example, if we examine studies of cooperative learning that included both group goals and individual accountability, we find significant positive achievement effects. Of these studies, 37 out of 44 (84 percent) show significant positive achievement affects. Only four of 23 studies (17 percent) of cooperative learning methods that did *not* use these components found significantly positive effects on student achievement. Group Investigation in Israel was the subject of two of those four studies.[13] In this classroom organizational plan, students in each group are responsible for a discrete part of the group's overall assignment, ensuring individual accountability. It seems as though a group evaluation took the place of group rewards, and so Group Investigation was perhaps operating with both components. The evidence, then, suggests that group goals and individual accountability are critical components of effective cooperative learning strategies.[14] In other words, groups must be working to achieve a common preset goal, reward, or recognition, and this recognition must rely on individual learning by each group member.

When cooperative learning is considered without group goals and individual accountability, it becomes clear why these components are so important. For example, in some forms of cooperative learning, students work in groups to complete a single task or product. Under such circumstances, it is unclear what might motivate more able students to invest time and energy in explaining material to be learned to less able group members. It is unclear whether any mechanism would ensure that less able members participate or feel involved and valued. It is also unclear how teachers could be certain that learning was taking place for all students, when the sole purpose of the group is to complete something. A number of scholars have argued that social and or cultural variables may under some circumstances foster group norms which motivate such "group centric" behavior;[15] however, the evidence to date calls for a more pragmatic approach to motivating students.

When a cooperative learning group is tasked with ensuring that each member understands the material, there is an incentive for each group member to invest time and energy learning from and explaining to other members. Research on student behavior in cooperative groups has found that, in fact, those group members who gain most from cooperative work are those who give and receive expanded, or elaborated, explanations.[16] Webb's research consistently found that when students gave or received answers without explanation, there was a negative impact on achievement. When groups are given clear goals, and group members are individually accountable, students are motivated to take each other's learning seriously.

All types of students benefit from cooperative learning methods. Teachers are sometimes concerned that cooperative learning will hold back their high achievers, but research on cooperative learning does not support this belief. Although occasional studies have found particular benefits for high achievers or low achievers, boys or girls, etc., most studies find equal benefits for all students involved. Research has shown that in cooperative learning classes, high achievers gain as much as average and low achievers.[17]

Most research on cooperative learning has involved students in grades 3-9. However, studies of outcomes at the senior high school level are generally as positive as studies at the earlier levels. Studies at the postsecondary level also generally show positive effects; however, there is a need for more rigorous studies of cooperative learning beyond the ninth grade, and in colleges and universities. In addition to showing positive results across educational levels, cooperative learning methods have proven to be equally effective in urban, suburban, and rural schools, and with students of various ethnic groups. Some studies have actually found particularly positive effects for African-American students.[18]

The positive effects of cooperative learning in social studies mirror those reported in other subject areas. In 9th grade geography, Allen and VanSickle found that Student Teams-Achievement Divisions produced strong positive effects.[19] U.S. history classes experienced similar effects when DeVries, Edwards, and Wells studied the use of Teams-Games-Tournament in this setting.[20] Students in Learning Together classes, studied by Yager, Johnson, Johnson and Snider retained more information from a unit in transportation, than did students who were taught in a traditional setting.[21]

Group Investigation has had particularly positive effects in the social studies. The most positive research study followed Israeli eighth graders studying geography and history in an eighteen-week experiment.[22]

For Jigsaw, achievement effects seem to be related to the form of the program used. Few achievement effects were shown for the original model.[23] Jigsaw II (i.e., Jigsaw with expert groups as breakout groups), which uses group goals and individual accountability, has had positive achievement effects. This research includes two social studies examples. Mattingly and VanSickle studied an integrated unit on Asia that was taught in a U.S. high school in Germany.[24] Ziegler studied the achievement of Toronto students on units about the Inuit people and the history and geography of Newfoundland.[25]

## B. Intergroup Relations

Research has consistently shown that cooperative learning methods have a positive impact on intergroup relations. Most of this research involves students listing their best friends at the start of the study, and again at the end. "Intergroup relations" was determined by the number of friends that a student listed from outside his or her own ethnic group. Student Teams-Achievement Divisions, Teams-Games-Tournament, Jigsaw, Learning To-

gether and Group Investigation have all shown positive effects on intergroup relations.[26]

Improving intergroup relations is central to the overarching agenda of social studies. Social studies curricula are designed to foster better understanding among diverse communities and cultures around the world and among groups that exist side by side. Traditional social studies curricula promote such understanding through content and factual knowledge. According to current research on intergroup relations, improved relations among groups are best achieved through contact, and only through contact where members of different groups are of equal status and have shared goals.[27] Traditional classroom practices allow for little direct, supervised contact, and where this contact exists, it is usually competitive in nature. Cooperative learning techniques can enrich social studies by encouraging children to develop skills and attitudes which facilitate understanding while providing them the opportunity to interact with others in the types of circumstances known to enhance intergroup relations.

Studies of cooperative learning and intergroup relations in the US have involved African-American, European-American, and, in some cases, Hispanic students. In one of these studies, which focused on Student Teams-Achievement Divisions, and in a Toronto study of Jigsaw II that involved Anglo-Canadians and children of recent European immigrants, intergroup friendships were determined several months after the studies' conclusion.[28] In both studies, students who had been in cooperative learning classes continued to name significantly more friends from outside their own ethnic groups, compared to students who had been in control classes. In two studies of Group Investigation conducted in Israel, friendship patterns between Jewish students of European and Middle Eastern backgrounds were examined.[29] Results showed that the improved attitude and behavior of students towards classmates of different ethnic groups extended beyond just those classmates who had been involved in the cooperative group work.

## C. Inclusion

Research on academically-handicapped children has been the focus of research on cooperative learning and inclusion or mainstreaming. In a study of Student Teams-Achievement Divisions in which students performing two years or more below peer level were integrated into the classroom social structure, there was a significant reduction in the degree to which normal-progress students rejected their mainstreamed peers. In addition, academic achievement and self-esteem increased for all students.[30] One study of social studies in a self-contained classroom for emotionally disturbed adolescents found that positive interactions and friendships among students increased when Teams-Games-Tournament was used as a teaching strategy.[31] Five months after the conclusion of the study, students who had been in Teams-Games-Tournament classes continued these positive interactions more often than in control classes. Janke conducted a study in a similar setting, in which he found that emotionally disturbed students in Teams-Games-Tournament classes were more often on task, better behaved, and had better attendance, compared with similar students in control classes.[32] As with inter-ethnic/cultural group relations, cooperative learning provides equal status, shared-goal interactions among normal-progress students and their academically handicapped peers. Thus again, an important social studies agenda can be served with the implementation of cooperative learning methods.

## D. Other Outcomes

Not only has research found positive effects of cooperative learning on achievement, intergroup relations, and acceptance of mainstream students, but effects have also been found on other important outcomes. Several researchers who study cooperative learning methods have noted an increase in self esteem. In particular, there have been significant improvements in self esteem for students in Teams-Games-Tournament and Student Teams-Achievement Divisions classrooms, Jigsaw classrooms, and for classrooms in which the three methods were combined.[33] Other outcomes affected positively by cooperative learning include enjoyment of school, developing peer norms in favor of doing well academically, feeling that the individual has control over his or her own fate in school, time on task, cooperativeness and altruism.[34]

Research has shown that Teams-Games-Tournament and Student Teams-Achievement Divisions have positive effects on students' time on task.[35] One particularly encouraging study followed students in 7th through 11th grades, with low socioeconomic status, and at risk of becoming delinquent. Results from this study found that those students who worked in cooperative groups had better attendance records, fewer contacts with police, and more positive behavioral ratings by teachers, compared to control students.[36] Another study which implemented various forms of cooperative learning with students starting in kindergarten and continuing through the 4th grade, found more effective resolution of personal conflicts, more support expressed for democratic values, and higher scores on measures of supportive, friendly, and prosocial behaviors among students who had

participated in well-structured cooperative groups.[37]

## Balancing the *Social* and the *Studies* within Social Studies Classrooms

Students in social studies, as in other disciplines, can benefit from cooperative learning. Research on cooperative learning in social studies and other settings has demonstrated the potential of this strategy to help students learn content and, at the same time, improve social skills and prosocial attitudes. It is important to note, however, that grouping students and telling them to work together is not enough. Furthermore it is not enough to assume that if any learning of any kind or amount occurs within a group setting, that is sufficient to consider the activity a cooperative learning activity or group. While a wide variety of cooperative learning methods have shown positive social outcomes, genuine academic achievement gains appear to rely on group academic learning goals; on a sustained, deliberate and concerted effort by all group members to attain the academic goals; and on individual accountability. It is imperative that group success depends on the actual academic learning and performance outcome abilities of every student.

Social studies is a particularly appropriate forum for cooperative learning, because explicit social goals are often included among desirable outcomes for this curriculum area. Teaching civic values and democracy to rows of passively listening students does not make sense. Different forms of cooperative learning can work in the social studies classroom to accommodate a wide variety of purposes. For example, Student Teams-Achievement Divisions or Learning Together can be used to teach information and skills; Jigsaw with expert groups can help students learn from texts; and Group Investigation can be used for group projects and reports with students selecting appropriate subtopics to investigate and learn about. Creative teachers can develop any number of variations of these strategies to align student group-learning activities and academic outcomes with social studies objectives.

Cooperative learning, when used in a thoughtful and informed way, can fill a social studies classroom with students who are debating, exploring, listening, reaching group consensus, questioning, teaching, tutoring, assessing, experiencing and constructing knowledge and practicing skills—in other words, students who are actively-engaged and academically-focused learners. A classroom like this embodies the *social* and the *studies* that are essential and integral parts of a comprehensive social studies curriculum and sound, integrated social studies instruction. 🔳

## NOTES

1. Michael J. Puma, Calvin C. Jones, Donald Rock, and Richard Fernandez, *Prospects: The Congressionally Mandated Study of Educational Growth and Opportunity*, interim report (Bethesda, MD: Abt Associates, 1993).

2. Robert E. Slavin, "Student Teams and Achievement Divisions," *Journal of Research and Development in Education* 12 (June 1978): 39-49; *Using Student Team Learning*, 3rd edition (Baltimore: Center for Social Organization of Schools, Johns Hopkins University, 1994); *Cooperative Learning: Theory, Research, and Practice*, 2nd edition (Boston: Allyn & Bacon, 1995).

3. See Quinton Priest, "Student Teams-Achievement Divisions (STAD): Applications to the Social Studies Classroom," in *Cooperative Learning in the Social Studies: A Handbook for Teachers*, edited by Robert J. Stahl (Menlo Park, Calif.: Addison-Wesley, 1994): 154-88.

4. David L. DeVries and Robert E. Slavin, "Teams-Games-Tournaments," *Journal of Research and Development in Education*, 12 (Fall 1978): 28-38; Slavin, *Cooperative Learning: Theory, Research, and Practice, op. cit.*

5. Elliott Aronson, Nancy T. Blaney, Cookie Stephan, Jev Sikes, and Matthew Snapp, *The Jigsaw Classroom* (Beverly Hills, Calif.: Sage, 1978); Elliott Aronson and Shelley Patnoe, *The Jigsaw Classroom: Building Cooperation in the Classroom* (New York: Longman, 1997).

6. Spencer Kagan, *Cooperative Learning* (Boston: Charlesbridge, 1995).

7. Slavin, *Cooperative Learning: Theory, Research, and Practice, op. cit.* See also Ronald L. VanSickle, "Jigsaw II: Cooperative Learning with 'Expert Group' Specialization," in *Cooperative Learning in the Social Studies: A Handbook for Teachers*, edited by Robert J. Stahl (Menlo Park, Calif.: Addison-Wesley, 1994): 98-132.

8. John E. Steinbrink and Robert J. Stahl, "Jigsaw III + Jigsaw II + Cooperative Test Review: Applications to the Social Studies Classroom," in *Cooperative Learning in the Social Studies: A Handbook for Teachers* edited by Robert J. Stahl (Menlo Park, Calif.: Addison-Wesley, 1994): 133-153.

9. David W. Johnson and Roger T. Johnson, *Learning Together and Alone: Cooperative, Competitive, and Individualistic Learning*, 4th edition (Boston: Allyn & Bacon, 1994).

10. See David W. Johnson and Roger T. Johnson, "Conflict in the Classroom: Controversy and Learning," *Review of Educational Research* 49 (1979): 51-61; *Cooperation and Competition: Theory and Research* (Edina, Minn.: Interaction Book Company, 1989); and "The Pro-Con Cooperative Group Strategy: Structuring Academic Controversy Within the Social Studies Classroom," in *Cooperative Learning in the Social Studies: A Handbook for Teachers*, edited by Robert J. Stahl (Menlo Park, Calif.: Addison-Wesley, 1994): 277-305.

11. See Herbert Thelen, *Dynamics of Groups at Work* (Chicago: University of Chicago Press, 1954) and *Education and the Human Quest* (New York: Harper & Row, 1960). See also Bruce Joyce and Marsha Weil, *Models of Teaching*, 2nd edition (Englewood Cliffs, N.J.: Prentice Hall, 1980), and two works by Shlomo Sharan and Yael Sharan, *Group Investigation: Expanding Cooperative Learning* (New York: Teacher's College Press, 1992) and "What Do We Want to Study? How Should We Go About Studying It?: Using Group Investigation," in *Cooperative Learning in Social Studies: A Handbook for Teachers*, edited by Robert J. Stahl (Menlo Park, Calif.: Addison Wesley, 1994): 257-276.

12. Kagan, *Cooperative Learning, op. cit.*

13. Shlomo Sharan, Peter Kussell, Rachel Hertz-Lazarowitz, Yael Bejarano, Shulamit Raviv, and Yael Sharan, *Cooperative Learning in the Classroom: Research on Desegregated Schools* (Hillside, N.J.: Lawrence Erlbaum Associates, 1984) and Shlomo Sharan and Chana Shachar, *Language and Learning in the Cooperative Classroom* (New York: Springer, 1988).

14. Slavin, *Cooperative Learning: Theory, Research, and Practice, op. cit.*; Angela M. O'Donnell, "The Effects of Explicit Incentives on Scripted and Unscripted Cooperation," *Journal of Educational Psychology* 88 (January1997): 74-86.

15. Ebony M. Dill and A. Wade Boykin, "The Comparative Influence of Individualistic, Peer Tutoring, and Communalistic Learning Context on the Text Recall of African American Children," *Journal of Black Psychology* 26 (2000): 65-68; A. Wade Boykin, Robert J. Jagers, Constance M. Ellison, and Aretha Albury, "Communalism: Conceptualization and Measurement of an Afrocultural Social Ethos," *Journal of Black Studies* 27 no. 3 (1997): 409-418; David W. Johnson and Roger T. Johnson, "The Internal Dynamics of Cooperative Learning Groups," in *Learning to Cooperate: Cooperating to Learn*, edited by Robert E. Slavin, Shlomo Sharan, Spencer Kagan, Rachel Hertz-Lazarowitz, C. Webb, and R. Schmuck (New York: Plenum Press, 1985): 103-123.

16. Noreen Webb, "Testing a Theoretical Model of Student Interaction and Learning in Small Groups," in *Interaction in Cooperative Groups: The Theoretical Anatomy of Group Learning*, edited by Rachel Hertz-Lazarowitz and Kathleen A. Miller (New York: Cambridge University Press, 1992): 102-119; Barak Rosenshine and Carla Meister, "A Comparison of Results with Standardized Tests and Experimenter-Developed Comprehension Tests when Teaching Cognitive Strategies," paper presented at the annual meeting of the American Educational Research Association, New Orleans, April 1994.

17. Robert E. Slavin, "Are Cooperative Learning and 'Untracking' Harmful to the Gifted?" *Educational Leadership* 48 (March 1991): 68-71.

18. Robert E. Slavin and Eileen Oickle, "Effects of Cooperative Learning Teams on Student Achievement and Race Relations: Treatment by Race Interactions," *Sociology of Education* 54 (July 1981): 174-80.

19. William H. Allen and Ronald L. VanSickle, "Learning Teams and Low Achievers," *Social Education* 48 (January 1984): 60-64.

20. David L. DeVries, Keith J. Edwards, and Elizabeth H. Wells, *Teams-Games-Tournament in the Social Studies Classroom: Effects on Academic Achievement, Student Attitudes, Cognitive Beliefs, and Classroom Climate* (Baltimore: Johns Hopkins University, Center for Social Organization of Schools. 1974).

21. Stuart Yager, Roger T. Johnson, David W. Johnson, and Barbara Snider, "The Impact of Group Processing on Achievement in Cooperative Learning," *Journal of Social Psychology* 126, no. 30 (1986): 389-97.

22. Shlomo Sharan and Chana Shachar, *Language and Learning in the Cooperative Classroom* (New York: Springer, 1988).

23. G. William Lucker, David Rosenfield, Jev Sikes, and Elliot Aronson, "Performance in the Independent Classroom: A Field Study," *American Educational Research Journal* 13 (1976): 115-123; Yisrael Rich, Yehuda Amir, and Robert E. Slavin, *Instructional Strategies for Improving Children's Cross-Ethnic Relations* (Ramat Gan, Israel: Bar Han University, Institute for the Advancement of Social Integration in the Schools, 1986).

24. Robert M. Mattingly and Ronald L. Van Sickle, "Cooperative Learning and Achievement in Social Studies: Jigsaw II," *Social Education* 55 (October 1991): 392-95. Teachers interested in reading how Bob Mattingly began using and continues to use cooperative learning strategies in his secondary social studies classroom should read his chapter in this volume.

25. Suzanne Ziegler, "The Effectiveness of Cooperative Learning Teams for Increasing Cross-Ethnic Friendship: Additional Evidence," *Human Organization* 40 (Fall 1981): 264-68.

26. Robert E. Slavin, "Cooperative Learning: Applying Contact Theory in Desegregated Schools," *Journal of Social Issues* 41, no. 1(1985): 45-62.

27. Victor Battistich, Daniel Solomon, and Kevin Delucci, "Interaction Process and Student Outcomes in Cooperative Learning Group," *The Elementary School Journal* 1 (1994): 19-32.

28. Ziegler, "The Effectiveness of Cooperative Learning Teams...", *op. cit.*

29. Sharan et al., *Cooperative Learning in the Classroom, op. cit.*; Sharan and Shachar, *Language and Learning in the Cooperative Classroom, op. cit.*

30. Maureen Ballard, Louise Corman, Jay Gottlieb, and Martin J. Kauffman, "Improving the Social Status of Mainstreamed Retarded Children," *Journal of Educational Psychology* 69 (October 1977): 605-11; Lucille Cooper, David W. Johnson, Roger T. Johnson, and Frank Wilderson, "Effects of Cooperative, Competitive, and Individualistic Experiences on Interpersonal Attraction among Heterogeneous Peers," *The Journal of Social Psychology* 111 (August 1980): 243-52.

31. Robert E. Slavin, "A Student Team Approach to Teaching Adolescents with Special Emotional and Behavioral Needs." *Psychology in the Schools* 14 (Fall 1977): 77-84.

32. Robert Janke, "The Teams-Games-Tournament (TGT) Method and the Behavioral Adjustment and Academic Achievement of Emotionally Impaired Adolescents," paper presented at the annual meeting of the American Educational Research Association, Toronto, Ontario, April 1978.

33. For Teams-Games-Tournament and Student Teams-Achievement Divisions classrooms, see Slavin, *Cooperative Learning: Theory, Research, and Practice, op. cit.*; for Jigsaw classrooms, see Nancy T. Blaney, Cookie Stephan, David Rosenfeld, Elliot Aronson, and Jev Sikes, "Interdependence in the Classroom: A Field Study," *Journal of Educational Psychology* 69 (April 1977): 121-28; and for classrooms in which the three methods were combined, see Robert E. Slavin and Nancy Karweit, "Cognitive and Affective Outcomes of an Intensive Student Team Learning Experience," *Journal of Experimental Education* 50 (Fall 1981): 29-35.

34. Slavin, *Cooperative Learning: Theory, Research, and Practice, op. cit.*

35. DeVries and Slavin, "Teams-Games-Tournaments," *op. cit.*; Slavin, "A Student Team Approach to Teaching Adolescents with Special Emotional and Behavioral Needs," *op. cit.*; Janke, "The Teams-Games-Tournament (TGT) Method and the Behavioral Adjustment and Academic Achievement of Emotionally Impaired Adolescents," *op. cit.*

36. Wynona S. Hartley, *Prevention Outcomes of Small Group Education with School Children: An Epidemiologic Follow Up of the Kansas City School Behavior Project* (Kansas City, Mo.: University of Kansas Medical Center, 1976).

37. Daniel Solomon, Marilyn Watson, Eric Schaps, Victor Battistich, and Jane Solomon, "Cooperative Learning as Part of a Comprehensive Classroom Program Designed to Promote Prosocial Development," in *Current Research on Cooperative Learning*, edited by Shlomo Sharan (New York: Praeger, 1990).

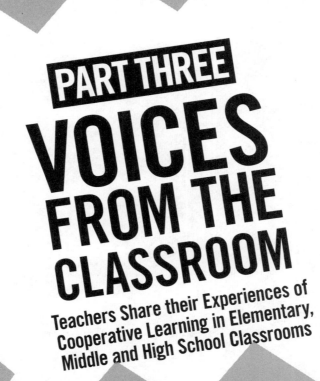

# PART THREE
# VOICES FROM THE CLASSROOM

Teachers Share their Experiences of Cooperative Learning in Elementary, Middle and High School Classrooms

# CHAPTER 6

# "Doing a Jigsaw" Can Be Very Different from "Doing Cooperative Learning"
## A Context for Using "Jigsaw Structures" in Classrooms

**Robert J. Stahl**, Arizona State University and **James Doyle Casteel**, formerly of the University of Florida[1]

**In social studies classrooms**, it is common for teachers to say that they are "doing cooperative learning" because their students are "doing a jigsaw." Teachers attending a workshop or conference session on cooperative learning are told that one of the easiest ways of *doing* cooperative learning is to get students into three-to-six member groups and have each group complete a jigsaw task. Staff developers might put teachers in small groups, have them complete a jigsaw task, and then declare that the teachers had *done* cooperative learning because they worked cooperatively in finishing their jigsaw task. It is common to read articles in journals and chapters of books whose authors refer to any jigsaw activity or a particular jigsaw activity as an example of cooperative learning.

The use of jigsaw structures often reinforces pervasive and strongly-held misconceptions, including the following: (a) any activity where students are working together and cooperating to complete a task or assignment is cooperative learning; (b) any group activity where individual students are assigned or volunteer to do a part of the work and where students eventually get together to "put together their different parts of the puzzle" to complete the task is a cooperative learning jigsaw activity; (c) any jigsaw activity *is* cooperative learning; (d) having students complete a jigsaw activity is having them *do* cooperative learning; and (e) any group activity where students might or do learn something—even when what they learn is only a small portion of the content and abilities they were suppose to learn—is a cooperative learning activity.[2]

The above misconceptions are not confined to the various group structures that have been labeled "jigsaw." Nor are they limited to K-12 social studies teachers. They are also prevalent among teacher educators at both the undergraduate and graduate levels, who are partly responsible for passing them on to pre- and in-service teachers. Three primary focuses of this chapter are correcting these misconceptions, providing more appropriate ideas, and describing a sample of the various forms that "Jigsaw" tasks may take.

### Important Concepts and Requirements for Optimal Cooperative Learning

As pointed out in Chapters 1 and 2, group activities and group structures, even those that are labeled "cooperative learning" by their inventors and advocates are *not* in and of themselves "cooperative learning" activities or structures. Cooperative learning requires that the focus of student involvement in these group structures must be on all students maximizing their own comprehension, retention, later recall and mastery of a particular set of content and abilities while completing assigned activities and tasks. The focus must also be on all students doing their utmost to ensure all their teammates achieve perfect or near perfect comprehension, retention and later recall and use of the same content and abilities—so that each student, as an individual, can score very high on the individual academic achievement test he or she takes *after* the team's cooperating efforts have ended. Any effort or activity that has another focus or that falls short of these high levels of academic achievement outcomes for all team members is *not* cooperative learning.

*No jigsaw group structure, group project or group activity is or ever can be cooperative learning in and of itself:* cooperative learning is not a structure or a structured activity; it is a type of learning whose quality must be demonstrated by the individual achievement scores of students.

## Table 1: Essential Elements of Optimal Cooperative Learning*

1. A set of clear, specific student academic outcome objectives that describe clearly and exactly what information and abilities students are to construct, rehearse, master and retain.

2. Students complete their academic study within maximally heterogeneous teams.

3. Students have a clear notion as to what particular academic content and abilities they are to learn and master in their teams —and what they must be able to do on their own after their group has stopped meeting.

4. Students feel assured that what they are assigned to learn in their groups will indeed be what will be on their after-group individual test.

5. Students accept that their primary task as individuals and as team members is to maximize their own academic achievement and the achievement of all teammates.

6. Students accept the notion that the awards for academic success come to the team rather than to individuals independent of the team.

7. Students have a clear and complete set of directions or instructions as to the academic tasks they are to complete to optimize their academic achievement.

8. Students in each team believe they have an equal opportunity for academic success.

9. Students have a sense of and engage in behaviors consistent with positive and academically-productive interdependence.

10. Students must test one another and provide appropriate feedback and feedforward information regarding each other's academic progress.

11. Students engage in productive "face-to-face" interaction and appropriate "knee-to-knee" posture.

12. Students demonstrate positive social interaction roles, behaviors and attitudes.

13. Students demonstrate positive task-completion roles, behaviors and attitudes.

14. Students demonstrate positive group-maintenance roles, behaviors and attitudes.

15. Students have and must spend sufficient productive time learning

16. There is an absence of structured competition within and among teams.

17. Each student is held individually responsible and accountable for his or her academic success by taking an individual academic test after the team has stopped meeting.

18. The awards and the award structure are linked directly and solely to academic achievement of all team members as determined by the individual academic tests.

19. Teams receive timely and adequate public recognition and awards for their academic achievement.

20. Students complete structured post-team "reflection" (or "debriefing") tasks concerning their within-team behaviors.

21. Students actually use the do-and-don't results of their debriefing tasks by employing the behaviors in future group activities.

---

\*    This Table incorporates a selection of the 38 elements of optimal cooperative learning outlined in Robert J. Stahl, "The Essential Elements for Optimal Cooperative Learning," paper presented at the annual meeting of the American Educational Research Association, Seattle, Washington, April 2001.

Four important ideas from previous chapters in this book are:

1. Cooperative learning requires a primary focus on the learning, retention and mastery of particular content and abilities rather than on increasing the quality and amount of cooperation within a group or team;

2. While students may or must learn to cooperate in productive ways, within cooperative learning their major concern must be to cooperate continuously and productively to ensure that all members of their team learn, retain and maintain their mastery of the academic content and targeted abilities;

3. The cooperation is productive and meaningful to the extent it enables all students to maximize their academic achievement; and

4. A high level of academic achievement is the only acceptable evidence of the degree of learning that occurred within each team and by each team member, and this evidence is based almost exclusively on the scores on individual outcome-aligned tests taken a day or more *after* the cooperation in formal settings has ended.

These are just four of the reasons why cooperative learning is a unique approach to instruction and is substantially different from traditional and alternative instructional efforts that use groups. Cooperative learning is not different from traditional groups and approaches to groups because of the group structures; rather cooperative learning is different because of its primary focus on enhancing and ensuring that all students of each group master the required academic content and abilities and by the requirement that all members of each group take a rigorous academic test to provide evidence as to the kind and extent of academic achievement each achieved. Optimal cooperative learning requires the establishment of "academic achievement teams" rather than "groups" of students.

Table 1 provides a selective list of elements that must exist prior to, during and after each team's cooperative activities in order to establish, monitor and maintain the required conditions for optimal cooperative learning.[3]

## "Jigsaw" Group Structures and Tasks: Attributes and Alternatives

Table 1 does not specifically mention "Jigsaw" group structures and activities. This is due to the fact that no jigsaw is an essential element of cooperative learning. Jigsaw structures are blueprints for organizing students within groups, arranging what each student will or will not get at the start of these groups, and making such decisions as whether students are to remain in their original groups during their entire time together or can break off to meet with other members of other groups to complete their work. jigsaw structures and activities can be completed even if only a few of the essential elements of optimal cooperative learning are met.

Each individual in a jigsaw group needs to have a specific set of items, materials, information or abilities that at the start is unavailable to other group members. To complete the overall task of the group successfully, or at least to the best of the abilities of the combined, cooperating individuals, each group member is expected at a particular time or in a particular situation to share or provide his or her materials, information or abilities while cooperating with the others to complete their group's work. All else being equal, the primary focus of the basic jigsaw is to cooperate to complete the task or project—and is *not* to learn and master the content and abilities associated with the task or project.

For instance, imagine three students are formed into a three-member group to assemble a 300-piece puzzle of a map of the 48 contiguous states in the United States of America. Each student is given 100 pieces, which only that student can place during the group's effort to form the complete map. In this instance, each student has a set of items (i.e., 100 puzzle pieces) that is deliberately made unavailable to others in the group and these items are needed for the entire group to be successful in its final product. If the students are to complete the map, all must contribute their pieces and work cooperatively to assemble the puzzle.

In another situation, imagine students are placed in a four-member group, with each student assigned a different article to read, and required to share the information from that article with other members of the group. The group's task is to answer a set of 20 questions, with answers to five questions found in each article. Once again, students cannot be successful in answering all 20 questions correctly unless each one provides information for five answers from the article that each read. So they agree to split up the questions, answer the ones they have, and assemble the questions and answers.

In yet another instance, students are placed in groups of three with the assignment to answer the questions at the end of the chapter. The teacher, wanting to create a jigsaw activity, assigns each student to answer six of the questions, with each set of questions linked to one-third of the chapter. Each student reads his or her third of the chapter, answers the questions, and contributes these to the group's final project, which is writing each question followed by its correct answer.

An instance of a jigsaw with a more extreme division of labor may occur when students are instructed to do some research and assemble a power-point presentation of their work and conclusions. If one student does the research and finds resources and information, another takes this information and puts together a report, and a third takes the report and creates the PowerPoint slide show for the group's presentation, the three have completed a jigsaw, with each contributing one-third of what was required to complete the assignment. In this latter situation, the teacher did not set up the project to be completed as a "jigsaw," but students created a jigsaw division of labor in order to complete the tasks assigned in a manner that felt comfortable to them.

The instances in the above paragraphs are useful in pointing out how jigsaw and other group tasks may be completed without the requirement that all participants learned and mastered any of the content or abilities they personally contributed, much less all the content and abilities each of the others contributed to their group effort. Consequently, none of the above "jigsaw" activities comes remotely close to cooperative learning. These instances reveal that while individuals may cooperate and contribute their part to the overall task, they may do so without having learned or mastered the information that they and others contributed. For example, without a focus on retaining and mastering the information about different states on his 100 puzzle pieces, it is entirely possible for a student who put in all 100 pieces of the puzzle to have concentrated solely on putting the puzzle together and, as a consequence, to remember almost nothing about the information on the different states that was included on his or her puzzle pieces. Therefore, teachers on all levels should never assume that, because two or more students successfully cooperated and completed a particular task, all members of the group learned and mastered all the important information and abilities that were collectively and cooperatively contributed to complete that task. Reiterating this point from a learning perspective, *thinking that focuses on completing an assignment or task will not achieve the same results as the thinking required for learning and mastering all the important content and abilities that were encountered while successfully completing the assignment.*

## A Brief Context for "Jigsaw" and "Jigsaw-like" Group Structures and Activities

Decades before "cooperative learning" emerged as a distinct philosophy and concept in the late 1960s and early 1970s, educators and human development trainers generated a variety of ideas about forming and organizing groups.[4] The initial focus

was for participants to achieve and maintain positive states of mind, attitudes, self-concepts, and abilities to deal with others. A secondary focus was to discover the effect of particular roles, group settings, group interaction activities, and behaviors on the achievement of positive results. These leaders assumed that positive, long-lasting effects would result as individuals cooperated with others and completed particular tasks and roles within group settings. Over time, many in the movement took the easier path and promoted the idea that certain group settings, activities, etc. were automatically good and effective in and of themselves. Their misconception was reflected by the oft heard statement that "It is the process that it important, not the product." In this switch of priorities, the actual "learning" and long term effects of the "processes" and "processing" gradually fell by the wayside in the pursuit of more interesting, entertaining and easy to use processing activities.

Another group of advocates experimented with different ways to form and structure groups and tasks within group settings. Some promoted the value of forming groups to play a game. In other situations, individuals were paired up or placed in larger groups as part of a sensitivity training or trust-building environment. The incorrect assumption was that having one individual fall back to be caught by another in a "trust building" activity and seeing others do the same automatically taught the individuals to extend this "trust" to others they did not know outside the group setting. While no sound research studies found that these trust-building activities resulted in significant changes in the degree, way or frequency that participants trusted others beyond the group, the lack of research support did not keep advocates of these activities from promoting their use. One author of this chapter, Robert J. Stahl, witnessed these trust-building activities during workshops on "peace education" in several countries in Eastern Europe in this decade given by internationally-known workshop leaders and authors in this field. Each leader promoted these activities as essential to building the "trust" needed to bring about world peace, break down cultural and ethnic barriers, and stabilize relationships with others that were based on trust. Other than personal testimonials they remembered that supported their position, they had no sound research evidence to support their assumptions and claims—but still the participants fell back to be caught by others in the name of trust and peace.

## The Origin of Jigsaw as a Formal Structure and Sequence of Student Activities

The label "jigsaw" was first assigned to a particular group structure and set of group tasks by Elliot Aronson in the 1960s.[5]

Aronson assumed that under particular conditions, students working and cooperating within groups might be able to focus their efforts and interpersonal abilities to help each other achieve higher levels of mastery of academic content and abilities than could each student working alone. In effect he assumed that under the right conditions, students could channel their cooperation not just to complete academic tasks and assignments but to significantly increase the amount of time and quality of their study together so that most if not all students in each group learned and retained the subject matter content and abilities they were to master.

He set out to invent a group structure and to isolate conditions that would help students to motivate themselves to increase their own academic achievement and that of other students within their group. He explored, refined and put into practice a number of devices, structures, activities and reward systems; researched them in classrooms; and found what consistently worked to enhance and to hinder or prevent students from studying and increasing their academic achievement while cooperating with peers in small groups.

The result of years of work was what he called "Jigsaw." His Jigsaw consisted of forming students into academic learning groups, having these groups break out into small, temporary "expert groups," and then breaking up these expert teams so that students returned to their original home teams or home groups to teach one another the content and abilities at which they had become "experts."

The original "Jigsaw" with a capital "J" was the structure and set of complementary instructional variables that Aronson and his colleagues invented, assembled and field tested with a number of studies in classrooms. Aronson's jigsaw is far more complex and oriented toward academic outcomes than what is usually thought of or advocated as "jigsaw" today.

## Slavin Investigates the Elements of Aronson's jigsaw

Seeing the impressive increases in academic achievement by Aronson's jigsaw structure and accompanying conditions, Robert Slavin and his colleagues in the late 1970s began investigating the use of this jigsaw group structure while simultaneously searching for those elements that were directly responsible for leading to or hindering high levels of individual student's academic success. In other words, they inquired as to whether it was (1) the group structure itself that led to significant increases in student achievement, or (2) something else that led to these results, or (3) the group structure *and* something else—in combination—that jointly were responsible for the high levels of student achievement

Aronson's students had demonstrated. Working primarily in inner city schools with at-risk and other low-achieving students, Slavin[6] discovered

- ▶ Aronson's jigsaw group structure (i.e., jigsaw with expert groups) was a powerful and robust way to arrange students into academic study teams and groups and to give individual students a specific set of academic-oriented tasks that, when executed correctly, could significantly increase their personal academic achievement and that of their entire home team;

- ▶ Aronson's jigsaw group structure (i.e., what is typically referred to today as "jigsaw with expert groups") provided students with opportunities to cooperate in new ways, to cooperate with others outside their original teams, and to cooperate with a focus on enabling each teammate to become an "expert" at a particular set of academic content and abilities;

- ▶ To maximize academic achievement, students needed to be organized into teams, encouraged to view themselves as members of a team, and have a well-structured reward system that awarded teams worthwhile "bonuses" on the basis of increases in the academic achievement of individual team members taken collectively. Consequently, a group is only elevated to the status of a team when a reward structure is put into place where teams can only be rewarded on the basis of the collective scores of individual members on a closed-book-and-notes individual test administered one or more days after all formal meetings of the team have ended;[7]

- ▶ Slavin concluded that (a) a particular set of conditions and requirements was definitely needed to complement any group structure if the focus was on academic achievement by all group members; and (b) the inclusion or absence of each of these conditions or requirements directly and dramatically affected the types and extent of academic achievement each member of each group or team achieved. Slavin referred to these conditions or requirements as "essential elements of cooperative learning."[8] In other words, like Aronson, Slavin found that when these essential elements were executed *to complement* Aronson's jigsaw group structure, significant academic achievement scores resulted for the vast majority of students in classrooms at all levels and regardless of the location of the schools. Furthermore, when Aronson's jigsaw was used and when one or more of these essential elements were missing or of poor quality, the amount of academic gains by students was correspondingly less. For instance, it was not because students were assigned to "expert groups" that they learned more. Rather, they learned more because students in these expert groups had clear guidelines as to (1) what they were to learn and remember, (2) what their specific jobs were within these expert groups, and (3) what each expert group member was responsible for doing once he or she returned to his or her home base team. In part, these students learned more because they felt a strong sense of belonging to their team, and they wanted to contribute what they could to help the team earn a bonus reward that could only be earned by each student scoring high on the individual tests taken after the team had finished its studying together. Slavin's research reconfirmed that the gains in student achievement were not due simply to the structure of Aronson's jigsaw (with expert groups) but to the several requirements (or "essential elements") that Aronson and later Slavin *added to his jigsaw structure*;

▶ Aronson's requirements, which Slavin examined and verified as "essential elements of cooperative learning," can and must be used with any group structure and cooperative activity in order to ensure that the cooperative activities within each team result in high levels of academic achievement in nearly all instances for all or nearly all team members.[9]

Slavin furthered his "fine tuning" of Aronson's original model by requiring all students at the start to read individually all the text assigned to the team. He added team rewards to the model, along with guidelines for determining which teams earned particular types of rewards. One important factor that differentiated both Aronson's and Slavin's model from other group structures and activities is that both required as one of their essential elements that the teacher should alert students to exactly what each had to learn and master rather than to tasks they had to complete.

## Misconceptions Arising from Slavin's Creation of "Jigsaw II"

Slavin was so emphatic about the power of these "essential elements," which now included his additional requirements, that about 1983 he introduced the name "Jigsaw II," with the "II" signifying those jigsaws with expert group activities that included all the essential elements required to ensure high levels of student achievement. The "II" distinguished his Jigsaw from that of Aronson. Using his system, a "jigsaw" described Aronson's group structure and an activity that included "expert groups" but did not include all of the "essential elements" to make this

structure effective. However, by that date the label "jigsaw" was being used to refer to a number of different structures and activities that were "like a jigsaw"—none of these being even remotely close to Aronson's model.

Two major misconceptions grew from Slavin's use of the name "Jigsaw II." One was that "Jigsaw II" was the name for any jigsaw with expert groups, whether or not the jigsaw being implemented met all of Slavin's essential conditions for optimizing academic achievement. A second was that educators saw the number "II" as a notation of a more complex form of a "jigsaw" structure rather than as a means of distinguishing jigsaw structures and activities that included all the essential elements.

Another result of Slavin's use of the 'II' was that educators began adding more numbers to the 'II' to signify group structures with more tiers of groups or group tasks. Hence, a Jigsaw III denoted a more complete set of groups and tasks than a Jigsaw II, and a Jigsaw IV would necessarily be more complex than a Jigsaw II or III. Jigsaw III[10] and Jigsaw IV[11] were introduced for structures that included additional meetings of the base or home teams. What got lost in Slavin's numbering system was that teachers started to concentrate on simply having students complete group tasks using these more complex structures and lost the necessary focus on ensuring that all the essential elements that significantly contributed to maximizing students' academic achievement were also implemented.

## A Modest Proposal

The word "jigsaw" in an educational context has come to mean many different things. This section provides a taxonomy of jigsaw-like activities as well as jigsaw structures and tasks within instructional settings. The taxonomy is intended to provide a useful identification system with accompanying descriptions. A jigsaw may emerge as individuals decide to complete a task but not as members of a group. jigsaw structures, activities and tasks may emerge from individuals who voluntarily form groups or voluntarily create a jigsaw structure to complete their tasks. jigsaw structures and activities may be deliberately set up and assigned by teachers with specific tasks for group members to complete individually and as and in a group.

The first section of the taxonomy, designated as "Voluntary Jigsaw Structures and Activities," labels and describes instances of jigsaw-like situations, structures and activities that could occur in contexts where a teacher has not assigned students to a group and specific tasks to complete. The second section, designated as "Instructor-Assigned Jigsaw Structures," include jigsaw structures and activities that are assigned by an instructor, with students given specific tasks to complete, first as individuals and then in conjunction with members of their respective groups. The taxonomy presents the great variety of activities that can be described using the word "jigsaw," and allows teachers to distinguish them from each other and identify those most likely to advance the goals of cooperative learning.

Readers should note that none of these jigsaw structures is by itself a cooperative learning structure or task. All can be used or engaged in to complete a task, project or assignment. Those desiring to elevate any of the activities and work by group members to achieve the conditions for optimal cooperative learning must add the essential elements described earlier.

## TAXONOMY OF JIGSAW-LIKE SITUATIONS AND JIGSAW GROUP STRUCTURES AND COMPLEMENTARY ACTIVITIES

### 1. Voluntary Jigsaw Structures and Activities
In these activities, two or more individuals voluntarily share particular items, materials, information, or abilities in order to complete a particular task or achieve a particular goal.

### Jigsaw-Like Situations W – Non-Structured Jigsaw-like Activities Within Casual Non-Group Settings
Situations in this category are not formally "structured" and do not follow any formal organization for cooperation among the individuals involved. Rather, individuals who do not see themselves as a group decide informally what they want to do together, agree to help out, and participate when and as they are able, all of which is done voluntarily. In these situations, each individual usually accepts at the outset that he or she is not likely to be able to successfully complete the entire task or achieve the entire goal without the assistance of one or more others.

Examples of a non-structured jigsaw-like situation include two or more individuals who do not see themselves as a group or team attempting to solve the same crossword puzzle; two or more students in the same course at the school library informally helping one another to complete the same homework assignment; two or more individuals who happen to stop their cars alongside the road to help the driver of a third vehicle pull out of a ditch or get the engine running; and two or more students in the same classroom passing the answers they found to some of the questions for an assignment while copying the answers others found to other questions so that all eventually have all the answers to all the questions.

### Jigsaw-Like Situations X – Self-Structured Jigsaw-like Activities within an Assigned Task Completion Group
Situations in this category typically occur when two or more individuals who are placed in a "team" or "group" without formal directions engage in cooperative efforts and create their own structure for accomplishing a goal. Group members divide up the task, assignment or project into segments each can or wants to work on, and then cooperate to complete it.

One example of this self-structured jigsaw occurs when students are organized into groups by the teacher with a project to complete, and students among themselves decide how they are going to divide up the work, complete the work (mostly independent of the others), and then put the products of their work together so that they have a completed project. In these instances, they create their own division of labor, complete their parts to the best of their ability, and contribute the product of their work in conjunction and cooperation with the other group members.

### Jigsaw-Like Situations Y – Self-Structured Jigsaw-like Activities within a Self-Formed Task Completion Group
Situations in this category occur when two or more individuals who are not members of a structured group openly and deliberately view themselves as a "team" or "group" and engage in cooperative efforts. Group members divide up the work into segments that each works on and then cooperate to complete the task, assignment or project. In these situations, each individual accepts that he or she may not be able to successfully complete the task without the assistance of others. There may be little direct contact among the group members and little face to face interaction as the focus of the work is the completion of the task or project they all view as important to themselves.

### Jigsaw-Like Situations Z – Self-Structured Jigsaw-like Activities within a Self-Formed Group or Team with a Focus on Learning-to-Master
Situations in this category occur when two or more individuals who are not members of a structured group openly and deliberately view themselves as a "team" or "group." Each individual accepts that he or she may not be able to successfully complete the task without the assistance of one or more others and so these individuals form a group in which each individual is committed to doing his or her individual share of the work and cooperating with others so that everyone has an optimal chance of success. As in the previous jigsaw-like situation, they divide up the work, task, assignment or project into segments that each works on,

and then cooperate to complete the task, assignment or project. What typically occurs in these situations is that the individuals teach others and expect to be taught by others so that they all have a chance to retain or even master the content and abilities that are the focus of the assignment, task or project.

One example of this self-structured jigsaw occurs when students in a class deliberately organize themselves as a "study team" or "study group." Members of the group share their resources while doing their best to teach others the content and abilities aligned with their part; and each student becomes a student of other group members when the latter are teaching their respective content and abilities. In these situations, students may exclude or expel individuals from the group or team who are viewed as not doing their part. In many instances, students form a strong emotional bond with others in their group or team, as well as with the group or team itself, and view the success of others in the group or team as something of a victory for themselves.

## 2. Instructor-Assigned jigsaw Structures

In these jigsaw structures, groups or teams are formally set up by the teacher, who provides each student with a set of items, materials, questions to answer, and information that are often unavailable at the start to all others in the group or team and that are needed for the group or team to be successful.

Jigsaw Structure A — Jigsaw Within Intact Groups or Teams
During these activities, members cooperate and contribute what they have to their group without being directed to leave the group or team to meet with others from another group or team.

There are three subcategories of this type of Jigsaw within instructional settings:

1. *Jigsaw with a Non-Academic Focus within Intact Groups or Teams.* Here the teacher provides time for group or team members to cooperate with the primary focus of achieving one or more non-academic goals. For instance, the teacher might direct students in each group to complete one or more tasks for the purpose of "team-building" or enhancing their abilities to cooperate effectively with one another, to hone their interpersonal skills, or to improve their abilities to communicate more clearly and effectively. The teacher judges the success of the endeavor by the behavior of students, the products they generate or some other indicator. With rare exceptions, students are not formally tested on the extent of their learning and retention of the content and abilities associated with completing these tasks.[12]

2. *Jigsaw with a Focus on Academic Task Completion within Intact Groups or Teams.* Here the teacher sets up groups or teams formally in the same way as in the last example, but with a focus on achieving one or more assigned academic tasks or goals. The teacher then provides time for group or team members to cooperate with a primary focus on completing one or more academic task or projects assigned by the teacher.

For instance, the teacher might announce that each group is responsible for coming up with correct answers to all the assigned questions. Each student is to read the text and find answers to his or her set of questions before sharing these with others as the group assembles all the questions and their respective answers. In these settings, students view their efforts and the focus of their work almost exclusively as *completing the task* of getting acceptable answers to all the questions. Learning, retaining and mastering some of the content associated with the assignment is more incidental and coincidental. Typically the teacher evaluates the final product of each group's work, usually assuming that the final product is sufficient evidence of all that the students in the group "learned" while completing the assignment.

3. *Jigsaw with a Focus on Academic Mastery within Intact Groups or Teams.* Here the teacher provides time for group or team members to cooperate with a primary focus on students in each group or team learning and mastering the academic content and skills required by the assigned project.

In the same way as in the previous examples, the teacher forms students into groups where each student has a set of questions to answer. The teacher announces that each group is responsible for coming up with correct answers to all the questions, that all students are to focus on learning the content and abilities associated with the questions and answers, and that students will take an individual test that will include a number of questions they are answering within their group or team. Merely getting answers to all the questions is the first step of their work. The major task is to help each other learn the questions and answers so that all will score high on a test in which books, notes and computers are closed; each student will take this test after their work in groups or teams is done. The teacher directs each student to first find answers to his or her set of questions before sharing these with others as the group assembles all the questions and their respective answers. In these settings, the major focus is to cooperate productively, teach one another and learn from one another so that all achieve the highest level of mastery of the content and abilities related to all the questions that were given to the group.

### Jigsaw Structure B — Jigsaw with One Tier of Breakout Groups

Activities using this jigsaw structure include situations where the teacher formally places students in groups or teams, in which each group member has a set of items, materials, information, or questions to answer that are often deliberately made unavailable at the start to all others in the group or team and that are needed for the group or team to successfully complete its tasks. At a time determined by the teacher, all students are directed to leave their initial or home group or team and to form temporary breakout groups consisting of students from other groups or teams in order to cooperate to gain greater expertise or information to bring back to their home group or team. Membership in these breakout groups is predetermined by the teacher. At a time determined by the teacher, students depart from these temporary groups and return to their home groups or teams, where they contribute what they gained and cooperate to accomplish the goals established for the group by the teacher.

There are two subcategories of this type of Jigsaw within instructional settings:

1. *Jigsaw with a Focus on Academic Task Completion with One Tier of Breakout Groups.* The teacher provides time for group or team members to begin their initial cooperation by focusing on completing one or more academic tasks or projects. The teacher allows students in each group to talk about their task, what is needed for all to complete the task, and to share some of their questions so all have a sense of what the scope and nature of the questions are. The teacher announces that each student is first to read the text and find answers to his or her set of questions before sharing these with others as the group assembles all the questions and their respective answers. In these settings, students view their efforts as aimed almost exclusively at *completing the task* of getting acceptable answers to all the questions.

When directed by the teacher, students leave their home groups or teams to form temporary breakout groups consisting of students from other groups or teams. For example, students who have the first set of questions to answer are placed with students who have the same questions to answer. In these groups, students first read the text and work together to arrive at agreed upon answers to each question. They cooperate productively so that each member gets all the correct information for each question to take back to his or her home group or team.

When students depart from these temporary groups, they return to their home groups or teams, where they share their questions and answers and cooperate so that their respective home group or team has answers for the complete set of questions—the

task established for them by the teacher. While some may learn, retain and master a little of the content associated with the questions and answers, this kind of learning and mastery is more incidental and coincidental. Typically the teacher evaluates the final product of each group's work, usually assuming that the final product is sufficient evidence of all that all students in the group "learned" while completing the assignment.

2. *Jigsaw with a Focus on Academic Mastery with One Tier of Expert Groups.* The teacher formally sets up the groups and provides each student with an "expert sheet" that describes in clear language what tasks students are to complete and the specific content and abilities they are to learn and master as they complete the tasks. The teacher provides time for group or team members to begin their initial cooperation, with their primary focus on learning and mastering the content and abilities so they can all score perfect or near perfect on the test consisting of questions and tasks written on the expert sheets available in each group.

In this case, the focus of the cooperative work is not just getting acceptable answers to all the questions, but for students to learn and master all the content and skills associated with the task.

At a time determined by the teacher, all students are directed to leave their initial or home group and to form temporary breakout groups consisting of students from other groups or teams in order to cooperate productively so that each member becomes an "expert" on the content and abilities specified on his or her expert sheet. In this case, students who have the first set of questions to answer are placed with students who have the same questions to answer. In these groups, students first read the text and work together to arrive at agreed upon answers to each question. They cooperate productively so that each member gets all the correct information for each question to take back to his or her home group or team. They then teach and test one another to ensure that all have correctly learned and have a high degree of mastery over the content and abilities their group was assigned. They also take time to help each other to prepare materials and plan the way they will teach the members of their home group what each of them is now an "expert" at.

At a time determined by the teacher, students depart from these temporary groups and return to their home groups or teams, where they contribute what they gained, teach one another, and learn and master all the content and skills that others in their group mastered in their respective expert groups. Students are expected to teach and test one another on the content and skills associated with all the expert sheets. Their aim is for each student to do very well on the individual test that all will take a day or more after their home team meetings have ended. In this setting, high levels of learning and mastery of the content and skills are not incidental or coincidental, but are the expected results of the academic study of all group or team members during all phases of cooperation and work together, whether in the home groups or expert groups.

### Jigsaw Structure C — Jigsaw with a Focus on Academic Mastery, One Tier of Breakout Groups and Additional Group Task(s)

Activities using this jigsaw structure include the same as those described in the jigsaw structures in the last section, with the addition of one major task by a group. This additional task makes the structure and its related activities more complex than those just described.

There are two subcategories of this type of Jigsaw within instructional settings:

1. *Jigsaw with a Focus on Academic Mastery, One Tier of Expert Groups and an Expert Group Test.* The teacher organizes the jigsaw with a focus on academic mastery in the same way as in the last section, but also administers an individual test to students when they have nearly completed their phase of academic study and cooperation in the expert groups. This test helps ensure that students focus on learning and retaining the content and abilities that are the responsibility of their expert team. The teacher grades these tests and provides them to students, who are still in their expert groups. Students use these test results to determine who needs additional assistance in comprehending and mastering particular content and abilities. When this re-teaching is done and after students informally test one another again on the content, members of each group continue their work in the manner and sequence that will be used in teaching their home group members. Holliday has presented a good example of this structure in practice.[13]

2. *Jigsaw with a Focus on Academic Mastery, One Tier of Expert Groups, and Test Review Session.* The teacher organizes the jigsaw with a focus on academic mastery in the same way as in the last section (subcategory B.2), but adds a test review session. After students have completed their study with expert groups and have informed their home groups of what they have learned, the teacher reconvenes each home group or team a day or two prior to the large unit or term test and assigns its members to review the content and abilities studied during their previous group or team meetings. Group members can use this opportunity to cooperate

not for the purpose of learning new content and abilities, but to review what they were to have learned during previous group or team meetings and individually in preparation for a major test that is to be taken within a day or two. Steinbrink and Stahl have provided a good example of this structure in practice.[14]

### Closing Comments

This chapter has made it clear that "Jigsaw" is not a single or simple group structure or activity. In the classroom, jigsaws may be set up very informally, with students assigned to cooperate to complete one or more group projects or tasks. While these activities would be jigsaws, they are far cries from all the formal steps and conditions that have to be met for a jigsaw activity and team effort to achieve the status of being optimal cooperative learning.

The different jigsaw structures are usually not difficult and time consuming to implement. Rather it is somewhat difficult and time consuming to organize all the essential elements of optimal cooperative learning that *must also be implemented along with and complementary to* the requirements for a jigsaw. This means that implementing a jigsaw structure as a cooperative learning activity is far from an easy task for the teacher. Teachers have a great deal to do before, during and after a jigsaw team activity to make sure that students operate within an optimal cooperative learning environment. The single most important criterion of the effectiveness of the cooperative work endeavor is the score each team member earns on his or her individual academic test taken a day or more after the teams have completed their work together. Only these scores serve as the measure of the learning that was accomplished during and over the period of the team meetings, regardless of the extent, quality and civility of the cooperation among team members.

A jigsaw structure or activity, like a lecture, or a discussion, or the use of a computer as a teaching or learning tool, is *not* in and of itself a model of teaching. Rather, a jigsaw structure, if combined correctly with one or more other activities, can be a major component of a model of teaching.

It is far easier to claim to be doing cooperative learning using jigsaw than it is to successfully execute all the decisions and activities that are required to transform a jigsaw structure and activity into a highly successful optimal cooperative learning activity. When educators simply use the language of "cooperative learning" without successfully carrying out these decisions and activities, one result is that most students in most groups will not come close to learning the content and abilities that they could achieve under optimal conditions of cooperative learning. A second result is that teachers will begin to assert that "cooperative learning" is only a theory and does not work in practice. However, those who comprehend and follow the information provided in this chapter, and implement jigsaw and other cooperative group structures complemented by the essential elements of optimal cooperative learning, will have a different experience. They will have sufficient evidence that *the "theory" of cooperative learning does work in practice* when and only when all aspects of the "theory" are implemented fully in their classrooms. 

## NOTES

1. Dr. James Doyle Casteel, formerly Full Professor and later Professor Emeritus of the College of Education, University of Florida, Gainesville, passed away on December 25, 1998. Dr. Casteel is included as a co-author here, as this chapter is an expansion of a manuscript that Robert J. Stahl and he started working on prior to his death. Inclusion of this chapter is also a tribute to Dr. Casteel from the co-author, who was privileged to have had Dr. Casteel as the Chair of his doctoral committee, as a colleague and beloved friend.

2. A number of misconceptions regarding group work and "cooperative learning" were noted in Chapters 1 and 2 in this book.

3. Space restraints prohibit the inclusion of all the essential elements that are needed to create the variables and environment to promote optimal cooperative learning.

4. Schmuck and Schmuck provide a very good overview of the history, models, leaders and research in groups and individuals in groups. See Robert A. Schmuck and Patricia A. Schmuck, *Group Processes in the Classroom*, 6th edition (Dubuque, Iowa: William C. Brown, 1992). For other contributions to the historical, practitioner and research literature about groups, see: Elliot Aronson, Nancy T. Blaney, Cookie Stephan, Jev Sikes, and Matthew Snapp, *The Jigsaw Classroom* (Beverly Hills, Calif.: Sage, 1978); Elliott Aronson and Shelley Patnoe, *The Jigsaw Classroom: Building Cooperation in the Classroom* (New York: Longman, 1997); Robert E. Slavin, *Cooperative Learning: Theory, Research, and Practice*, 2nd edition (Boston: Allyn & Bacon, 1995) and *Introduction to Cooperative Learning* (New York: Longman, 1983); and David W. Johnson, Roger T. Johnson, Edythe J. Holubec, and Patricia Roy, *Circles of Learning: Cooperation in the Classroom* (Alexandria, Va.: Association for Supervision and Curriculum Development, 1984).

5. See Elliot Aronson, Nancy T. Blaney, Cookie Stephan, Jev Sikes, and Matthew Snapp, *The Jigsaw Classroom, op. cit*; Elliot Aronson and Shelley Patnoe, *The Jigsaw Classroom: Building Cooperation in the Classroom, op. cit.*

6. Robert E. Slavin, *Introduction to Cooperative Learning*, op. cit., and in *When and Why Does Cooperative Learning Increase Achievement? Theoretical and Empirical Perspectives* (Baltimore: Johns Hopkins University, Center for Research on Elementary and Middle Schools, OERI no. G86-0006 1986, 1989).

7. Robert J. Stahl has referred to groups established for the primary purpose of maximizing the academic achievement of all members as "structured academic learning teams." Like Aronson and Slavin, Stahl has pointed out that the primary criterion for determining whether the cooperating, studying and learning within each team warranted the title of "cooperative learning" is the score of each individual team member on a test taken one or more days after the team has completed its formal work together. In other words, because "cooperative learning" is a process that is expected to achieve a product—i..e., high levels of academic achievement for all team members—the product, i.e., the individual test score of each team member, is the ultimate standard as to whether the process was successful. Consequently, teachers who use means to evaluate individual student and team achievement other than a closed-note and closed-book individual test are not collecting the evidence that is needed to determine the group or team's academic achievement.

8. Robert E. Slavin, *When and Why Does Cooperative Learning Increase Achievement?, op. cit.*

9. It should be noted that Slavin attended to and described six essential elements, to which Johnson and Johnson added in their writings regarding the essential elements. In Chapters 1 and 2 of this book, Stahl expands upon their foundational work by breaking apart some of the original essential elements and adding a number of others based on his work with undergraduate and graduate teacher education students and especially feedback from teachers who tried to achieve optimal cooperative learning in their own students at levels ranging from grade 3 to graduate level. The majority of these teachers insisted that Stahl should stress with his pre- and in-service teachers that when any of his essential elements are not included, the quality of the student's behavior and cooperation in teams goes down, as well as the scores on student's individual tests.

10. John E. Steinbrink and Robert J. Stahl, "Jigsaw III + Jigsaw II + Cooperative Test Review: Applications to the Social Studies Classroom," in *Cooperative Learning in the Social Studies: A Handbook for Teachers*, edited by Robert J. Stahl (Menlo Park, Calif.: Addison-Wesley, 1994): 133-153.

11. Dwight C. Holliday, "The Development of Jigsaw IV in a Secondary Social Studies Classroom," paper presented at the annual meeting of the Midwest Educational Research Association, Chicago, April 2000.

12. In cases where the learning and mastery of specific techniques for effective cooperation, effective interpersonal relations or clear and effective communications are aligned with targeted national, state or district standards or major student outcome objectives posited by the teacher, then a focus on helping students encounter, learn and master the application of these techniques would be considered instances of an academic mastery focus. If the teacher is committed to ensuring students learn and master these techniques and purposely tests each student to determine his or her degree of mastery of each technique, then the jigsaw activity to master these techniques would be the third discussed in this section, "Jigsaw with a Focus on Academic Mastery within Intact Groups or Teams."

13. Dwight C. Holliday, "The Development of Jigsaw IV in a Secondary Social Studies Classroom," *op. cit.*

14. John E. Steinbrink and Robert J. Stahl. "Jigsaw III + Jigsaw II + Cooperative Test Review: Applications to the Social Studies Classroom," *op. cit.*

# CHAPTER 7

# An Elementary Classroom Where Students Learn to Cooperate and Cooperate Effectively

**Robert J. Colomb**, Sunset View Elementary School, Provo, Utah with **George W. Chilcoat**, Brigham Young University, Provo, Utah and **Nancy N. Stahl**, Constructivist Learning Associates, Chandler, Arizona

**Like many teachers on all levels**, elementary social studies teachers expect their students to learn to interact with their classmates, get along with others, and take responsibility for themselves. This expectation, however, is not always followed up with instruction on how to accomplish these goals. A classic example is a silent primary or elementary classroom. Many teachers in these classrooms sincerely believe that silence is golden. But is it? Does silence promote proper communication between the teacher and students or between students? Do periods of silence result in improved thinking, higher achievement, and greater acceptance of personal responsibility? We think not.

One problem with such ideas about silence is that we do not live in a silent society. We live in a society where mass communication demands that we be interdependent. In fact, no single group can exist without the active and continuous interaction of its members. If teachers must prepare students for the world outside the classroom, they must help them to succeed in a world that communicates, that cooperates, and that views responsibility in the context of social meanings. If students are to do this beyond the classroom, teachers then have an obligation to make sure students learn how to interact, to cooperate, to succeed, and to be responsible in the classroom.

Although we expect students to speak, we often forget that many need to learn how to speak. They need to learn such things as how to articulate their thoughts, when to speak, how to control the level of their speech, and what kinds of language are appropriate and inappropriate in particular situations. Many students learn these things through trial-and-error experiences, but many are unsuccessful. These unsuccessful students either avoid speaking or often speak in ways that are inappropriate. In the classroom, we need to help students learn the art and skills of speaking, especially of academic, interpersonal, and cooperative speech.

We must not automatically assume, however, that when students are talking and working in groups in the classroom, they are meeting the teacher's expectations. Students may be speaking with no one listening. They may be sharing ideas and information with no one learning. They may be working alongside others in a group without working as a group. These students may be interacting but not becoming skilled at interacting. They may assume responsibility for getting their portion of a project completed without learning to be responsible outside such projects.

As these possible results suggest, talking and silence in the classroom are not either-or choices. What occurs during the silence and during the talking is important.

Using cooperative learning techniques, elementary teachers rely heavily upon student speech and student silences to help large numbers of students meet the teacher's achievement and affective expectations. When used appropriately, cooperative learning theory and strategies can be powerful tools for teaching social studies.

The following section emphasizes the perspective and experiences of Bob Colomb, while he was a second grade teacher at Sunset View Elementary School. Written in the first person, this next section creates a personal sense of the nature of learning to cooperate and cooperative learning from one elementary teacher's perspective.

## My Cooperative Learning Experience as It Evolved in My Elementary Classroom

My elementary teaching experience has consisted of involvement in various grade levels from 1st through 6th. For years I had used student groups for all kinds of reasons. I never really felt as though I had used groups very well, but students did seem to enjoy being in them and groups did change the routine of the class activities,

In other words, I had used groups to do things but had not paid much attention to their structure and organization. During this time I also felt that the sense of cohesion and teamwork I always thought would evolve from students working in groups never emerged. Students formed groups, did their group work, and left their groups as though the groups had never existed. What I felt was missing was a way to organize the students and groups so they could accomplish what I thought they could.

For years I tried various kinds of group activities, even using commercially produced materials and those given out by presenters at conferences to enhance the quality of my students' group work and the benefits that I thought should result. Although these provided a greater variety of group tasks and activities, they still fell short of what I wanted and what my students needed.

When I first heard about cooperative learning I was both excited and wary. The initial information sounded too good to be true. Could groups really accomplish all that I heard and read they could accomplish? Was it really that easy to transform my class into a cooperative learning environment? Could something that effective be that simple to learn to use? My caution was partially an outgrowth of the attitudes of so many elementary teachers that cooperative learning was only a theory that wouldn't work in their classrooms. Some of my colleagues suspected that this was another theory from university professors who hadn't been in real elementary or secondary classrooms for decades. There were also concerns that cooperative learning was a new fad that would come and go like so many others in recent years.

I was curious and concerned about how I could improve my teaching. I also felt that, as a professional, the least I should do was find out more about cooperative learning to determine whether I should use it in my classroom.

## I Had to Start Somewhere, or How I Became Involved

When an opportunity arose, I volunteered to travel from Utah to Southern California to see cooperative learning in action. I wanted to find out whether the rumors about its effectiveness were true.

I visited the ABC School District (not its real name) where Spencer Kagan's cooperative learning methods were being implemented.[1] I observed 1st, 3rd, 4th, and 6th grade classes. In every classroom, students were using their peers in various ways to teach themselves. At first I was not impressed and was not sold on what I saw. I had expected to visit classrooms in which students had had extensive experience using cooperative learning, were almost "super learners," and had teachers who were veteran users of these strategies. Instead I found teachers and

students who were just past the starting line themselves. These teachers were in the early stages of becoming better implementers of cooperative learning teams.

With this perspective, my interpretations of what I was watching changed. Coming to understand that these students were just getting started, I became impressed with what they were learning, how well they stayed on task in their small groups, and how well they interacted with one another. If I could get my students to do many of these things by the end of the year, I would be pleased. If this is what students could accomplish early in their use of cooperative learning, I started to imagine what they could do when they really became experienced users of these strategies. This visit whetted my appetite enough to investigate and read all I could find about cooperative learning.

## What I Found in the Literature on the Philosophy, Theory and Research on Cooperative Learning

What proof was there that cooperative learning did what people claimed it could do? More than 530 classroom studies on cooperative learning have been reported.[2] These research studies reveal that structured cooperation with others consistently produced higher achievement and productivity than when individualistic or competitive structures were used. Furthermore, students did better in many affective areas (such as getting along with both peers and the teacher), in the quality of their talking with one another, and in the time they spent voluntarily on task.[3] In short, these research studies reveal that cooperative learning done well improved the whole child in nearly all the areas of concern to elementary teachers.

What also impressed me was that what I found in the professional journals and textbooks was not just theory and research: I discovered that countless studies were done in classrooms like mine where teachers were using cooperative learning with their own students. I found that cooperative learning could work in my classroom if I wanted to put in the time and effort necessary to implement it as it should be implemented. I also discovered that there were a number of very technical steps that I needed to follow so that I could create genuine cooperative learning groups and activities rather than traditional group activities.

The philosophy of cooperative learning promotes cooperation and collaboration so that students' energy can be channeled by specific instructional strategies to promote positive academic, affective, and social interaction goals. I learned that appropriate cooperative learning apparently would enable my pupils to achieve higher academic results and productivity.

This was what I was after!

The closer I looked at cooperative learning and its basic elements, the more convinced I became that this could be an effective way to teach social studies. I had to try it in my own classroom. I felt that at last I had something I could adapt and use to enhance student learning of academic and social skills. I decided I would put this new philosophy of cooperation and interaction to the test.

## My Early Frustrations Led Me to Further Exploration and Additional Strategies

Well into my second year of using cooperative learning I remained frustrated with the lack of whole-group inclusion activities. Up to that time I had applied nearly all the basic elements of cooperative learning and was using them to the best of my ability. Still, something was lacking. A colleague and I decided that we needed more whole-group inclusion before we formed our students into small groups. We eventually labeled the element missing in the original list of basic elements "diversity of grouping procedures." I believe this element is critical if the elementary classroom is to evolve into an effective cooperative learning environment.

This diversity, one of the most important elements of cooperative learning, is often ignored. Many educators begin cooperative learning in small-group learning situations, forming their classes into small groups before students practice cooperative skills. In the whole-class group activities I started using, my students learned and improved individual cooperative skills that enabled them to work together in small groups like well-oiled machines. When students fail to achieve acceptable levels of cohesion and skill before placing them into small groups, a major result of using cooperative groups will be frustration for the students and teacher alike. When students acquire the skills and get the practice they need, however, frustration is rare.

To ensure quality team achievement, I first created a cooperative atmosphere within my primary level classroom through whole-group inclusion or class-building activities. I find that during the class inclusion activities the cooperative philosophy is modeled for all students. Teacher and students alike are able to see the philosophy and theory behind cooperative learning in actual practice. They also observe the guidelines, expectations, rules for behavior, and attitudes demonstrated and reinforced. Various rewards are used to praise appropriate behaviors and attitudes.

I advise teachers just getting started with cooperative learning in their classrooms to start here. Based on my experience, I believe elementary students will achieve their potential fully only after whole-group inclusion is attained.

After I came to realize how important class-building activities were to maintaining a cooperative atmosphere, I continued to use these activities all year long, using a different social goal, content area goal, or academic skill as the focus of each new activity. For instance, I might use math, science, literature, or reading tasks in addition to my social studies topics. Many of my colleagues here at Sunset View agree on the importance of the skills and attitudes that result from these class-building tasks. By continuing cooperative efforts in the class throughout the year, my students reach levels of learning never achieved in my pre-cooperative learning classroom.

Cooperative learning is not a panacea for the problems in education. It is, however, a philosophy and an approach to teaching in which I fully believe.

## For Me, Cooperative Learning is a Philosophy Underlying My Approach to Teaching

Cooperative learning is first and foremost a philosophy. Of course, a philosophy without effective implementation strategies has no power—just as a set of strategies with no philosophical context will have little effect. They are interdependent. The philosophy of cooperative learning through the theory was appealing to me and led me to investigate and then to use many strategies. While using these strategies, I never lost sight of the philosophy-theory behind them. I have observed many teachers use these strategies unsuccessfully because they expect the strategies to work with any philosophy they choose. These strategies work to the extent that their practice is guided by consistent theory and philosophy. I encourage all teachers to spend at least as much time studying and learning to use the philosophy-theory of cooperative learning as they do learning the strategies. Neither will work well without the other.

How can elementary teachers use this philosophy in their classrooms? They must learn the theory, structure the class tasks, get students talking and working together, play down competition, and increase students' positive interdependence. In other words, elementary teachers must use cooperative learning.

Students love to talk. They get excited about moving about in the classroom. They get excited about finding out what others think. They want to share what they know. They are interested in hearing about and studying new things. They tend to get turned off in classrooms where the activities result in one student after another saying the same thing or where the teacher goes around the room or circle and each student says something. In addition, many students have learned that when they get too excited while talking about what they are studying or learning, the teacher will insist that they be quiet to cut down the noise level.

I have found that students have not been taught how to be quiet and how to talk within extended interaction situations. They are directed to be quiet but not taught how to be quiet.

In my classroom, I hear structured noise or on-task noise generated from on-task conversation that allows other students and me to listen to the learning that is occurring at that moment. For students to achieve quality-structured noise, I teach them how to come face-to face with one another so that all they need are their twelve-inch voices rather than their typical twenty-four inch voices.

Elementary students need to learn how to be quiet and also how to be good listeners when they are quiet. In other words, they need to learn that being quiet means they have a number of jobs to do that do not require talking—that being quiet means far more than merely shutting up.

## My Classroom as You Would Find It

Many of my classroom activities start out with whole-group inclusion activities before we move to specific small-group work and then finally to individual work. When the individual work is completed, the product is brought back to the small-group level again and then to the whole group for presentation and interaction. I consider this type of cooperative learning an advanced form. Ideally, for me, a teacher would want to take a class from whole group to team, from small group team to individual or competitive, then back to the small group, and finally from the small-group learning teams to the whole group. This shift must be made slowly at first.

On a typical day, the first thing we do in the morning is form a big circle on the floor so everyone faces each other. After some initial conversation and sharing, student groups begin to complete their assigned tasks. One group may work on the calendar for the month, another the science bulletin board, another the social studies project display, and so forth. Each group knows it is responsible for one of these classroom routines each month. Their particular routine changes each month. Early in the year we spend time in our whole-class group learning what it means to be responsible and learning how to carry out each routine so that it is acceptable.

Instead of having a room with fancy, commercially produced bulletin board materials or materials that I spend hours cutting and pasting and my students essentially ignore, my room now has relevant and fact-filled boards that get attention from nearly every student on a daily basis. Students now observe what other groups put on their boards. They now seem to learn a lot from what is posted.

As the months go by, the student groups get better at completing these routines and improving the quality of their projects.

In that first week we also spend time learning how to interact and work in groups and how to work as a group. The various roles students may need to carry out are explained along with examples. We talk about why these roles are important and what might happen if a role is not carried out. We also share some of our feelings about these roles and why those in the class need to do their jobs in the groups. Some time is spent helping students to feel they are important to the success of the group they are in. We even talk about the ways students can use the groups to learn the material. After the first few weeks, my students have a good sense of what they are to do in their learning groups. We review and continue to work on all these things throughout the year.

From the beginning, I assign specific roles to specific students in each group. This assignment ensures that the same students are not in the same role all the time. Later, students are allowed to pick the major roles they will play, once again with the restriction that they cannot play the same role all the time.

Helping students think about guidelines for their attitudes and behaviors in these groups takes a lot of time at the beginning. What is gained in student achievement, on-task behavior, and improved social skills, however, more than makes up for the time spent helping them become good cooperative group members.

Usually by the end of the first month of the year, I have determined the membership of the base groups where each student will remain throughout the year. Except in rare situations, this is each student's permanent group. Because these are permanent, I am very careful in my selection of which students are to be together for this length of time. From time to time, however, new but temporary groups are formed. These groups are used for different reasons, one of which is to ensure that students work with more of their peers of different gender, race, or ethnic backgrounds.

Small groups with the same and different student membership are used in math, science, reading, language arts, and social studies. Students may remain in their base groups or be reassigned to new groups for one day or several weeks. They may be in one, two, or three different groups on some days depending on what we are studying in the different subject areas. We are not in cooperative learning groups all the time.

I also use various group strategies. Using jigsaw, for example, students placed in teams may choose to study a particular time period of history but different incidents within this period. Two girls and two boys in a group together once decided to study and learn about the Vietnam War era. The girls did not want to write or study about the war itself, but were interested instead in the hippie movement. They each took a different approach to the hippie movement. The boys investigated two different aspects of the war. One looked at the military situation; the other at the political. The four students then met together and brought back all that they had learned to the group, put it together as a group, and presented a fantastic informational project to the class.

In this same class, each group was also responsible for completing a large section on a historical time line that covered all the walls of the room. This complete project took us about two months and encompassed research, presentations, writing, art, science, reading, and cooperative skills. As students found specific information, they placed it in their section of the time line once their group had confirmed its relevance, importance, and accuracy. At the end of the unit, students shared with the class what they had learned in their particular section of investigation.

I found that students need not always complete all of the assignments each day just to have it done. For instance, if they are given fifteen questions to answer as part of their social studies group task, I would much rather they answered ten correctly for the day's work, and that they all really knew the correct answers to those ten questions, than have partially correct answers for all fifteen. In part, this decision reflects my acceptance of my role as facilitating optimal student learning as opposed to having students merely finish assignments regardless of what they learn or do not learn. To ensure that students are working on task and are helped in their learning efforts, the class has adopted the use of the raised hand which is the universal sign in cooperative learning that it is time for everyone to be quiet. This quiet time functions as a time-out during which new directions can be given, points of uncertainty can be clarified, and specific questions can be answered. Students learn early that once the hand is raised, everyone is to take time out in his or her group work and stop in silence. I am still amazed at how well this signal works and how fast students catch on to the meaning of the raised hand.

Many of the students in their small groups exchange phone numbers to make sure that their groupmates have done their parts of one or more assignments outside of class. After a while, it is not uncommon for them to call each other at home in the evening and on weekends. They share information and make sure that their groupmates have the assignment when they are not in class for one reason or another. On more than one occasion, two or three members of a group have called a fourth who had missed several classes to tell him or her that they were concerned about the student's absence and about the student generally. They also told the absent groupmate that he or she was part of a team and the team couldn't succeed when not all its members were there in class working together.

When some of these absent students arrive back in class they often report that the members of their groups had called many times to see how they were doing. I now find fewer students voluntarily missing class as the year goes by and students are better informed about what they missed while they were absent.

One day I received a phone call from a parent informing me that the phone at his house had rung at 6:30 that morning. The call, made by a student in my classroom, was for his child. The parent was concerned that his child had been awakened too early in the morning and that the caller was a student in the class. I investigated the matter and found out that this particular student's group was working on a major part of its project and needed everyone in class on that day. The student had missed the day before and his group was concerned he would not be there on that day. So one member of the group volunteered to call the absent student that morning to urge completion of the assignment and attendance at school. The student was in class and was prepared. I find it hard to express my reaction to finding out that the cohesion and mutual concern fostered in this cooperative learning environment would result in second graders actually calling each other at 6:30 in the morning to encourage attendance, to extend personal support, and to insist upon completion of the homework assignment. What is more remarkable is that these are not overachievers; they are children of varied socioeconomic and ethnic backgrounds who have emerged as students within this cooperative learning environment.

## Overcoming Concerns: Two Cases

Implementing effective cooperative learning has implications beyond the classroom walls. A number of situations have arisen that generated concern by people other than the teachers and their students. These situations were handled in ways that promoted the preservation and growth of the cooperative learning environment. The two cases below illustrate how particular concerns were successfully managed.

One problem that emerged from the use of cooperative learning concerned substitute teachers who came into my classroom. These teachers usually expect to have a quiet classroom and maintain total control. In part, they tend to view a quiet classroom as one that meets the absent teacher's expectations. In addition, they don't want anyone to have the impression that they have no control over the students. With cooperative learning, you give the power of learning to the students and they help with the teaching. Over time, the cooperative teams produce many higher-level thinkers and active learners.

Students become accustomed to interacting to help each other learn. Consequently, some of these students will have a difficult time making the transition back to the old way of life, B.T. (i.e., before talking was acceptable). To head this problem off, the same substitute teachers are assigned to cooperative learning classrooms. To further relieve this problem, in-service training sessions in the cooperative learning model should be required of all substitute teachers assigned to these classrooms.

Another problem encountered was that of parents who, for many reasons, did not understand what I was doing with their children in my classroom. This problem was resolved by having a back-to-school night. Parents were given a two-hour training session on the cooperative model and how it was being used in the school. The session included discussion of the research findings along with activities so the parents could have practical experience with cooperative learning. The parents were also given some guidelines and ideas they could apply in their own homes. Many parents requested that follow-up parent training classes be provided so they could be better users of the cooperative models at home. These training sessions have been held. Many parents in our district are now familiar with the cooperative learning philosophy and its basic elements.

## A Final Reflection

As I reflected upon that first experience in these classrooms I came to realize that to do cooperative learning really well requires study, looking for and taking time to read books and articles on theory and research as well as the practical sides of cooperative learning, comprehending the material, thinking seriously as to what one needs to do to implement these ideas, concepts and ideas into one's own classroom, accepting a number of new ideas, breaking of old notions and habits, effort, and time. Facilitating and incorporating cooperative learning is not a quick fix and does not come without its share of frustrations, anxiety and hard work over time. Johnson and Johnson say that it usually takes a teacher at least three years to really get into the groove of doing cooperative learning efficiently and easily in his or own classroom, so don't expect overnight success. Believe me, what I do in my classroom was years in the making. But I would not trade the environment in my classroom, the excitement and activity of my students, or the high levels of academic success we now achieve together for anything. The teachers I observed

during their early stages of using cooperative learning are to be commended for their work and for their courage in opening up their classrooms to cooperative learning.

## Additional Points for Guiding New Teachers in Successfully Implementing "Cooperative Learning"

Appropriate cooperative learning is not easy to start and not easy to achieve. I have trained with Spencer Kagan and with Roger and David Johnson. David once told me that when he came to visit, he would ask me how my cooperative learning model was going. He said he would not ask how his cooperative learning model was working in my class. Because cooperative learning is a philosophy, theory, and set of practical strategies, elementary teachers must take and use what really works for them as long as it is consistent with the essential elements of this theory. The most difficult part of putting cooperative learning into practice is just to begin. After students begin working for themselves and using their energy for educational purposes, being in a cooperative learning classroom becomes fun. I have more fun and more success with each new month of the school year.

When I travel, presenting cooperative learning workshops, I constantly run into teachers who have been using parts of groups for their entire careers. What they lacked, however, was a guide to direct them with well-structured yet flexible methods that would help their students achieve the affective, social, and cognitive learning they desired. I point out that just having groups whose members "cooperate" with one another is a good sign, but that they need to add other things in order to elevate these groups into effective cooperative learning teams. I inform them that I found that cooperative learning gives names to many of the things teachers do or need to do. The cooperative group structures, such as Jigsaw, Teams-Games-Tournament, and Share-Pair provide concrete strategies for them to refine existing things they do and provide guidance for new group structures and tasks. I remind them that they need to develop a philosophy of cooperation and cooperative learning and to use the how-to guidelines to provide structure and organization to this philosophy.

I also point out that even though their students were in groups doing group projects of one kind or another, they may have been using ideas and guidelines that actually prevented or impaired appropriate cooperative learning from occurring. They realize that even though they would like to believe it, they may not be using cooperative learning in their classrooms.

## Final Comments and Encouragement to Teachers to Use Cooperative Learning

Bob's experiences are those of one elementary teacher. Each teacher's experiences will be different in many ways from those in this Provo, Utah, classroom. We want to point out, however, that there will be many similarities. To make cooperative learning work in any classroom, teachers will need to read the theory, research, and practical how-to literature on cooperative learning; accept the research findings that cooperative learning can generate the numerous positive results claimed; use the guidelines and organizational plans for cooperative groups; and develop a philosophy of cooperative learning that will guide decisions and behaviors in the classroom. In forming a personal conception and philosophy of cooperative learning aligned with the theory and research, teachers will evolve their own personalized versions of cooperative learning. Consequently, they will apply their own cooperative learning philosophies rather than a verbatim copy of Kagan's, Johnson and Johnson's, or Slavin's philosophy.[4]

We caution that these individualized philosophies must remain aligned with major features of those that have proven themselves on countless occasions in classroom settings. For instance, a cooperative learning philosophy should not allow the teacher to have a half-hour cooperative learning activity three or four times a week as though cooperative learning was a subject like math, science, or language arts. Cooperative learning is a way of teaching and learning, not a subject to teach or activity to complete. A cooperative learning philosophy should not allow just any group work to be accepted as bona fide cooperative learning in practice. Although many teachers do some things consistently with cooperative learning, many group activities we have observed in classrooms are not compatible with appropriate cooperative learning theory or practice.

Social studies is the most natural subject to be learned in a cooperative mode because social studies, when taught properly, requires active discussion and discovery. The very name, social studies, should be a clue to what our students need to be doing every day in our classrooms. This name also should be a clue to teachers for ensuring students are engaging in social study.

Cooperative learning done well will create a mood of cooperation in your classroom and among your students that will most likely lead to at least four benefits: students will enjoy social studies more than under conventional teaching strategies; their retention of knowledge will increase; their social and interpersonal skills will improve; and their relationships with students different from themselves will improve. Finally, social studies education should provide experiences that encourage students to want to learn and to achieve their maximum potential. Cooperative learning is a proven way to accomplish these goals. 🔯

### NOTES

1. Spencer Kagan, *Cooperative Learning Resources for Teachers* (San Juan Capistrano, Calif.: Resources for Teachers, 1989); *Cooperative Learning* (San Juan Capistrano, Calif.: Kagan Publishing, 2000).

2. See, for example, David W., and Roger T. Johnson, *Cooperation and Competition: Theory and Research* (Edina, Minn.: Interaction Book Company, 1989) and *Cooperative Learning in the Classroom* (Alexandria, Virg.: Association for Supervision and Curriculum Development, 1994); Robert E. Slavin, *Cooperative Learning: Theory, Research, and Practice* (Englewood Cliffs, NJ.: Prentice-Hall, 1990), and "Synthesis of Research on Cooperative Learning." *Educational Leadership* 48 (February 1991): as well as the contributions to this book by Robert E. Slavin, Anne M. Chamberlain, and Eric A. Hurley (Chapter 5) and Ronald L. VanSickle (Chapter 4).

3. David W. Johnson and Roger T. Johnson, *Learning Together and Alone: Cooperative, Competitive, and Individualistic Learning*, 2nd edition, (Englewood Cliffs, N.J.: Prentice-Hall, 1987) as well as *Cooperation and Competition, op. cit.*, and *Cooperative Learning in the Classroom, op. cit.*

4. See Kagan, *Cooperative Learning Resources for Teachers, op. cit.*; Ronald Brandt, "On Cooperative Learning: A Conversation with Spencer Kagan," *Educational Leadership* 47 (January 1990): 8-11; David W. Johnson and Roger T. Johnson, *Learning Together and Alone, op. cit.*, and *Cooperation and Competition, op. cit.*; and Robert E. Slavin, *Cooperative Learning: Theory, Research, and Practice, op. cit.*

# CHAPTER 8

# Cooperative Learning in Middle School Social Studies Classrooms
## A Method to the Madness

**Dwight C. Holliday**, Murray State University, Murray, Kentucky
in collaboration with
**Janet McKenna**, Donald E. Gavit Middle School, Hammond, Indiana
**Joel Johnson**, Joseph L Block Jr. High School, East Chicago, Indiana
**Trudy Floyd**, Henry W. Eggers Middle School, Hammond, Indiana
**Victor Vazquez**, Henry W. Eggers Middle School, Hammond, Indiana

**The self-perceptions** middle school students have of their own maturity run the full gambit from being too old for the "artsy-craftsy" student-centered elementary methodology, to being too young for the rigors of the content-focused secondary curriculum. Middle school students have simultaneous needs for both nurturing and freedom to explore. Likewise, they seek both to please and to rebel against those in authority. Middle school students primarily attend school to socialize—not for academic study or achievement. These same students prefer active to passive learning activities. They tend to be curious and inquisitive. They prefer interacting with peers during learning activities as well as participating in problem-solving situations. They tend to be very impatient and resist sitting still for an extended period of time. Internally, their bodies are undergoing great physical changes and metabolic fluctuations. In addition, most of these students are concrete operational, highly inquisitive and always searching for creative reasons to explain larger phenomena.[1]

During this stage of their development, these students are expected to learn in environments that are often not conducive to the ways they learn. Many experience feelings of alienation that lead to a decline in their academic achievement, absenteeism and an increased likelihood of finally dropping out of school.[2] Yet, knowing these factors exist, many teachers still attempt to teach in traditional ways rather than adopt methodologies that are more conducive to middle school students. With this being the case, how can teachers hope to accomplish their lofty academic goals for their middle school students?

The general focus of the middle school is on the developmental needs of the early adolescent student. Since the 1980's, the middle school reform movement has provided many very valuable designs to accomplish the tasks at hand. Two important designs are: (a) the Model Middle School concept, and (b) block scheduling. The Model Middle School concept employs teams of teachers who teach the four core courses (science, math, language arts, and social studies) to the same students. To do this well, teachers in the same team are given the same planning period and are expected to work as a team to handle all disciplinary and academic concerns and conferences.[3] When done well, team teaching provides greater opportunities for pupil self direction.[4] Team teaching allows teachers in grade-level interdisciplinary teams multiple opportunities to address the diverse personal, social and academic needs of individual students. Cooperative learning in the core classrooms can make their tasks easier by putting the responsibility of academic learning on the shoulders of the very ones who need it—i.e., the students.[5]

Block scheduling in its many forms was introduced to the middle school level over the past several years as a means of extending the time allowed for serious academic study of each subject area. Depending on the type of scheduling system, the average time increase is from a 50-minute to approximately a 90-minute class period that meets from three to five times a week. Few teachers can maintain the attention of their students by lecturing for 90 minutes. Teachers can thus break up their 90-minute periods into segments and use cooperative learning groups. When planned well, having different activities during these segments provides students a change of pace, allows them to stay on task and increases the chances that they will be more attentive to their academic work. The purpose of this chapter is to show how either or both of these designs, with the help of cooperative learning, can improve middle school students' academic achievement.

## A Context for Using Cooperative Learning Methods

In order to decrease alienation and to foster success, the Carnegie Council recommended that teachers create small learning communities through which students could develop fundamental interpersonal-relationship skills and be known individually by at least one adult in the school. Cooperative learning is a methodology that allows teachers to accomplish these tasks. The role that teachers are expected to play in the Model Middle School concept is one where the core group works as a "teaching team" to educate the 100-130 students under combined tutelage. They must find ways to keep students on task and more attentive in order to complete their academic work.

But whether working alone or in their teams, teachers seeking to establish cooperative learning activities need to incorporate the essential elements of cooperative learning. Five of these essential elements are described here. The first element is *face-to-face or knee-to-knee interaction*. The second is *individual accountability*, wherein each student is to provide evidence of his or her academic achievement. In order to make their group function effectively and efficiently, all students must use *group-processing skills*, the third element. However, in many instances, these skills must first be formally taught and then monitored. The fourth element is *positive interdependence*, which means that all members of each group must rely on each other to complete the tasks and to ensure each other's academic learning. A fifth element is that students must have and accept a common academic goal or task that requires the combined effort of all teammates to complete.[6]

## Likely Consequences of Effective Implementation of Cooperative Learning

The research on cooperative learning reveals that the effective use of cooperative learning methods promotes numerous benefits that are important to the development of middle school students' academic achievement. Cooperative leaning methods have been found to:

- Develop higher level thinking skills.[7]
- Stimulate critical thinking debate and help students clarify ideas through discussion and debate.[8]
- Build skills and reduce the tediousness of class activities.[9]
- Develop oral communication skills.[10]
- Improve students' recall of information and retention of material learned.[11]
- Create an environment of active, involved, exploratory learning.[12]
- Encourage student responsibility for learning and involve students in developing curriculum and class procedures.[13]
- Help students wean themselves away from considering teachers as the sole source of knowledge and understanding.[14]
- Allow students to exercise a sense of control while on task.[15]
- Promote higher achievement and class attendance.[16]
- Enable more students to stay on task for longer periods of time.[17]
- Reduce the disruptive behaviors of students.[18]
- Foster modeling of problem-solving techniques by student peers and allow students to explore alternate problem solving solutions in a safe environment.[19]
- Enable weaker students to improve their performance when they are grouped with higher-achieving peers.[20]
- Address learning style differences among students.[21]

## Four Middle School Teachers Meet the Challenges of Using Cooperative Learning

The challenge for middle school teachers is: how can we utilize cooperative learning in order to take advantage of our students' strengths and counteract their weaknesses? This challenge is currently being met very successfully by four northwest Indiana middle school teachers: Janet McKenna, at Donald E. Gavit Middle School; Joel Johnson, at Joseph L. Block Jr. High School; and Trudy Floyd and Victor Vazquez, both at Henry W. Eggers Middle School. Their work and classroom environments are the focus of the remainder of this chapter.

Janet McKenna, an eighth grade social studies teacher in an urban school, teaches as part of a teaching-team within an extended-block (i.e., a 90-minute class period) format. Joel Johnson also teaches eighth grade using the team concept, but within 50-minute class periods and six periods per day. Victor Vazquez, a 7th grade social studies teacher, and Trudy Floyd both operate within the Model Middle School concept and the block-scheduling format. The amount of cooperative learning employed by these teachers varies according to their own confidence level in their skills. The gauntlet runs from once or twice a month for Johnson, to two or three times a week by Vazquez and Floyd, to once a day by McKenna.

Janet McKenna uses cooperative learning to break up her modified block scheduled class period. She first heard of cooperative learning in college. However, when she was hired at Gavit Middle School, she was placed on a team that did not encourage or utilize cooperative learning in the core classes. Almost immediately she felt a need for more diversity in her teaching and in the activities she assigned for her students. She did not like to lecture continuously and needed a strategy that would allow her to employ other techniques in her class. She attended workshops to further her own desire to develop and use cooperative learning in her classroom. Outside the math teachers, she was an exception in her school because she utilized cooperative learning. She was excited to have a tool that would stimulate her students to stay on task and work more positively with their classmates. One way in which she has accomplished this has been to have her higher-achieving students assist their lower achieving classmates. She utilizes cooperative groups while students work on their nine-week interdisciplinary projects. Janet assigns students to heterogeneous groups according to their academic rank in the class. She formally assigns each student a role. She also has each student evaluate each teammate's performance within the group.

During her first 40-minute period, her "Homeroom," Janet starts the class by having her students write in their journals or do some other assigned individual task. While they do these tasks, she takes care of her normal daily routines. The students then proceed to the group interdisciplinary-project portion of the period. Here students in cooperative groups work on their assigned group projects. Her colleagues on her team use this time to assist individual students as needed. This format for class activities occurs four times a week during the first period. The rest of the day is divided between the two blocks on alternating days. She breaks the 75-minute periods up to allow her students time to work and have a change of pace in their activities. The Friday schedule involves all social studies classes that meet throughout the day. The teachers on her team work together to coordinate all activities so that classroom instruction is not interrupted by outside work.

Janet, as the facilitator, and her students, as those responsible for the learning process, like the format of multiple and mixed activities that allows for formal instruction, class discussions and group work. This variety of activities corresponds with the research that reveals that middle school students prefer more active learning and to interact with peers during learning experiences.

She is confident that her cooperative learning activities create an environment of active, involved exploratory learning.[22] She agrees that these activities allow her students to take personal responsibility for their own learning. She believes that, to be successful, her lessons using cooperative learning must be well organized and highly focused, and include clear, well-established directions for students to follow. Janet believes that each student's role must be well defined and that all students must understand the role and task expectations for each student and each group. This is especially true for the term projects that she requires.

Janet has had her share of successes and failures using cooperative learning, but has always learned from the experience, as have her students. She considers it a failure when the activity or project has not gone well or achieved the desired academic results. As much as she is conscious of it, one of her most common problems is providing clear and precise instructions, the lack of which confuses and frustrates her students. However, when things go well her students enjoy the lessons and learn at the same time. Quite often, the social skills and on-task behaviors of her students are reinforced through their participation in their cooperative learning groups.[23] Janet's successes are the product of hard work and her personal determination to be successful and make an important difference in her middle school classroom.

Joel Johnson also teaches at a predominantly inner-city school. He first encountered cooperative learning in the 1980s during his graduate studies. When he saw that cooperative learning had positive implications for helping minority children, Joel decided to implement it in his classes. In making the step to use groups in his classroom, he found that he had two major adjustments to make. One was getting used to the amount of freedom and responsibility it gave to students. The second was the requirement for him to change roles from being an instructor to being a facilitator. At the beginning, and even today, he has found that certain topics are far more conducive to cooperative learning than are others.

At the beginning of the school year Joel uses cooperative learning during his first unit on Native Americans to introduce his students to the methodology. He has each of the five or six groups choose a different Native American culture and learn all the cultural artifacts associated with each culture. Students are informed that at the end of the term, they are to make a presentation to the class of details about their respective cultural group. After the presentations, students are given a test in which they match the correct cultural item with the correct cultural group. The team getting the most correct answers wins a reward. Setting up a unit in this way allows him the opportunity to train his students initially in the cooperative learning skills that they will use about once a month later in the semester and throughout the year.

Joel has found that in cooperative learning there is no front or back to the class but only different areas of the room that are utilized by the students to work in their groups. Noise, usually a problem for teachers and administrators, is not a problem for him because of the social and communicative skills learned by the students in his class. He believes his students can use these skills for the rest of their lives.

Trudy Floyd teaches in a culturally-diverse school in northwest Indiana. Besides being a classroom teacher, she is coordinator of the urban teacher education program at her school's PDS (Professional Development Site). She became aware of cooperative learning and its implications for improving student learning during her work as a staff developer. She liked the cooperative learning approach of making each student more directly responsible for his or her learning. Trudy's enthusiastic approach to cooperative learning allows her to implement the methodology about two to three times a week. The major adjustments she had to make by using cooperative learning were negligible because, as she states, "I am not a lecturer" and "My lessons and instruction have always been student centered." Her students enjoy the lessons, and she found that careful and thoughtful preparation rendered many of her group activities successful. Over the past few years, she has found that many staff members use what they "think" is cooperative learning but that they sometimes struggle in an effort to make it successful.

According to Trudy, knowing about and then using the details of cooperative learning correctly significantly increases the chances of success. She designs her room to be cooperative-learning friendly by having the room well lit, having supplies ready and easily accessible, and having the seating arranged so that group seating is the norm. Many of her lessons center on group projects and group investigations and end with groups presenting their findings orally to the class or in displays in the class or hallway. Her day consists of seven periods, five of which are designated for academics. The majority of her teaching team uses cooperative learning correctly and agrees that when everybody is on the same page, it is easier to make a difference in the classroom. More on task time, greater problem solving skills, higher student achievement, the development of social and communication skills and the ability to reach all levels of learners are all products of cooperative learning in her class. Trudy is confident that many of these skills will last a lifetime.

Victor Vazquez, who teaches with Trudy, is also a baseball coach in his urban middle school. He uses cooperative learning about once or twice a week. Like his baseball teams, his students learn to work well together to accomplish their group tasks. Victor learned his cooperative learning during several in-service training sessions, which he attended at the request of his principal who stated it would be an effective teaching tool for new teachers. Besides the encouragement of his principal, Victor credits his team teachers for encouraging his use of cooperative learning. He believes that his coaching background put it in perspective for him by tying it into his philosophy of "everyone works together to get better."[24] His major adjustment in using cooperative learning was pairing high achieving students with low achieving students and then being able to balance the groups equally.

Victor's classroom is similar to his ball practices in that there is a lot of activity going on at once. In fact, his classroom looks disorganized to the untrained eye. However, in spite of the appearance, the classroom has lots of "good" noise, is organized and work is getting done. These students debate, negotiate and reason through the details needed to complete their tasks. The lessons Victor uses help make his students winners in and out of the classroom. The development of problem-solving skills and the exercising of some control over how they learn are important for the development of middle school students.

Cooperative learning is effective in Victor's class because his students take responsibility for their learning just as his baseball teams take credit together for winning or losing when they take the field. Victor found that like his baseball teams, "chemistry" plays a major role in how well his classroom teams work together. However, with proper training and practice—repetition, like ball practice, makes perfect—the students have mastered the skills needed for success in cooperating to learn in their groups. The breaking down of larger units to smaller mini-units also helps make it easier for students to do their individual and group work with a high level of success. According to Victor, his students enjoy the classroom structure and are definitely more academically successful than when other activities are used. He believes that a cooperative classroom is like a well-trained team in that all members know their job, attend to their jobs, and achieve success when the team wins or succeeds.

These teachers, all urban teachers in a diverse population, sought ways to reach their inner-city students, who many feel are unreachable in traditional classroom settings. They use cooperative learning to stimulate their students to become active participants in the learning process and to succeed where many have not succeeded. These teachers have moved away from traditional teaching methods. They adapted their classrooms to meet the needs of the students rather than having the students adapt to the way they taught. They wanted to make their students lifelong learners. They may not have always been successful but the students are the winners because these teachers dared to try new approaches in order to help their students "get better together."

## Conclusions and Some Comments

These teachers were introduced to cooperative learning either through staff development, college course work or watching other teachers utilize the methodologies. The underlying rationale for their exploration and later use of cooperative groups was to improve instruction in their middle school classrooms. For instance, research on cooperative learning reveals that students can learn appropriate social skills and how to work together to complete a task.[25] These outcomes fit well with the mentality of middle school students, as they are social animals who like working with their peers to solve problems.[26] Anyone who has seen students working in cooperative groups knows that students enjoy these activities because they are more active and more social. The most important outcome of the research reveals that under appropriate conditions academic achievement can improve for students as a direct result of their cooperative work.[27] Cooperative learning seems to work well with students whose social skills, self-esteem and acceptance in school are limited. Furthermore, some students who work cooperatively have been found to be more attentive in class, to come to school more frequently, and to like school and other students better than those who do not work cooperatively.[28] One explanation for these changes in student behaviors is that the peer pressure imposed upon students by their teammates and the fear of being ostracized have led many students to be at school and have their work ready rather than run the risk of letting down their teammates.[29]

The benefits of cooperative learning for students are well documented. Cooperative learning caters to the middle school students' need for sociability and a very active learning process. Cooperative learning allows middle school students to investigate and problem-solve in an environment that is conducive to their learning styles. When done well, cooperative learning takes advantage of middle schoolers' strengths and works on their weaknesses toward improving learning within the classroom. Cooperative learning may not be the cure for all the ills that plague middle schools and the students who attend them, but it is a step towards teaching these adolescent learners in a manner that is more in tune with the way they want to and can learn. 📖

## NOTES

1. Conrad F. Toepfer, Jr., "What to Know About Young Adolescents," *Social Education* 52, no. 2 (1989): 110-112.

2. Carnegie Council on Adolescent Development, *Turning Points: Preparing American Youth for the 21st Century* (Washington, DC: Carnegie Corporation, 1989).

3. Donna E. Alvermann and Denise K. Muth, *Teaching and Learning in the Middle Grades* (Boston: Allyn & Bacon, 1992).

4. Daniel Tanner and Laurel N. Tanner, *Curriculum Development: Theory Into Practice*, 3rd edition (Upper Saddle River, N.J.: Merrill/Prentice Hall, 1995).

5. Robert E. Slavin, "When and Why Does Cooperative Learning Increase Achievement? Theory and Empirical Perspectives," in *Interaction in Cooperative Learning Groups*, edited by Rachel Hertz-Lazarowitz and Kathleen A. Miller (New York: Cambridge University Press, 1994): 145-173.

6. Roger T. Johnson and David W. Johnson, *Learning Together and Alone: Cooperative, Competitive and Individualistic Learning*, 5th edition (Boston: Allyn and Bacon, 1999).

7. Donald L. Scwartz, James B. Black and Johanna Strange, "Dyads Have Fourfold Advantage Over Individuals Inducing Abstract Rules," paper presented at the annual meeting of the American Educational Research Association, Chicago, April 1991.

8. Sally J. McCarthy and Susan I McMahon, "From Convention to Invention: Three Approaches to Peer Interactions During Writing," in *Interaction in Cooperative Groups*, edited by Rachel Hertz-Lazarowitz and Kathleen A. Miller (New York: Cambridge University Press, 1992): 116-135.

9. Josh Tannenberg, "Using Cooperative Learning in the Undergraduate Computer Science Classroom," paper presented at the Midwest Small College Computing Conference, Sioux City, S.D., 1995.

10. *Ibid.*

11. Angela M. O'Donnell and Donald F. Dansereau. "Scripted Cooperation in Student Dyads: A Method for Analyzing and Enhancing Academic Learning and Performance," in *Interaction in Cooperative Groups*, edited by Rachel Hertz-Lazarowitz and Kathleen A. Miller (New York: Cambridge University Press, 1992): 136-155; and Alexander W. Astin, *Four Critical Years: Effects of College Beliefs, Attitudes, and Knowledge* (San Francisco, Calif.: Jossey-Bass, 1977).

12. Slavin, "When and Why Does Cooperative Learning Increase Achievement?", *op. cit.*

13. Melissa Sue Kort, "Down From the Podium," in *New Directions for Community Colleges*, edited by Linda C. Stanley and Joanna Ambrose (San Francisco: Jossey-Bass, 1990): 98-102.

14. Felder, *op. cit.*

15. Shlomo Sharan and Yael Sharan, *Handbook of Cooperative Learning Methods* (Westport, Conn.: Greenwood Press, 1977).

16. Felder, *op. cit.*

17. Robert J. Stahl and Ronald L. VanSickle. "Cooperative Learning as Effective *Social Study* Within the Social Studies Classroom: Introduction and an Invitation," in *Cooperative Learning in the Social Studies Classroom: An Introduction to Social Study*, NCSS Bulletin No. 87, edited by Robert J. Stahl and Ronald L. VanSickle (Washington, DC: National Council for the Social Studies, 1992): 1-7.

18. Stahl and VanSickle, *op. cit.*

19. K. E. Sanberg, "Affective and Cognitive Features of Collaborative Learning," *Review of Research and Developmental Education* 6, no. 4 (1995): 2-4.

20. Elizabeth G. Cohen, "Restructuring the Classroom: Conditions for Productive Small Groups," *Review of Educational Research*, 64, no. 1 (Spring, 1994): 1-35.

21. Ruby B. Midkioff and Rebecca Davis Thomasson, *A Practical Approach to Using Learning Styles in Math Instruction* (Springfield, Ill.: Charles Thomas, 1992).

22. Slavin, "When and Why Does Cooperative Learning Increase Achievement?" *op. cit.*

23. Josh Tannenberg, "Using Cooperative Learning in the Undergraduate Computer Science Classroom," paper presented at the Midwest Small College Computing Conference, Sioux City, S.D., 1995.

24. David W. Johnson, Roger T. Johnson and Edythe Holubec, *The New Circles of Learning: Cooperation in the Classroom and School* (Alexandria, Virg.: Association for Supervision and Curriculum Development, 1994); Robert J. Stahl and Ronald L. VanSickle. "Cooperative Learning as Effective *Social Study* Within the Social Studies Classroom," *op. cit.*

25. See, for example, Johnson, Johnson and Holubec, *The New Circles of Learning, op. cit.*

26. Conrad F. Toepfer, Jr., "What to Know About Young Adolescents," *Social Education*, 52, no. 2 (1989): 110-112.

27. Slavin, Robert E. "When and Why Does Cooperative Learning Increase Achievement?" *op. cit.*

28. *Ibid.*

29. Dwight C. Holliday, "The Development of Jigsaw IV in a Secondary Social Studies Classroom," paper presented at the annual meeting of the Midwest Educational Research Association, Chicago, April 2000.

# CHAPTER 9

# Theory into Practice
## A Cooperative Learning Success Story in Middle Level Classrooms

**Eric F. Luce**, The University of Southern Mississippi, Long Beach, Mississippi
in collaboration with
**William McKendry**, Social Studies Teacher
**Dennis Dool**, Social Studies Teacher
**Michael Smith**, English Teacher
**Myra Wolpert**, Mathematics and Reading Teacher
Bala-Cynwyd Middle School
and
**Philip Selim**, Assistant Principal, Lower Marion High School, Lower Merion School District, Pennsylvania

**The co-authors of this article** studied, collaborated and first implemented cooperative group structures and cooperative learning at Bala-Cynwyd Middle School in the early 1990s. Our initial successes with this approach were described in the chapter we wrote for the first edition of this Bulletin, published in 1992.[1] The present chapter reports on our initial efforts as well as on the continued success we have had over the 13 years since our story was told in 1992. Over this period, Phil Selim moved on to become Assistant Principal of Lower Merion High School; Mike Smith and Myra Wolpert retired, and other faculty have been added to a Social Studies Department that still values and uses cooperative learning within the majority of the classes. However, with all these changes, we, the authors of the original chapter, still feel a sense of "ownership" in the success story that continues at Bala-Cynwyd Middle School today. So we have joined forces once again through this collaborative effort to share our experiences. This chapter begins with much of the opening background information in our earlier chapter and then describes how our program and its successes have continued for more than a decade. The fact that William, Dennis and Mike and the new faculty have continued this emphasis is itself testimony to how powerful this approach is for both students and teachers involved when it is implemented correctly and completely. We had a good story to tell then, and we have an even greater story to share now.

## Context of Middle School Education

Conflicting expectations for schooling are common among middle school students, parents, and educators. Middle school parents want their children to be physically and psychologically safe. They expect their children to know adults well enough to confide in them. They want schools to foster constructive friendships among students. They want their children to be involved in school activities and to have enough positive experiences in school to want to return to school the next day.[2]

Middle school students are malleable and impressionable. Variability in social, emotional, and intellectual development is common. Their growth and development varies and they navigate the transition between childhood and adolescence at various times and at various rates. Teachers and parents can become models and significant others for them.[3] Yet, middle school students also experience the need to feel independent and self-sufficient. At times, they seem to be quite capable of finding their own way in life; they may, therefore, resent rather than appreciate unsolicited attention and advice.[4]

Middle school educators do not always know how to do all that is expected of them. Caught in the middle, some have been trained in the traditions of elementary education whereas others are more comfortable in secondary schools. Elementary schools are commonly thought to be normative and nurturing places (student-centered) in which the students still feel the influence of parents. In secondary schools, on the other hand, compliant student conduct and deportment may seem less important than successful academic performance. Although schools might not encourage the questioning of basic authority, breaches of decorum are more commonly viewed as obstacles to the acquisition of desired subject matter than as threats to the social order.[5]

The Secondary School Recognition Program of the United States Department of Education developed a list of fourteen attributes, drawn from research on effective schools, that it uses as criteria to identify unusually successful public secondary schools. These attributes include

- ▶ clear academic goals,
- ▶ high expectations for students,
- ▶ order and discipline,
- ▶ rewards and incentives for students,
- ▶ regular and frequent monitoring of student progress,
- ▶ opportunities for meaningful student responsibility and participation,
- ▶ teacher efficacy,
- ▶ rewards and incentives for teachers,
- ▶ concentration on academic learning time,
- ▶ positive school climate,
- ▶ administrative leadership,
- ▶ well-articulated curriculum,
- ▶ evaluation for instructional improvement, and
- ▶ community support and involvement.

The Bala-Cynwyd Middle School, a suburban school district adjacent to west Philadelphia, was included on the Department of Education's list of successful public secondary schools.[6]

Philip Selim, who was Bala-Cynwyd's Assistant Principal in the early 1990s, worked with a staff of teachers, some of whom had been trained in elementary education while others had been trained for the secondary level. Selim's experience building a distinctive middle school ethos and tradition with these teachers led him to observe that elementary school teachers focused more on the whole child, whereas secondary school teachers tended to view themselves more as content-matter specialists. Even today, the compartmentalized structure of instruction in many secondary schools hides natural links between content areas that are more easily identified at the elementary level and that add relevance and meaning to learning.

Phil actively supported the inclusion of cooperative learning approaches across the curriculum, believing that this would enable teachers and students to notice the natural links between content areas and to establish and build on their knowledge bases.

## Guess What? The Research Findings Actually Helped Convince Us to Try This Cooperative Approach

One popular perspective held by teachers and by the public at large was that effective teaching is the steady, clear transmission of new information to passively receptive students who come to understand this information as knowledge.[7] Consistent with this perspective, many educators view shortcomings in academic achievement as characteristics of children rather than as failures of the education system.[8] Furthermore, according to the research, teachers on all levels consistently tend to take personal credit and responsibility for student successes, and rarely take the blame when students fail to achieve the teachers' expectations. Yet we know that students who fail to learn according to their potential do so because they are academically behind and lack content and skills that other children, who are better prepared, possess.[9]

The curricular flexibility of middle schools was one response to the diversity that exists among middle school students. Appropriately flexible curriculum approaches should provide continuous assessment of an individual student's needs. Teachers are responsible for providing appropriate programs of study. The instructional environments they create must stress interrelationships among various disciplines and facilitate the acquisition of learning, thinking skills, and problem-solving skills.[10]

Using cooperative learning approaches, students can benefit from the expertise of other students as well as that of teachers. Scribner and Cole revealed that the acquisition and use of reading and writing skills are greatly enhanced by socialization into cultural activities requiring reading and writing for specific purposes.[11]

When used correctly, cooperative learning activities are capable of improving the academic achievement of all students,[12] as well as the social integration and self-esteem of students from varied ethnic and racial backgrounds.[13] To be most effective in raising students' academic achievement, these activities require clear group learning goals and individual student accountability. These two requirements are powerful factors that affect both individual and group achievement. Slavin and Stahl have proposed additional explanations for the successes associated with cooperative learning.[14]

No single model for the conduct of cooperative learning exists. The models that work best require students to achieve academic goals following specified plans that ensure individual and group productivity, content learning, and on-task interaction. The success of groups in attaining their goals depends upon each member's development of the expertise required to contribute to the group. The structures these models provide serve to ensure that students work *in* groups *as* groups—better yet, *as academic teams.* Leaders in the cooperative learning movement highly recommend that teachers provide extrinsic rewards recognizing accomplishment of goals to each member of each successful student group. Cooperative learning also requires individual student accountability through evaluation of independent learning performances through end-of-unit testing.[15]

## A Report from the Classroom: Cooperative Learning Still Going Strong After All These Years

At Bala-Cynwyd Middle School, social studies teachers Bill McKendry and Dennis Dool, along with a team of teachers from other subject areas, are using cooperative learning approaches in their classes. Since 1989, when he participated in in-service activities and workshops supported by the school district, McKendry tried a variety of cooperative group structures and activities within a cooperative learning context. His success has had a ripple effect; other teachers are now giving cooperative learning a try.

From the beginning, McKendry and Dool agreed that "some people are traditional teachers; cooperative learning may not be for them." They agreed, however, that using cooperative learning procedures does not always necessitate a radical departure from successful, established teaching practices. Effective cooperative learning activities neither replace all direct instruction nor eliminate student accountability.

In the beginning, Myra Wolpert, then a Bala-Cynwyd reading and mathematics teacher, was convinced that cooperative learning was not a radical departure for her. As she put it, "I probably used cooperative learning before I heard the term. It is a matter of personal philosophy with me. We live in a high achieving society, but we also fight wars! It is important for children to learn to get along with each other."

McKendry observed that when using cooperative learning strategies, classes are sometimes noisier, discussions are heated, and distractions are more common than when he used traditional approaches. Positive experiences and high levels of student involvement in academic study activities, however, led him to believe that teachers can achieve positive results with middle school students.

McKendry has observed insecure students become more confident. He has seen academic discussions develop among students while they are working cooperatively on individual and team assignments. He has been surprised that the initial resistance of loners to cooperative learning teams typically fades away. It is his conviction that, in working cooperatively with his students, more advanced, upper-level students acquire greater quantities of background information instead of rote facts. Students gain depth and breadth of understanding through discussing facts in context, rather than simply understanding facts as facts. They come to understand how facts can help to form and illustrate concepts.

The teachers at Bala-Cynwyd have personally seen cooperative learning raise the academic achievement of social studies students, while helping them improve literacy skills enabling students to increase their participation both in and beyond school. Students learn to develop and refine their own ideas. As they gain experience and security in doing so, they are not as afraid to fail as they were in conventional teaching settings.

McKendry agrees that it is generally true that when students interact in cooperative learning activities, they spontaneously raise and negotiate task-relevant topics. Students discuss the meaning of questions, the content of good answers to questions, and how to find answers to questions. They discuss grammar and the meaning of words, phrases, and sentences. Students discuss their progress in completing assignments and the relationship of social studies content material to their background knowledge— unwittingly, but naturally, employing metacognitive strategies for organizing and directing their learning while acquiring expertise in content.

McKendry has found that even in cooperative learning environments students need a teacher's guidance. For example, a set of rules for noise levels has evolved in his classes: hands up means attention, thumbs down means that a behavior is unacceptable, and a hand signal forming a zero means that silence is called for.

McKendry also employs a bonus point system that provides rewards for completion of assignments in a timely manner and for cooperative behavior marked by the absence of derogatory comments directed at peers. Students can earn bonus points at the end of each social studies unit. McKendry has found that this reward system motivates students in powerful ways.

Clear group goals and individual student accountability have positive effects on students' achievement. With early guidance, including teacher-provided structure for lessons and assignments and close teacher monitoring of student progress, nearly all students will be successful in dividing up jobs, in discussing what they have learned with one another, in giving one another feedback, and in hearing and seeing what others have to offer the group. Students have to be taught not only the content but also how to work in a cooperative group. In far too many classrooms, the most successful students have learned to work independently or competitively. Learning to work cooperatively requires guidance, practice, and feedback.

Team-developed composition projects in which students investigate topics and contribute findings to their teams in their writing have been popular with students. In these projects, group reports are compiled in which data are used to back up student opinions and conclusions. Topics such as "The Revolutionary War: Evolutionary or Revolutionary?" have served well in stimulating student cooperative inquiry. Teachers need to select team gatekeepers who can coordinate and compile the individual work of group members as they complete tasks. Cooperative learning forces students to analyze and verify opinions with evidence, as opposed to reporting facts and generalizations without challenge. Furthermore, cooperative learning and social studies go well together because both value discussion and personal opinions.

Teachers need to convince students about the merits of working and learning together cooperatively. And students need to accept that good things can happen to and for them as a result of this participation. Students articulate their resistance through questions such as, "What's in it for me?" and "What am I going to get out of this?" Student resistance to cooperative learning activities and to staying on task is sometimes hard to overcome. Skeptical students will no doubt become convinced, however, that one of the best ways to learn a thing is to teach it and that when students help each other to learn, their abilities to express their own ideas improve. Perhaps the sincerity of these explanations is what convinces students to try to work cooperatively: it works because it makes sense to students.

For outside observers, or even for the teacher in charge, it may be unnerving to see middle school students interact casually and informally as they participate on task in group activities. The sight of students laughing and joking as they speak to one another and the sound of conversational asides might appear to be inconsequential to learning and might discourage some teachers from implementing cooperative learning strategies. From the beginning of the move towards cooperative experiences until he moved to another school, Phil Selim noticed that the social studies classrooms he visited were noisier and student behavior initially appeared more disorganized during cooperative learning lessons. Selim was very aware that appearances can be deceiving.

When Phil Selim visited Bill McKendry's classes, he found student attention focused in sustained ways on social studies course objectives to an extent that was surprising and worthy of note. He asked McKendry's students what they were learning and checked to find out how much they were actually learning. Invariably, students answered that they were learning, and their answers about what they were learning varied. Students often told him that the work in Mr. McKendry's class was worthwhile yet more difficult than in their other classes. They had to work with others, work on their own, be accountable to other people, divide up work, make decisions, and resolve conflicts. Students also told Assistant Principal Selim that they learned more in Mr. McKendry's class than they did in others.

Selim realized that such information was not easily quantifiable. With support and encouragement from the Lower Merion School District through in-service training and staff development activities, other teachers at Bala-Cynwyd, like McKendry, began to implement cooperative learning across the curriculum. Cooperative learning was not, however, the dominant model for instruction in the district. At present it is far more pervasive than it was in the early 1990s, and we can say that it directly accounts for a great deal of our recent high student performances on standardized tests of academic achievement.

For Selim, strict standardized multiple-choice tests do not assess students' ability to interact with each other, nor do they adequately measure thinking skills such as analysis and synthesis. In the long run, skills developed through cooperative learning, such as the ability to work with people whose backgrounds and experiences are different from one's own and to work with others as part of a team, might be more important in the workplace than the ability to do well on standardized tests.

Mike Smith, a now-retired English teacher and a member of the team of teachers that began working with McKendry in the early 1990s, believed that cooperative learning lent itself well to teaching social studies because it made it possible to look at content in many ways. Smith used cooperative learning approaches in his English classes. For him, middle school students needed more than lectures from their teachers. He also believed that for students to work well in groups cooperatively it was necessary to teach them how to work effectively in groups and as a group. Students, he believed, "work best if there is a natural atmosphere that is not restrained," but achieving this atmosphere took a lot of knowledge, newly-learned skills, hard work and time.

We found that when asked to work cooperatively with other students, achieving students did not automatically share what they knew and what they had learned. They did not automatically become teachers and leaders in their groups. Over time, the reluctance of brighter or more capable students to share their work with other, less able students can be overcome. Smith found that by using essay assignments that students must complete by participating in cooperative groups, attitudes sometimes changed. Students became interested in listening to what other students had to say. The process also became more interesting to students when they found that to complete their work they must both present their findings to their classmates and defend their personal judgments.

Smith agreed that cooperative learning probably promotes the development of higher-level thinking skills. In cooperative groups, students are less likely to assume that all their teacher expects of them is to take notes from lectures so they can reconstruct information at a later time to pass a test. When a teacher plans cooperative learning activities, students must become more active in their learning. They need to make decisions about what is important and what is not. Students also have "more opportunities to develop and kick ideas around."

Smith also found that he had to learn to work cooperatively *with* students. Wanting to work cooperatively, however, does not automatically translate into cooperative learning. He had to work to develop a "comfort level" that took into account that kids have to be kids. He still had to leave room for exercising leadership and direction in his role as teacher. He learned how to do these through trial, error, and practice: "Just because you know the principles and the research doesn't mean you can make it work. That takes time!"

Social studies teacher Dennis Dool still believes that cooperative learning activities offer his students more time and opportunity to process information. He has noticed that one of the ways his students communicate and process information as they work cooperatively is through "kidspeak"—using their own language. As a result, active verbal student interactions are improved. When the opportunities emerge, students record kidspeak in written form. Dool accepts and encourages students to use their language and idioms "when it shows understanding."

Partly because of McKendry and Smith's enthusiasm for cooperative learning, Dool has decided to integrate cooperative learning activities into his teaching. Dool is convinced that to teach effectively at the middle school level it is necessary to vary instructional activities. The variety of cooperative learning strategies allows him to do so. Dool tries to use at least three activities in teaching a lesson. He has found that strategies such as the Jigsaw method evoke high interest from his students and involve them in classroom activities as teachers and experts.

Dool has also used cooperative approaches effectively to bring closure to a unit and to promote review and practice. He sometimes uses three-day blocks of class time for this purpose. On the first day, he will teach a mini lesson, emphasizing key concepts, vocabulary, and questions of importance. Then the sharing begins. On the second day, cooperative work groups are organized. The group's tasks are to create quizzes on the unit and to refine and improve their questions by trying them on their group members. Thus prepared, on the third day Dool stages review contests using student questions. The winning team members each receive two points that he adds to their grades on the subsequent test.

After all these years, Dool and others still are sharpening their knowledge, skills and attitudes with cooperative learning. They attend in-service activities and go to workshops on the subject. Dool is convinced that teaching is an art and that it takes time for artistic expression to mature. He is convinced by the scientific case that can be made for cooperative learning. He is familiar with research on cooperative learning and with the leaders in the field. He is willing to try it, but for now he often finds that he must rely on his own motivation to try something new in order to convince his students that they have something to gain by cooperating and learning together with him. He knows that good things will not automatically happen simply because he has planned a cooperative learning lesson.

### Challenges

Implementing cooperative learning concepts and strategies effectively is a challenge for even the best of teachers. Teachers must replace many traditional practices and assumptions with others that are consistent with this approach. To be successful it is necessary, but not sufficient, to have willing teachers. Knowledge and training need to be provided. Teachers also need freedom to learn new skills and to know that they will receive support while they risk trying something new.

Becoming comfortable with noise and commotion is one adjustment teachers might need to make. It also takes time to develop the finesse and expertise to know the difference between student conversations that are merely social and those that relate to the lessons. Knowing how and when to intervene and to refocus student conversations without getting angry or destroying student interest also requires skill and tact that a teacher can probably learn only through trial and error.

Teachers need to learn how to support team-building processes. It is one thing to assign students to work in groups. To get them to work together as a team is a much more complicated matter. This requires not only planning interesting and engaging learning assignments, but also making decisions about how to structure group activity and motivating groups to act like teams.

For cooperative learning to work, teachers need to instruct students on how to examine evidence and opinions. They need to learn where they can find information, but they also need to learn how to ask for information. Teachers may need to learn how to mediate disagreements and negotiate working arrangements between and with students as cooperative learning unfolds.

One of the more difficult impediments to using cooperative learning successfully in middle school classes is absenteeism. It is hard to motivate groups of students to cooperate and to share learning when they feel that members of their group are not pulling their weight and are dragging the group down. Students who are regularly absent make it difficult for members of their group to share learning tasks and responsibilities. Group members cannot depend on these students to support the group's work. Students who are absent infrequently and who take school seriously are sometimes resentful that they are, or might be, expected to help slackers catch up. Students do not always think it fair that they have to do another student's work or that they should be penalized for others' shortcomings. Yet once the groups begin to function as groups, students really work hard to help each other and develop a strong sense of obligation to help their groupmates succeed.

Over a period of time, fewer students seem to miss fewer classes when cooperative learning is used successfully and students' achievement in academic learning continues to grow.

Students need to believe they will benefit personally and substantively from working cooperatively. Most students expect to work individually and competitively in school. These expectations may cause students to resist cooperative learning. To overcome this resistance, teachers not only must be excited by the promise of cooperative learning, they also must be actively committed to making it work. Teachers might need to learn how to modify assessment practices so they can recognize individual and group achievements.

## Epilogue

As noted earlier, Michael Smith and Myra Wolpert have retired from teaching, but remain active lifelong learners. They are missed in the classrooms and hallways of the Bala-Cynwyd Middle School and are envied a bit in the faculty lunchroom when talk turns to imagining what life might be like after middle school. Phil Selim also has moved on from his position of leadership at Bala-Cynwyd Middle School to be Principal of the Merion Elementary School and now is Assistant Principal

at the Lower Merion High School. Bill McKendry and Dennis Dool "soldier on" as social studies teachers at Bala-Cynwyd Middle School.

McKendry and Dool have experienced change, as well as continuity, at Bala-Cynwyd in the decade since this chapter first appeared. Inclusion, heightened academic and student accountability in the form of standardized assessments, and the introduction and integration of new technologies across the curriculum have brought changes, but cooperative learning approaches and strategies have not been crowded out or faded away as the educational landscape shifted. McKendry, now in his 36th year as a social studies professional at the middle school level, has tasted most of the in-service "flavors de jour" that one might imagine, but when asked about the current relevance of cooperative learning approaches and strategies for teaching and learning he still remains animated and excited about both theory and practices that "encourage creative flair" in teachers and students and which provide "scientifically based" rationales for "thinking out of the box"

McKendry and Dool seem both to have taken Inclusion in stride by drawing on their experiences in planning and organizing cooperative learning environments that adjust and accommodate to student groups which include diverse learning styles and wide ranges of skill and interest levels. Dool thrives on the challenges and opportunities for encouraging and exciting student involvement in social study while also addressing benchmark curriculum objectives and standards. McKendry has not lost his enthusiasm for "involving students to exercise their social skills to find answers to questions and to ask and answer new ones that they have formulated." They agree that working and learning cooperatively with students does not jeopardize the academic standing of their school. It is their observation that their students will hold one another accountable for performance up to high standards when "given the chance to make decisions and be responsible for their own learning and the learning of their classmates" and that they "thrive when allowed to devise their own assessments and plans for sharing their learning experiences and performances."

The advent and availability of new technologies can support cooperative learning too. With such information tools and resources available, Dool's answer to student questions about Sacajawea's life is now "Go find out and share with us what you discover!" McKendry does not hesitate to offer that cooperative learning "has helped" to address the new accountability of the "No Child Left Behind" era. It has been his experience that "cooperative learning gives kids choices for learning that hold them accountable" for their own, and their classmates', learning.

Many barriers can make it difficult for middle school teachers to collaborate about curriculum and instruction, but some of these obstacles can be mitigated, as the Bala-Cynwyd case has demonstrated. Ideally, adolescents would be expected to practice inquiry, to question, to reflect, and to transform information in all content areas. Middle school social studies teaching and learning experiences can provide adolescents with opportunities to summarize, to contextualize, to infer, and to monitor. The natural curiosity of adolescents about the world and their technological savvy may be more sophisticated than that possessed by their teachers, which could make middle-level students ideal participants in new types of teaching and learning arrangements.[16]

Cooperative learning has established itself in our middle schools. It (and new technologies) may not be a prescription for instant middle school success. It takes serious work and places serious demands on both teachers and students. But, cooperative learning and new technologies are not just fads in our schools. Because of the results that have been obtained, cooperative learning continues to contribute to middle school education generally, and to social studies education specifically. Cooperative learning groups free students and teachers alike to notice and discover "natural links" that add relevance and meaning to learning. 🖳

## NOTES

1. See Chapter 6 of *Cooperative Learning in the Social Studies Classroom: An Introduction to Social Study*, NCSS Bulletin No. 87, edited by Robert J. Stahl and Ronald L. VanSickle (Washington, DC: National Council for the Social Studies, 1992): 32-37.

2. James P. Garvin, "What Do Parents Expect from Middle Level Schools?" *Middle School Journal* 19 (November 1987): 3-4.

3. John H. Lounsbury, "Middle Level Education: Perspectives, Problems, and Prospects," *Educational Horizons* 68, no. 2 (Winter 1990): 64.

4. Gary K. Clabaugh, "Educators Caught in the Middle," *Educational Horizons* 68, no. 2 (Winter 1990): 60-61.

5. *Ibid.*

6. Bruce L. Wilson and Thomas B. Corcoran, *Successful Secondary Schools: Visions of Excellence in American Public Education* (Philadelphia: The Falmer Press, 1988).

7. John Goodlad, *A Place Called School: Prospects for the Future* (New York: McGraw-Hill, 1984, 2004); Larry Cuban, *How Teachers Taught: Constancy and Change in American Classrooms, 1890-1980* (New York: Longman, 1984).

8. Richard P. Duran, "Cooperative Learning and Language Minority Students," paper presented at the annual meeting of the American Anthropological Association, Chicago, November 1991.

9. Benjamin S. Bloom, *Human Characteristics and School Learning* (New York: McGraw-Hill, 1976); John B. Carroll,. "The Carroll Model: A 25-Year Retrospective and Prospective View," *Educational Researcher* 18 (January/February 1989): 26-31.

10. Sylvester Kohut, "A Quality Middle School: What Makes the Difference?" *Educational Horizons* 68, no. 2 (Winter 1990): 107-8.

11. Sylvia Scribner and Michael Cole, *The Psychology of Literacy* (Cambridge, Mass.: Harvard University Press, 1981).

12. Spencer Kagan, *Cooperative Learning Resources for Teachers* (Berkeley: University of California Press, 1985); Roger T. Johnson, David W. Johnson, and Edythe J. Holubec, *Structuring Cooperative Learning: Lesson Plans for Teachers* (Edina, Minn.: Interaction Book Company, 1987); Robert E. Slavin, *Cooperative Learning: Theory, Research and Practice* (Englewood Cliffs, N.J.: Prentice-Hall, 1990).

13. Spencer Kagan, "Cooperative Learning and Sociological Factors in Schooling," in *Beyond Language: Social and Cultural Factors in Schooling Language Minority Students* (Los Angeles: California State University Evaluation, Dissemination, and Assessment Center, 1986).

14. Robert E. Slavin, *When and Why Does Cooperative Learning Increase Achievement? Theoretical and Empirical Perspectives* (Baltimore: Johns Hopkins University, Center for Research on Elementary and Middle Schools, OERI No. G86-00061986, 1989); Robert J. Stahl, "The Essential Elements for Optimal Cooperative Learning," paper presented at the annual meeting of the American Educational Research Association, Seattle, Washington, April 2001.

15. Richard P. Duran, "Cooperative Learning and Language Minority Students," paper presented at the annual meeting of the American Anthropological Association, Chicago, November 1991.

16. Katherine A. O'Connor, Amy J. Good,, and Eric F. Luce, "Making Long Distance Relationships Work," *Meridian: A Middle School Computer Technologies Journal* (Raleigh, N.C.: North Carolina State University), 7, no. 2 (Summer 2004), accessible at http://www.ncsu.edu/meridian/sum2004/relationships/ : 1.

# CHAPTER 10

# My Personal Experience Using Cooperative Learning in My Secondary Social Studies Classroom

**Quinton G. Priest**, University High School, Tucson, Arizona

**In 1974**, I enrolled in a graduate seminar on the Scientific Revolution. This course changed my ideas about teaching. The professor kept us interested and involved through lectures, discussions and individual student presentations. Subsequently, I took the History of Science as a field of graduate study. As I look back on the experience, I realize I decided to become a teacher because of the excitement and intellectual stimulation I felt in that graduate program: I wanted to instill in my students the same sense of excitement and involvement that I felt in those history of science courses. Was it possible to replicate such an experience in a secondary school setting? The trick, I concluded, was to find the level of language and the type of teaching style that would get the academic information and ideas across to high school students. But, as importantly, I needed to find an approach and structures that would engage students while improving their academic content and abilities.

I have spent much of my professional life learning how to implement such a vision in the classroom. Like the student of the martial arts master in *Karate Kid*, I was to learn that powerful social studies teaching would require a commitment of time, technical skills and pedagogy as well as energy and enthusiasm.

## In the Beginning: Idealism Confronts Reality

As a new teacher, I tried to incorporate lectures with group activities in such a way that students could understand the larger issues and then personally come to grips with primary sources. The idea was that they should learn something of the subject and then act as historians to draw conclusions about it. To say that they were not enthused with my lectures would be an understatement: they were bored. To make matters worse, the students seldom cooperated with one another to complete the activities. At best, they divided up the material and each did his or her share. Sometimes they self-segregated into smaller groups of friends and little or nothing got done. Often, one or two students would do all the work, and the others would just "hitchhike." Not only did projects lack the power, depth, and commitment to understanding that I had hoped, students did not seem to extend themselves beyond meeting the minimum requirements. What I wanted, I realized, was an environment where students were pushing one another to extend themselves intellectually as far as they could. I wanted them to leave my classroom at the end of the year better prepared for college and careers, and with a greater ability to work with others. Clearly some rethinking and restructuring of my teaching methods was in order.

Finally, I sought to gain a better understanding of the thoughts and attitudes of my students. I could then use that knowledge to craft learning experiences that would draw students together in a positive learning environment. Fortunately, my school was conducting a longitudinal survey of student attitudes as a part of its North Central Accreditation Improvement Plan. So, I had much evidence to draw upon.

Naïve as this may seem, I learned that most high school students come to their course of study with a different set of attitudes than do most college students, much less than do graduate students! First, most high school courses are mandated as graduation requirements. As a result, students feel they have few choices about which courses they take. As a consequence, they are less committed to learning the content of any individual course beyond what is necessary for earning the desired grade. The result is that they develop an attitude that one merely needs to do the assignments, take the tests and earn the grade. Second, little thought is given to why they are taking a particular sequence of social studies courses—often there is no sequence, but rather a specified number of units are required. Third, students do not have active subject-based knowledge to draw on during a lecture.

If their mind is actively involved in what the teacher is saying, it is to acquire new information, not to synthesize and analyze. This is especially true as students seldom read the assigned materials ahead of the lecture, with the idea of interacting with the teacher. Most students value courses where they are allowed a certain involvement in shaping the course of study and to work with their peers on projects. For example, informal group work outside of class was the means by which most students completed homework assignments. In many cases, they split up the task or assignment and did their work alone and independently and then, almost at the last minute, they assembled the pieces into a whole paper or project to be handed in for an individual grade. In effect, they cooperated and shared, but they weren't cooperating to learn or help their peers learn.

I could see that within these sets of attitudes lay the key to my problem. Students were asking for meaningful work; they wanted to participate in their learning; they wanted to be actively engaged in academic pursuits that made sense to them; and they had developed certain survival skills that could be shaped to meet their needs. The answer, then, was to organize groups that would have the same mechanism of accountability that the informal groups had. This meant that each group's work had to reward individual members for meeting standards of achievement. This, in turn, meant creating group activities and reward structures that required both interdependence and individual accountability. I needed to find a method of linking lectures, readings, and group work to achieve a common end. Finally, I needed clear, practical concepts, guidelines and structures that would allow me to manage learning without me being a pervasive part of these structures. This all seemed like such an overwhelming task.

## An In-Service Opportunity That Paid Off

A neighboring school district offered a six-session in-service workshop on cooperative learning, and invited members of our school to participate. I had scarcely heard of the term, but as department chair I arranged to have some of our teachers, and myself, enrolled in the workshop. As the workshop progressed, I caught a glimpse of cooperative learning's potential for structuring an exciting new approach to teaching. For me, this approach addressed many of the problems with which I had been wrestling.

The workshop took us through the theory and practice of cooperative learning using *Cooperation in the Classroom* by David Johnson, Roger Johnson and Edythe Johnson Holubec and *Using Student Team Learning* by Robert Slavin.[1] I followed

this workshop with a second. This time we focused on structures using works by Spencer Kagan and another volume by Johnson, Johnson and Holubec.[2]

From the start, it was obvious to me that there were significant differences among their approaches to cooperative learning group work. Slavin stressed equalizing opportunity and individualizing accountability. Kagan emphasized the use of flexible cooperative learning structures, allowing the teacher to implement cooperative learning in a number of ways. Johnson, Johnson and Holubec stressed the development of social and interpersonal skills. All the well-known experts in this field concurred that the acquisition of adequate social skills and effective group interaction were basic ingredients in the successful cooperative learning strategies.

By this time I was convinced that I was on to a method—rather a variety of methods—for restructuring my classroom learning environment. Previously, I had made the students individually responsible to each other for getting the work done. What I had failed to do was make students individually accountable for their contribution to the group's success. What was missing was a reward structure for the groups with clearly-stated, preset standards of academic achievement beyond merely completing the work. But awarding points would not be enough. It was obvious that in addition, I would have to help them acquire the social skills to make the structures a meaningful part of the learning process, to commit them to the larger goals of the group as a whole. Also, I needed to know which structures were appropriate for each particular learning situation.

Before I embarked on such a seemingly arduous restructuring process, I needed to answer some larger questions. It occurred to me that students' test scores were the same whether they worked in groups or individually prior to the test. Would cooperative learning structures significantly improve their test scores? Would they like school better? Would students with low self-esteem see improvement and, hence, gain a better self-image and higher standing among peers? An opportunity to answer some of these questions presented itself when I enrolled in a course titled "The Foundations of Education." I decided to investigate the literature on cooperative learning and academic achievement for my research paper. Using the Educational Resources Information Center (ERIC) database and resources at the College of Education at the University of Arizona, I was able to compile a rather long list of resources. I set about my research and found that most of the research was focused on elementary and middle school classrooms. Thus, I had to make some broad assumptions about its applicability to the secondary school classroom. The result was a 25-page paper whose primary conclusion was that students benefit in reading, writing, and social skills through the expertise of their peers and teachers.[3] Cooperative learning structures "offered greater promise for student achievement."[4] Student accountability "was retained and addressed at more levels in the learning process than with traditional structures." Finally, "teachers' roles were more those of resource manager and learning facilitator than of expert disseminator of information."[5]

At the end of this search, I decided that three structures had the greatest potential for the secondary social studies classroom: *Student Teams-Achievement Divisions* (*STAD*), *Teams-Games-Tournament* (*TGT*) and *Jigsaw II* (Jigsaw with Expert Groups). My research revealed that Student Teams-Achievement Divisions and Teams-Games-Tournament produced consistently positive academic outcomes. While Jigsaw II did not fare as well academically, it was a structure that seemed to have potential for certain project-oriented outcomes at the secondary level.[6] Including a testing component to Jigsaw II, termed Jigsaw III, it seemed possible to add the achievement component of Student Teams-Achievement Divisions.

I began with Student Teams-Achievement Divisions and Teams-Games-Tournament in my World Geography courses. Basically, Student Teams-Achievement Divisions follows a seven-step process that emphasized individual accountability and personal and team-improvement points. The Student Teams-Achievement Divisions structure can be used to teach any set of content or abilities in which questions with one right answer can be posed. This is an excellent structure for teaching when a presentation, practice and a quiz or test are included in a unit or for a chapter. Similarly, Teams-Games-Tournament can be used to teach any set of content or abilities in which questions with one right answer can be posed. In Teams-Games-Tournament, however, all students on the team can earn "game points" for their team during a tournament. Both structures have the objective of mastery of and ability to use specific academic content. My experiences with Student Teams-Achievement Divisions and Teams-Games-Tournament have been very positive. Compared to classes in which I did not use either of these two structures, student grades following Student Teams-Achievement Divisions and Teams-Games-Tournament are always higher by a minimum of 6.8 points.[7] Below, I will discuss my experiences with Jigsaw II[8] and Jigsaw III.[9]

## Organizing My Thoughts: Criteria for Cooperation in the Classroom

I realized that before implementing my cooperative learning structures I needed to develop some clear guidelines for myself as well as my students. I then used these guidelines in class-building exercises and to guide students through the cooperative learning structures. If cooperative learning was to succeed in my classroom, these guidelines needed to be comprehended and followed by every student. I first formulated the general elements of cooperation. Each student needed to understand

- the academic and social objectives for the unit they were to study;
- the ways students were to achieve the expected academic and social objectives;
- the expected group participation behaviors or roles;
- the nature and value of positive interdependence in a cooperative learning environment;
- that they would be held individually accountable for all academic assessments, content and abilities and group skills—and that this accountability would be measured by an individual test each would take after the groups finished working as groups; and
- the criteria for group success that would enable groups to earn rewards.

I felt it was necessary to create a checklist of items in order to present these six general "understandings" in concrete form to students.

Four overheads were created that graphically represented the cooperative skills and behaviors I wanted students to acquire and use for a Jigsaw II-III activity: These four were entitled: (a) "A Brief Description of 'F-Words'—Forming, Functioning, Formulating and Fermenting;" (b) a flow chart that related the "Four Phases of Jigsaw II & III;" (c) the "Procedures for Expert Groups;" and (d) a "Collaborative Skills Checklist."[10] Each of these overheads is addressed below.

The "A Brief Description of F-Words" overhead describes the types of behaviors every member of every group must strive for in order for the group to be maximally successful. The contents of this overhead are shown in Table 1.

The overhead with the names and definitions of the four phases of Jigsaw II and Jigsaw III that I use is provided in Table 2.

One overhead concerned desired roles of individual group members in both Home and Expert Groups. Four roles and their functions were described next. These were:

Table 1: **Behaviors that Facilitate Maximal Group Success**

## A BRIEF DESCRIPTION OF F-WORDS

**1. Forming**
- a. move without noise
- b. stay with your group
- c. use quiet voices
- d. encourage everyone's participation
- e. use names and look at the person speaking

**2. Functioning**
- a. direct the group's work
- b. express support
- c. ask group for help and clarification
- d. offer to explain or clarify
- e. paraphrase other's work
- f. energize the group
- g. describe feelings when appropriate

**3. Formulating**
- a. summarize out loud
- b. seek accuracy by correcting and summarizing
- c. seek elaboration
- d. seek ways to remember ideas and facts
- e. demand vocalization when appropriate
- f. ask other group members to plan out loud

**4. Fermenting**
- a. criticize ideas, not people
- b. differentiate when there is disagreement
- c. integrate ideas into single positions
- d. ask for clarification
- e. extend other members' answers
- f. probe by asking in-depth questions
- g. generate further answers
- h. test reality by checking group's work

---

Table 2: **Names and Definitions of the Four Phases of Jigsaw II and Jigsaw III**

**Phase One:** Home Base Teams
Students meet as heterogeneous Home Teams, consider cooperative roles, and are introduced to what they are to learn. They are aware that each team member has a part of all that everyone on the team must learn. Students are encouraged to commit themselves to mastering the content and skills, and to make sure they help everyone else on their team master these as well. They also are very aware that their team can only earn an award if all members of their team score well on the test each member will take alone after their team work is done.

**Phase Two:** Expert Groups
Students form into heterogeneous "expert groups" to cooperatively study the important content and skills and learn from one another so that each student becomes an "expert" in the area each is to study. They also take time to test one another and to plan how they will teach their particular part to their teammates on their Home Teams.

**Phase Three:** Home Teams Re-form
Students return to their original Home Teams, with each student required to teach all members his/her area of expertise and monitor their success. In addition, each team member is expected to learn all that his or her teammates teach. All students know that in a few days, each student will take an individual test alone to measure how much he or she learned.

**Phase Four (For Jigsaw III only):** Home Teams Reassemble as Cooperative Test Review Teams
Students reassemble in their original Home Base Teams and help each other review for the unit/lesson test.

The *Coordinator*—checks for understanding, agreement, and helps set long- and short-term individual goals.

The *Recorder*—keeps records of ideas, decisions, processing, and products.

The *Taskmaster*—checks for on-task behavior and participation, and praises effort.

The *Gofer*—gets materials and checks with group members when in Expert Groups.

Table 3 describes the 12 procedures for each member of each expert group that I project on the overhead and review with the class.

The "Collaborative Skills Checklist" can be used to monitor individual and group behaviors. It also can be used by students to evaluate their own behaviors within their group. It consists of a five-by-four matrix. In the first column is listed the collaborative skills to be observed: share materials; encourage all members to participate; summarize and read aloud; criticize ideas without criticizing people; and integrate different ideas into single positions. At the top of the next three columns are always, seldom, and never. Of course, the collaborative skills can be varied depending on those you wish to emphasize.

I then formulate my responsibilities, which are in addition to describing the roles and responsibilities of students. I need to

- Select a precise set of academic objectives that my students are to achieve
- Prepare a lesson plan that focuses on what students need to learn to achieve these academic objectives within the framework of the Jigsaw with expert groups strategy
- Construct the "expert sheets" which will serve as the study guides for members of each Home Team and respective Expert Group
- Determine a method for designating membership for each Home Team and Expert Group
- Determine the members for each maximally-heterogeneous Home Team[10]
- Determine the members for each Expert Group
- Determine the timeline of activities for Home and Expert Teams meetings
- Prepare and deliver an "anticipatory set" to open the lesson and prepare students for what they are to learn and how they are to go about learning it
- Assemble the members for each Home Team, distribute the expert sheets, and provide time for them to meet
- Assemble the members for each Expert Group and provide time for them to meet so that they become "experts" in their part of the academic learning

---

### Table 3: Twelve Procedures for Members of Each Expert Group

1. You will be a member of an Expert Group.

2. You will meet in Expert Groups according to the nature of the assignment.

3. You represent your Home Team in your Expert Group, and are expected to learn and master the information and skills discussed so that you can teach your "expertise" to your Home Team members.

4. You will be told how much time your Expert Group has to complete the assignment.

5. You will read the expert sheet within your Expert Group and as a group decide the steps your group will take to generate accurate and complete answers to all the questions or items on your expert sheet. Agree on the research method members of this group are to follow.

6. You will individually do what is needed to generate answers to all the questions or items on your expert sheet.

7. You will share and discuss the answer to each item on the expert sheet with all the members of your Expert Group. Agree on the most accurate and complete responses.

8. You will write out your conclusions or answers to each item on the expert sheet.

9. You need to take the time to make sure that all members of your group comprehend the conclusions or answers so that they are all experts in the area stressed by your expert sheet questions. Find ways of testing one another to ensure each is an expert in all the areas.

10. You will jointly work on planning the way you will teach what you have learned to all members of your Home Team.

11. You will, as time permits, prepare specific materials you will use to help you teach your Home Team members. Do not forget to plan the questions or test you will use in your Home Teams to make sure that all members comprehend and have "mastered" all the information and skills designated on your expert sheet.

12. You will, as time permits, practice teaching your planned lesson with others in your Expert Group.

- Assemble the members for each Home Team to re-assemble and provide time for them to meet to teach one another
- Monitor student activities within their Home Teams and Expert Groups according to a shared standard
- Remind students they are to take an individual test over all the learning objectives from all the expert sheets
- Administer and grade all individual tests and/or products
- Pass back the graded individual tests and/or products
- Provide public recognition for teams whose members meet the criteria for earning rewards based on the academic achievement of team members
- Allow structured time for students to self-reflect and evaluate their use of assigned roles and other behaviors within the respective Home Teams and Expert Groups

Using works by Johnson, Johnson and Holubec, as well as by Kagan,[11] I compiled the details of these steps and articulated them to my students. By consciously paying attention to each of these steps and making them part of the expected outcomes, I am able to stay on track when planning and using Jigsaw II. The time spent going over the expected behaviors and outcomes pays huge dividends in improved organization and operation of cooperative learning practices. Of course, the social skills need to be practiced consistently over the school year for them to reach their maximum efficiency.

## Using and Testing Jigsaw II In My Classroom

To test the Jigsaw II structure, I compared its effectiveness against my typical whole-class method. Two of my 9th grade Western Civilization classes at University High School, a college preparatory public school in Tucson, Arizona, were included in this comparative study.[12] I assigned one class of 28 students to a Jigsaw II group activity and the other class of 30 students to my typical instruction. Both classes contained similar students and scored similarly on the pretest.

The first experiment was a four weeks' study of Ancient Greece. The textbook chapters conveniently allowed me to divide the subject into the Minoans and Mycenaeans (including Homer and Hesiod), the Lyric Age (including the rise of the *polis*), the Classical Period, and the Persian and Peloponnesian Wars (which framed the Classical Period). I thought that if this structure and the students' involvement were successful in increasing academic test scores on the Ancient Greeks, I would follow this unit with a unit on Republican Rome. The two classes proceeded through the unit. Both classes used the same text; received the same lectures, primary sources and computer lab time to visit

relevant web sites; and took the same tests.

I organized the cooperative learning class into home base teams and expert groups according to the Jigsaw II team model.[13] I created four-member teams selected for balance based on past achievement. The students met initially in their home teams to delegate duties and assignment schedules; they went over the learning objectives and the materials they would have to process during the unit. They then met in their expert groups within which they delegated duties and scheduled computer lab and library times. Following this, the students met several times in either their home teams or expert groups several times each week, depending on what they were studying or discussing.

All students read assigned portions of the chapter on Ancient Greece and a short background essay. Students then met in their expert groups, read, researched, and became experts. They then discussed how best to teach the material to teammates in their respective home teams. Experts returned to their home teams and taught their teammates. They then compared their information with the learning objectives and set about to prepare one another for the unit test. Students took the unit test individually and received two scores. The first score was their test score, and was entered in the grade book alongside the individual's name. The second score was their team score based on both their improved individual performances and my evaluation of their group participation.[14] The latter portion of the team score was derived by averaging the points I gave individuals during my observation of their group activities and the points given by their teammates. The maximum team points were 15. I compiled and posted team scores divided by improvement points and team participation points. Particularly strong team performances were acknowledged. We closed the unit by discussing the specific behaviors students thought they performed very well and those they thought should be improved in future group activities. I used the lists they generated to chart improvement goals for the next unit.

In the meantime, the control class received the same assigned readings, primary sources, lectures, and computer lab and library time. Lectures and whole-class discussion took up more time in the control class than in the cooperative learning class because with less small-group interaction more had to be presented and shown to them and discussed.

## Results of the Achievement Tests

Test score differentials were not as impressive as I had hoped. Students' test scores in the Jigsaw II class were statistically higher than those in the comparison class. The average scores of 76 for the 28 Jigsaw II students exceeded the average score of 71.3 by the 30-student comparison class. The 4.7-point difference in scores between the two classes mean scores may not have been due to differences in teaching structures, however.

I considered that four weeks was a short time for students to learn the various social skills and routines, get used to an entire new structure for academic learning, and master a set of new information on Ancient Greece. For me, this short period was just too short to determine once and for all the efficacy of the Jigsaw II structure. I also felt that the problems were not with the structure itself, but with many of the complementary factors that were associated with converting this structure into a true cooperative learning activity with real live students. Given that I did have higher scores and much higher levels of student involvement, I decided to follow this unit with one similarly structured on the Roman Republic. I employed the same procedures for this unit as I did on Ancient Greece. The differences were that the Jigsaw II class now had the "corporate memory" of the structure to draw upon, and they had new skills-building goals, thanks to the debriefing at the end of the previous unit. This time, the Jigsaw II students exceeded the average scores of the comparison class by 6.6 points.

This informal study convinced me that Jigsaw II was capable of producing higher levels of achievement than conventional teaching methods, at least in my social studies classrooms. This study correlated well with my knowledge of the research on cooperative learning and student achievement generally. It also showed that specific class-building procedures, accountability and skills need to be taught prior to introducing the cooperative learning structure. The guidelines for student participation and roles need to be revisited after each Jigsaw II activity by a debriefing-reflective activity to acknowledge what has been accomplished and to chart future improvement.

My experience also convinced me to end the experiment and convert my instruction in my comparison class to Jigsaw II. I began the class-building process in that class beginning with the next unit on the Roman Empire.

## Some Reflections on the Teacher-Student Relationship During Jigsaw II

I had improved student scores. But had I achieved my larger goals? Had I instilled in my students a sense of excitement and involvement that made learning more exciting? Was my classroom more of an environment where students were pushing one another to extend themselves intellectually? What had my role as a teacher become?

By the end of the first semester, students assumed greater responsibility for what and how much they learned. As they became more familiar with the new structure, they took greater responsibility for what each member contributed to the group. My role became more of a facilitator and consultant than a stand-up lecturer. Sure, there were times that students needed the guidance and details of a lecture. But their work shifted away from constructing the facts and chronology of the time period to developing the conceptual framework in which the material was to be understood. Jigsaw II allowed me to roam the classroom, and sit in on home team and expert group discussions. I could then re-direct their work by reminding them of the larger framework discussed in the lecture, or direct their attention to sources they overlooked or skimmed.

However, I would not solve problems or answer questions that they themselves could answer. Here, I imposed the "four-before-me" rule, requiring that all group members try to solve the problem before consulting with me. Each member had a card that, when placed in the center of the table, indicated he or she had tried to address the question before the group. Only when all four cards were showing, and the group was genuinely stuck, could they hold up a question card to call me into the discussion.

## Closing Remarks

As an experienced teacher, I found that an "old dog can learn new tricks," but my conversion to using cooperative learning and various group structures effectively did not come overnight. I had to work at it. I had to learn a new vocabulary, new guidelines, new ways of thinking about students and learning, and ways to make sure I was implementing the steps and essential elements of cooperative learning correctly. Each time I tried it, I found myself doing more and more things right. The results have been very positive, so positive that I am extending my use of groups and cooperative learning to my other classes, to other units, to begin earlier in the year, and for longer periods throughout the year.[15] 🔃

NOTES

1. David W. Johnson, Roger T. Johnson, and Edythe Johnson Holubec, *Cooperation in the Classroom* (Edina, Minn.: Interaction Book Company, 1988); Robert E. Slavin, *Using Student Team Learning*, 3rd edition (Baltimore: Center for Research on Elementary and Middle Schools, Johns Hopkins University, 1986).The workshop materials contained no citations and may have been disaggregated from published sources. An excellent source of blackline masters for making copies and transparencies for most cooperative learning structures is Spencer Kagan, *Cooperative Learning: Resources for Teachers* (Riverside, Calif.: Resources for Teachers. 1989).

2. Kagan, *op. cit.*; David W. Johnson, Roger T. Johnson, and Edythe Johnson Holubec, *Cooperation in the Classroom* (Edina, Minn.: Interaction Book Company. 1988).

3. Sylvia Scribner and Michael Cole, *The Psychology of Literacy* (Cambridge, Mass.: Harvard University Press. 1981).

4. Kagan, *op. cit.*

5. Quinton G. Priest, "Cooperative Learning: Educating Students for the Future," unpublished manuscript, 1990.

6. According to Newmann and Thompson, Jigsaw II raised academic outcomes in only 17% of the cases studied. However, the chapter by Slavin and his colleagues in this volume update the effectiveness of this model, when implemented properly, on student achievement. It is important to note that many people who use Jigsaw with expert groups fail to include many of the essential elements required for optimal cooperative learning, and hence their results will be much different and lower than those who met these requirements. Unfortunately, those who do and publish their studies rarely report enough about what they did to determine which, if any, of the essential elements were actually included and were used correctly. Until such reporting is standard, the results of such studies will always be much lower that what students could achieve had all the essential elements been included and done correctly as described. See Fred M. Newmann and Judith A. Thompson, *Effects of Cooperative Learning on Achievement in Secondary Schools: A Summary of Research* (Madison, Wisc.: National Center for Effective Secondary Schools, University of Wisconsin, 1987).

7. Details of my experiences with these structures are included in chapters by myself and by myself and Robert J. Stahl in *Cooperative Learning in Social Studies: A Handbook for Teachers*: Quinton G. Priest, "Student Teams-Achievement Divisions (STAD): Applications to the Social Studies Classroom," *Cooperative Learning in Social Studies: A Handbook for Teachers*, edited by Robert J. Stahl (Menlo Park, Calif.: Addison-Wesley Publishing Company, 1994): 154-188; and Quinton G. Priest and Robert J. Stahl. "Team-Games-Tournament (TGT): Applications to the Social Studies Classroom," *op. cit.*: 189-211.

8. Robert E. Slavin, *Cooperative Learning: Theory, Research, and Practice* (Englewood Cliffs, N.J.: Prentice Hall, 1990); Ronald L. VanSickle, "Jigsaw II: Cooperative Learning with 'Expert Group' Specialization," in *Cooperative Learning in Social Studies: A Handbook for Teachers*, edited by Robert J. Stahl, *op. cit.*: 98-132.

9. John Steinbrink and Robert J. Stahl, "Jigsaw III = Jigsaw II + Cooperative Test Review: Applications to the Social Studies Classroom," in *Cooperative Learning in Social Studies: A Handbook for Teachers*, edited by Robert J. Stahl, *op. cit.*: 133-153.

10. Guidelines and criteria for setting up maximally-heterogeneous Home Teams and Expert Groups and for determining improvement points as the basis for rewarding teams for high levels of academic achievement are beyond the scope of this book. Those seeking details may want to contact Robert J. Stahl for references to these guidelines.

11. See Johnson, Johnson, and Holubec, *Cooperation in the Classroom, op. cit.*; Kagan, *Cooperative Learning: Resources for Teachers, op. cit.*

12. I conducted a similar comparison of Student Teams-Achievement Divisions and Teams-Games-Tournament structures in my 9th grade World Regional Geography classes at Green Fields Country Day School, Tucson, Arizona. Those results were published in Priest and Stahl, "Team-Games-Tournament (TGT): Applications to the Social Studies Classroom," in *Cooperative Learning in Social Studies: A Handbook for Teachers*, edited by Robert J. Stahl, *op. cit.*: 189-211.

13. Spencer Kagan, *Cooperative Learning: Resources for Teachers, op. cit.*; Ronald L. VanSickle, "Jigsaw II: Cooperative Learning with "Expert Group" Specialization." In *Cooperative Learning in Social Studies: A Handbook for Teachers*, edited by Robert J. Stahl, *op. cit.*: 98-132.

14. I determined improvement points using a chart that takes into account the difference between each student's test score and base score. Slavin calls this method, "Equal Opportunity Scoring." See Robert E. Slavin, *Using Student Team Learning*, 3rd edition (Baltimore: Center for Research on Elementary and Middle Schools, Johns Hopkins University, 1986). It is described in detail in my chapter on Student Teams-Achievement Divisions (Quinton G. Priest and Robert J. Stahl. "Team-Games-Tournament (TGT): Applications to the Social Studies Classroom," in *Cooperative Learning in Social Studies: A Handbook for Teachers*, edited by Robert J. Stahl, *op. cit.*: 189-211). This system allows both low-achieving and high-achieving students to earn points for their respective teams at a rate consistent with their academic achievement as determined by growth over their respective base scores. As the minimum number of improvement points is "0," individual accountability is maintained.

15. For teachers who have colleagues in either science or language arts, there are excellent easy-to-follow descriptions with classroom examples of Jigsaw II, Student Teams-Achievement Divisions, TGT, Jigsaw III and a number of other cooperative group models in *Cooperative Learning in Language Arts: A Handbook for Teachers* and *Cooperative Learning in Science: A Handbook for Teachers*, both edited by Robert J. Stahl (Menlo Park, Calif.: Addison-Wesley, in 1995 and 1996, respectively).

# CHAPTER 11

# I Know It Works!!! Seeing a Cooperative Learning Structure Succeed in My Secondary Classroom

**Robert M. Mattingly,**[1] Fulda American High School, A Department of Defense Dependents School, Fulda, Germany

**Several years ago** as my rifle squad moved up a steep slope we witnessed a jeep with a trailer overturn. Without hesitation we moved to right the wrong. Ten of us organized ourselves to set the vehicles upright. It went like clockwork. Within minutes, we had the vehicles back on the road, ready to roll. Imagine the feelings we had! It was truly close to moving two huge "mountains."

I could never have righted that jeep by myself. Could you?

Would the results with the jeep have been the same if one or a number of us had not contributed? Was our effort actually a cooperative effort, or was it merely some form of accidentally successful group work, which may have allowed some members of the squad to be non-contributing hangers-on?

I don't think it occurred to any of us at the time that we had just participated in one of the great truisms: none of us is as strong as all of us. None of us, alone, can ever hope to be as strong or as smart as more of us working together with and for each other. Each of us that day readily recognized that we were successful collectively for that particular job because each member of the squad had contributed his best. While each one of us had particular strength capabilities, only our "best effort" *working together* enabled us to share the success none of us could have experienced had we exerted the same effort *alone*.

Is this also true in the classroom? To what extent might the analogy about our efforts with the jeep hold for secondary school classrooms? Is it actually possible that our students' "best efforts" *working together* could enable each of them to achieve the success few of them could attain were they to exert the same effort *alone*? More importantly, are there systematic ways that students, in their working together, can facilitate the learning and achievement of every other member of the group as well as themselves as individuals?

Research in many K-12 classrooms has revealed that appropriate cooperative group effort consistently produces very positive social, personal, and academic results.[2]

## In the Beginning: Before Cooperative Learning

As a new teacher, one of the first teaching strategies I tried to incorporate into my instructional repertoire was the use of cooperative group work. It soon became apparent to me that very often my groups were not working in a very cooperative fashion. Typically, unsuccessful group projects ended up with one or two members doing most or all of the work while the rest did little or nothing. Even groups that did successfully complete an assignment or report tended to follow this same pattern of some contributing much and others very little. Groups often splintered into self-segregated grouplets.

The majority of group projects that were turned in consistently lacked the power, depth, and polish which were possible had everyone in the group contributed his or her personal best effort. When some groups did prepare an excellent collective project I often found that it was the result of the work of one or two of the academically-oriented members while other members simply hung on, catching a free ride.

At times I was so discouraged that I considered abandoning group strategies completely. Still, the ideas of students working together, pooling their talents, and helping each other learn were powerfully attractive notions, in fact, too attractive to abandon.

I wanted more than just high quality group projects and groups that operated without me having to spend my time keeping them on task. I wanted more than groups where every member contributed his or her best personal effort just to get an assignment finished or report prepared. I also wanted more than individual group members being concerned solely with getting the task done. One of the things that I most wanted was that students would use these group tasks as a means by which each would actually learn more of the material better than each would likely learn it studying separately. I really wanted to find a way to make groups in my classroom operate so that students' attention, effort, and time were spent maximizing the learning of each member rather than operating merely to enable students to work together just to complete a project. In a real sense, I wanted more than cooperation, I wanted learning—lots of it by all my students!!! I wanted each of my students to actually learn a large part of the material that her or his group was responsible for studying.

Being committed to the goals of social studies education, I was aware that part of my responsibility was to enable students to leave my classroom at the end of the year with far greater abilities in the areas of social participation, interpersonal relations, and working with others. I was frustrated that my group activities were not producing the positive attitudes and behaviors in these areas I had hoped. I did not see noticeable advancements in these areas after the weeks and months of group activities in my classroom. Once the task was assigned and the groups met, the task continued to be subdivided among group members and each went about finishing his or her subtask virtually independently of the others in the same group. This occurred even when students were sitting next to each other as a "group."

Eventually, the members would put their separate parts together, smooth the transitions, and assemble the final report much like a small number of auto workers might do their individual jobs that eventually produce an assembled car. Instead of increasing the positive interactions and concern within each group, many students worked alone, often avoiding conversations with peers. This is a description of a relatively successful non-cooperative group. Many groups were not even this successful. Furthermore, most students didn't seem to care whether they or their group members learned the material. Clearly, my students were not moving toward the very goals that I valued and that I used group activities to help them attain.

As I reflected upon what occurred in my classroom, it was obvious that students, when put into groups, were seeing their tasks as getting done and getting a report or presentation cranked out. For the most part, what mattered was doing what was needed to get the task done. Since typically the members of the group all got the same grade for their joint project, nothing prevented them from splitting up the work, however that might occur. While they were responsible to each other in terms of getting their part of the project done, they were not individually accountable for what they were contributing or for what they learned or failed to learn. Under such conditions it was disappointing but not surprising that my students usually earned about the same scores on tests whether they had worked or not worked in groups on the same material prior to the test.

It seems strange to me now how I could have missed a key to my problem. One of the problems was that I had not included a means of holding each team member personally accountable for his or her contribution to the group's success. There had been no planned interdependence among group members for each other's success. The group task structures I had been using had no provision for rewarding the groups for meeting clearly stated, preset standards of academic achievement, and for publicly recognizing and rewarding individual improvement. Also missing from my early group activities were clearly defined task specializations where each member had a clearly defined, unique task within the group.

## To Change or Not To Change?

It became apparent to me that I had four choices: (1) I could discontinue using groups altogether; (2) I could use groups as I had used them primarily to break up the class routine dominated by my lectures and demonstrations; (3) I could continue using them merely as a device to get tasks done or to get longer reports assembled; or (4) I could find and use an effective model to organize and guide group work.

I decided to find an organizational structure for using groups which would allow me to manage learning and social skill development without me being a pervasive part of the structure. I hoped for a model that, once the groups got started, would run itself. I wanted a teaching strategy with a group task structure which would help all my students retain more information and increase academic achievement. The strategy should also help them refine a systematic approach for solving problems with others. If in the process I could help them to like school better and gain higher self-esteem, so much the better. While all of this was happening I wanted to be the teacher who wasn't there. I wanted to place the responsibility for learning where it belongs, with the students. At the same time, I accepted that it was my responsibility as a teacher to foster the best possible conditions wherein each student could be a highly successful learner. I wanted to motivate students to excel! These intentions, of course, were easier wished for than achieved, but I wanted it all!

This quest was not pursued free of apprehensions about what I might have to do were such a strategy found. Part and parcel with my search were a number of questions that needed to be answered.

How does one bring about such seemingly radical changes in a traditional teacher in a traditional teacher-dominated classroom without inviting bedlam? What was to be my role in a "new" environment where groups would actually work to achieve these goals? How different would these new roles be from what I have done in the past? How were the students to behave toward me and their peers? What rules would govern these new group structures and the new relationship between my students and myself? What would I have to do to ensure that everyone followed the rules? These are only a sample of the questions I asked — and sought to answer.

It became obvious to me that in addition to finding a new method of helping students study social studies content and materials, I was going to have to help them acquire and rehearse social skills as well. If I was ever to achieve anything close to the cooperation that was needed, I would have to clearly define, make students aware of, introduce, monitor, assess, and let every student practice every one of these social skills. Without these things, especially the clear definitions and practice, my students would not likely master these abilities to use in their groups or outside the classroom.

## The Search

While attending the University of Georgia I had the great good fortune to study with a professor who was also very interested in the academic achievement possibilities offered by cooperative learning and its related goal structures. He pointed me immediately in the direction of the Educational Resources Information Center (ERIC). ERIC had a lot to say. The list of researchers involved in cooperative learning was long, but some names appeared more often than others. Robert Slavin, Spencer Kagan, David Johnson, and Roger Johnson appeared at the time to be the most actively involved in this area. I began my investigation with these practitioners.

There were, to be sure, differences among the approaches to cooperative group work. Slavin emphasized equalizing opportunity and individualizing accountability. Kagan stressed the need for the use of flexible cooperative learning techniques, which would allow the teacher any number of ways to operationalize cooperative goal structures. Johnson and Johnson stressed the need for students to acquire and refine group processing and interpersonal skills. All agreed that it was important for students to learn and master appropriate social skills. Students needed to learn and become skilled at basic abilities to interact and communicate without which no cooperative strategy could be optimized.

After studying and very carefully considering these three approaches, I chose to concentrate on the three models, Stu-

dent Teams-Achievement Divisions (STAD), Teams-Games-Tournament (TGT), and Jigsaw II, proposed by Slavin.[3] They seemed to have the greatest potential for a secondary social studies classroom. Sharan and Hertz-Lazarowitz's version of Thelen's Group Investigation model also had the potential to be a powerful group strategy for social studies teachers.[4]

According to a study done by Newmann and Thompson, two of the three Slavin models, STAD and TGT, have produced consistently positive academic results.[5] Jigsaw II, however, was reported to have enjoyed only marginal success. Newmann and Thompson reported Jigsaw II positively affected academic achievement in only 17% of the cases studied. I was intrigued.

## My Search Ended: Jigsaw II Selected

Jigsaw II seemed perfect for the secondary social studies classroom. Why was it not more effective? It had all the critical elements of STAD and TGT, plus, when done appropriately, it offered the additional advantages of intense home team and specialized "expert group" interaction, in-depth analyses, and extended on-task discussions.

It seemed to me that its relatively poor performance could only be the result on one of two factors. Either the Jigsaw II model itself was flawed or the way in which it had been operationalized in the case studies was inconsistent with the model. The model seemed to be straightforward. It involved the following elements:

    a.    Whole-class teaching,
    b.    Student readings,
    c.    Expert group discussions,
    d.    Home team reporting,
    e.    Individual testing,
    f.    Team recognition.

It met all of the criteria universally agreed to be necessary to be an effective cooperative task structure. The results of studies Newmann and Thompson reported, I surmised, must have been due to the poor operationalization by those who attempted to use the model.

Ron VanSickle, of the University of Georgia, and I reviewed the Newmann and Thompson studies as well as a number of other published and unpublished studies. In all of the studies except one, the Jigsaw treatment was similar to Aronson's original Jigsaw.[6] The group strategy used in these classrooms did not meet Slavin's required group reward and individual accountability criteria.

The more I looked at Jigsaw II the more I liked it. I decided to test Jigsaw II in my classroom. The prospect was really exciting!

### Determining and Stating Clear Parameters for Classroom Operation

Before introducing this new organizational strategy to my classroom, I needed to organize my thoughts. I had to articulate some very basic operational guidelines. These were guidelines which I believed every student should understand and follow if we were to have any chance of achieving our primary goal of improving academic achievement. This list was very straightforward. I decided that each student needed to understand:

a. The academic and social objectives for this group strategy and for the academic content they are to study;
b. How they are to accomplish the expected academic and social objectives;
c. The expected group participation behaviors, what she or he is to do or say and how she or he is to behave toward others;
d. The nature of positive interdependence and its place within a cooperative learning environment;
e. That he or she will be held accountable for mastering materials or skills;
f. The criteria for success.

It also seemed a good idea to develop a list of rules that all members were to follow. This list would provide the do's and don't's to guide the activities within the group and among its members. I began collecting ideas from students in all my classes. We finally settled on the following working rules:

a. Follow directions.
b. Stay on task.
c. Help the group stay on task.
d. Give all necessary information.
e. Check each others' understanding and mastery of your information.
f. Seek information.
g. Paraphrase information given by others
h. State and seek opinions where appropriate.

We also agreed on a list of specific social skills students were expected to use at all times within the different groups they were placed. These included the following:

a. Practice active listening.
b. When you disagree, disagree with what has been said, not with who is saying it.

c. Encourage others to contribute.
d. Acknowledge and praise contributions.
e. Show appreciation for the work of others.
f. Express feelings.

Obviously, my students could not be expected to do all these things unless I acted in ways consistent with this model. In order to fulfill my responsibilities, I had to:

a. Select and state a precise set of academic objectives that made it quite clear what students were to learn in each unit;
b. Locate or develop a post-test that is aligned with the academic outcome objectives set for each unit;
c. Provide a description of the Jigsaw II model and of the roles and responsibilities of both students and teacher during its operation;
d. Determine group membership for each home team;
e. Administer and grade pre-tests;
f. Form the groups and establish time lines for activities within the unit;
g. Monitor student progress within the different groups;
h. Administer and grade post-tests;
i. Compare pre-test and post-test scores and determine improvement;
j. Provide public recognition for group and individual students who meet the criteria.

The details for these steps were provided in the literature describing this model and how to use it. I found that by *consciously paying attention to each of these steps*, I was able to stay on track during the time Jigsaw II was being planned and used. This conscious attention also prevented me from doing things in the classroom that were inconsistent with the model.

### Using and Testing Jigsaw II in My Classroom

I decided to test my understanding of the Jigsaw II model. To see how well it worked, I decided to compare its instructional effectiveness against a more traditional whole-class lecture method. Two of my ninth grade World Regions Geography classes at Fulda American High School, a Department of Defense Dependents Schools high school in Fulda, Germany would be used in this comparison study. One class was randomly assigned to Jigsaw II (23 students) with the other class to be given conventional, whole class instruction (22 students). Both classes were composed of students from a wide range of academic ability levels, including students enrolled in the school's learning disabilities program. Both classes were composed of very similar students.

The experiment lasted nine weeks and encompassed a complete nine-chapter study of Asia.[7] A typical chapter included the narrative description about its topic (e. g., "The Land and People of Southeast Asia"), as well as a social studies feature (e. g., "reading a weather chart"). From the beginning, the two classes proceeded through the three units (South Asia, East Asia, and Southeast Asia) at a rate of one chapter per week. Both classes used the same text, were provided the same enabling activities and materials (e. g., lectures, compass work, or map reading drill), and took the same tests that accompanied the textbook

In the one class, the cooperative groups were organized according to the Jigsaw II student team learning model.[8] Students were assigned to four-member teams balanced in terms of high, average, and low past achievement. The students met several times each week in cooperative groups. They either met in their "home" teams or their "expert" groups depending on what they were studying or discussing.

A typical textbook chapter followed the steps in the order that follows. (1) Students were given their general assignment and expert topics. They then read the assigned material consistent with the academic objectives. (2) Students met in their "expert" groups, became "experts," and prepared to teach the content to their respective "home" team members. (3) Experts returned to their "home" teams and taught their content to their teammates. (4) Students took the standardized chapter test individually and received two scores. The first score represented each student's individual test score for grading purposes, and the second was his or her contribution to the team score based on improved individual performance. (5) Team scores based on total improvement points were computed and posted. Strong team performances were then publicly recognized.

Improvement points were determined by using a system known as "Equal Opportunity Scoring" (EOS).[9] EOS awards improvement points based on improvement differences between test scores and base scores. I used a 10 point maximum. Each student's initial base score was his or her last unit test score. The ten point limit worked well in this study, allowing sufficient latitude for steady improvement by low and average achievers. High achievers were also able to score maximum points because a perfect score automatically earned 10 points. The minimum number of improvement points that could be earned was zero. Base scores were adjusted weekly.

Meanwhile, the other class received instruction in my more traditional format: assigned readings, enabling activities, whole-class discussion, and tests over the same materials and enabling activities. The Jigsaw II class spent less time in lecture and whole-class discussion than the comparison class because of the time required to work in cooperative, small groups.

## Results of Final Achievement Tests

When the post-test scores were analyzed the achievement scores of students in the Jigsaw II class were significantly higher than the comparison class at a statistically significant level.[10] Nearly 80 percent of the 23 Jigsaw II students *exceeded the average score* of the 22 comparison class students. I considered the 5.2% difference in scores between the two class mean scores to be practically significant; it was a big enough difference to make a difference to me!

For me this study and its consistency with the larger cooperative learning research base illustrate that Jigsaw II, when used as directed, can produce higher levels of academic achievement than conventional whole-class, non-cooperative instructional procedures in secondary social studies classes.

## My Roles Within My Jigsaw II Classroom: Reflections and a Look Ahead

My role in the cooperative classroom was pleasantly different from my usual roles. As the weeks passed and the class became more familiar with the new format and, as they became accustomed to their new relationships and responsibilities, the teams assumed greater overall responsibility for what and how much was learned by each of their individual members. It was beginning to look like a machine that could run itself! This allowed me a degree of teaching freedom I had not experienced before, especially with ninth graders. My role became more like a consultant or facilitator than a lecturer. As the students assumed more responsibility for learning I had more time to organize the material they were studying.

Jigsaw II allowed me long periods of uninterrupted time to work on specific problems with individual teams with little or no distraction. We had adopted the "four-before-me" rule which required intra-team consultation on questions or problems before calling on me. The differences in my roles between the two classes were really remarkable.

In the comparison class, work progressed as usual. I did hear some grumbling about why they couldn't do what first period was doing. However, we carried on in the traditional mode: whole-class instruction, everyone for himself or herself. The environment of this classroom aptly fit the individual "sink or swim" metaphor proposed by Johnson and Johnson.[11] It became

Table 1: **Worksheet for a Cooperative Learning Unit that May Be Used to Guide Planning in Alignment with the Jigsaw II Strategy**

Grade Level: _____          Course (Subject): _____

**Specific Behavioral Objectives relative to:**
1.   Academic content

2.   Academic/processing skill

3.   Social interaction skills

**Organization of Class:**
1.   Number of students in each "home team" group:

2.   Basis of assignment to groups:

3.   Description of special room arrangement(s):

**Materials/Resources To Be Used/Provided:**

**Format For First Class Period of the Unit:**

**Anticipatory set:**
1.   Teacher input:

2.   Cooperative group work structure:

   a.   Group interdependence to be determined by:

   b.   Individual accountability to be determined by:

3.   Guidelines/rules for participation in groups: *(These may be printed on handouts and distributed to each student)*

4.   Timeline of events from day to day throughout the unit:

**Test Questions Aligned With Objectives to Be Included on Unit Exam**
(May attach copy of final unit exam rather than list all items here.)

**Standard(s) for High Achievement by Individuals and Groups (following grading of final unit test)**

quite clear to me that I was working harder in this classroom, but definitely not smarter. While students in this class might have been working as hard as students in the cooperative learning class, they were neither working smarter nor getting smarter. In the Jigsaw II class I was able to see that the labor necessary for individual and group learning and success was equitably and reasonably divided. I was only one of the contributors to their success. I came to realize that for much of the time I was not necessarily the most important direct contributor to what each student learned.

## Students Within and After This Cooperative Venture

The students using Jigsaw II enjoyed improved academic achievement. However, that is not the whole story. While engaging in their new classroom roles, other equally important improvements occurred. Improvements in the quantity and, I believe, the quality of students' interactions with one another were evident. One reason for these improvements appeared to be that every student had the chance to belong to three distinct groups: (a) his or her preferred group of friends; (b) a Jigsaw II home team; and (c) a changing expert group.

I rejected my students' tendency to self-segregate by assigning them to heterogeneous teams that I created. These teacher-made team assignments brought together many students who probably would have passed the entire year without speaking to each other. After seeing the advantages of such assignments, I continued this practice and encouraged other teachers who use this strategy to do the same.

The "home team" and "expert group" features of Jigsaw II allowed each student both to give and receive direct and specific academic help. The Equal Opportunity Scoring procedure appeared to increase the perception that every student's contribution was valuable. Consequently, the necessary exchange of help and information among all students took place within a pleasant and supportive climate. Students of different academic backgrounds had, perhaps for the first time, reason for serious school-related dialogue.

Students enrolled in my school's learning disabilities program seemed to benefit most from the new environment, both academically and socially. They were encouraged to elaborate on their contributions and tended to receive explanations rather than curt, terminal answers from their teammates. Once the class "caught on" to the Jigsaw operations, these students were certainly the most enjoyable to watch and assist.

## Jigsaw II in Other Social Studies Classes

The format described earlier can be used, with modification, in any social studies class. Table 1 provides a "Worksheet For a Cooperative Unit," based on Lourie,[12] that can be used for planning and organizing a unit which follows the Jigsaw II strategy.

In addition to this Table and the guidelines described herein, additional detailed information on Jigsaw II and the other cooperative learning strategies that work in secondary classrooms can be found by referring to references listed in the notes to this and other chapters in this Bulletin.

I have tried to share my experiences with one cooperative group strategy. This initial success has excited me to continue to use and improve upon Jigsaw II. In addition I expect to explore other strategies in the weeks and months ahead. Surely Jigsaw II is not the only group approach that will work effectively in social studies classrooms.

This chapter is also more than a report of my efforts and successes with groups in my own classroom. I perceive myself as being student oriented. I clearly saw that I was not enabling students to attain the goals we value as social studies educators. It was because so many of my students were not achieving the success that I thought they were capable of attaining that I pursued my quest for a more effective way to use groups in my classroom. Today I am satisfied that *I am increasingly becoming the effective teacher I want to be.*

While cooperative learning is not the single answer to all my concerns, at the present time it offers me a far more powerful tool than what I had been using. It is a tool more secondary social studies teachers can use starting today. 🔳

### NOTES

1. This chapter was written while Robert was a full time teacher at this school. He continued to use Jigsaw with Expert Groups and other cooperative group structures until he retired. He is now settled in his new home in Georgia.

2. See, for example, Fred M. Newmann and Judith A. Thompson. Effects of *Cooperative Learning on Achievement in Secondary Schools: A Summary of Research* (Madison, Wisc.: National Center for Effective Secondary Schools, University of Wisconsin, 1987) and Robert E. Slavin, *Cooperative Learning: Theory, Research, and Practice* (Baltimore: The Johns Hopkins University, 1990). Also see the chapters by Johnson and Johnson, VanSickle and Slavin in this Bulletin for greater details about particular cooperative learning approaches, guidelines, and research findings.

3. See Robert E. Slavin, *Using Student Team Learning*, 3rd edition (Baltimore: The Johns Hopkins University, 1986). References to these are cited in this chapter and in the chapters by Quinton Priest and Robert Slavin in this Bulletin.

4. See Shlomo Sharan and Rachel Hertz-Lazarowitz, "A Group Investigation Method of Cooperative Learning in the Classroom," in *Cooperation in Education*, edited by Shlomo Sharan *et al.* (Provo, Utah: Brigham Young

University Press, 1980). See also Yael Sharan and Shlomo Sharan, "Group Investigation Expands Cooperative Learning," *Educational Leadership* 47 (December-January 1990): 17-21.

5. Fred M. Newmann and Judith A. Thompson, *Effects of Cooperative Learning on Achievement in Secondary Schools: A Summary of Research, op. cit.*

6. Elliott Aronson, Nancy Blaney, Cookie Stephan, Jev Sikes, and Matthew Snapp, *The Jigsaw Classroom* (Beverly Hills, Calif.: Sage Publications. 1978).

7. J. L. Swanson, *World Geography: A Physical and Cultural Approach* (River Forest, Illin.: Laidlaw, 1987).

8. Slavin, *Using Student Team Learning, op. cit.*

9. *Ibid.*

10. For details of this entire experimental study, especially a discussion of the statistical data generated, see Robert M. Mattingly and Ronald L. VanSickle,"Cooperative Learning and Achievement in Social Studies: Jigsaw II," *Social Education*, 55 (October 1991): 392-395. The intent of this chapter is to portray a teacher's use of cooperative learning strategy in his own classroom. It is not to report extensively on a study and its findings.

11. See David W. Johnson and Roger T. Johnson, *Cooperation and Competition: Theory and Research* (Edina, Minn: Interaction, Book Company, 1989).

12. Nancy E. Lourie, "How Do We Get There From Here? Implementing Cooperative Learning in the Classroom," *Social Studies Review* (1989).

# CHAPTER 12

# Implementing Complex Instruction in Heterogeneous Social Studies Classrooms
## A Case Study and Exemplars

**Elizabeth G. Cohen** and **Rachel A. Lotan**, Stanford University, Palo Alto, California and
**Jennifer Whitcomb**, University of Denver, Denver, Colorado

**As the curtain rises**, an institutional gray desk, a round table, carts loaded down with textbooks, and a sagging sofa take shape. Although it is September, the heat of August still lingers. Jean rises to open a window. The social studies teachers at Valleyview Middle School in West Los Palos, California, have gathered in their department office to share insights from summer workshops and travels and to plan for the upcoming year. They sit casually, some at the table, and some on the sofa.

Valleyview is a middle school with an untracked social studies department. In recent years, the school has had a dramatic influx of Spanish-speaking and Asian students. In the face of these changes, most teachers agreed that they could no longer continue with business as usual. Too many kids were shut out, got lost or were dispirited.

It was clear to the social studies faculty that they needed a new and different way to teach social studies in academically heterogeneous classrooms. A nearby campus of the California State University system was offering a two-week institute in Complex Instruction (CI) followed by a year of classroom support. CI focuses on the development of students' higher-order thinking. This approach is the product of over 20 years of research and development at Stanford University's School of Education, where educators worked to create equitable classrooms which have a wide academic range. At the institute, four teachers from Valleyview studied the principles of CI and practiced it with middle school students. During the following school year, these teachers tried CI in their classrooms. Staff developers visited their classes and provided feedback on implementation.

## Creating Equitable Classrooms

These four teachers, convinced that the approach would work, were eager to get all members of their department to move in the direction of more equitable classrooms, using Complex Instruction. Imagine that we are in the school when these teachers return from a summer institute for professional development. Imagine further that we are present at the first department meeting and these teachers are excited by what they have to share. As the action begins, the four Complex Instruction advocates are engaging in a dialogue with their skeptical but interested teacher colleagues—trying to persuade them of the value and practicality of the approach. We eavesdrop on their conversation.

## Managing the Classroom

**SIT (Skeptical but Interested Teacher):** I tried cooperative learning, and once was enough for me. What a disaster! The kids would not stay in their groups. Many were not doing their work. I ran from group to group putting out fires. Little if any academic learning was taking place.

**ECI (Experienced Complex Instruction):** Yes, this can definitely happen when the teacher shifts to small groups that are supposed to work on their own. Cooperative learning requires new behaviors for both the students and the teacher. The teacher, as you found out, can't be everywhere at once. With groupwork, a fundamental shift in the teacher's role is unavoidable: You need to delegate authority to students so they will take responsibility for their own behaviors and learning while in the groups.

**SIT**: How do you do that?

**ECI**: In Complex Instruction, an activity card lays out a different task for each group (e.g., see Figures 1a and 1b). Students as a group are responsible for completing their task. In addition, each student writes an individual report after completing the task.

**SIT**: Sounds pretty straightforward but that isn't going to control behavior by itself.

**Figure 1a: Activity Card**

## Unit: CRUSADES
## HOW DO HISTORIANS KNOW ABOUT THE CRUSADES?

**Activity 1: Crusader Castle, Crac des Chevaliers, Syria, 12th C**

Activity Card

Historians often turn to art, architecture, and craftwork of the period they are studying for clues about how people lived and what they wanted to remember.

As a team, look carefully at the photographs of Crac des Chevaliers and discuss the questions below.

1. Why would the Crusaders build a castle?

2. What does the architecture of this castle (the floor plan and interior/exterior structures) tell you about how warfare was conducted in the medieval times?

3. If you lived inside this castle, how would you defend it against enemy attacks?

4. If you were an enemy invader, how would you plan your attack of this castle?

5. What were the roles of men and women inside the castle?

6. What were the roles of children?

**Design and build a castle or a fortress to protect your group from adverse forces.**

**Present your castle to the class.**

© *Program for Complex Instruction/Stanford University School of Education*

---

**Figure 1b: Activity Card**

## Unit: CRUSADES
## HOW DO HISTORIANS KNOW ABOUT THE CRUSADES?

**Activity 6: Gesta and Raymond's Eye-Witness Accounts of the Siege, Attack, and Capture of Jerusalem**

Activity Card

An important resource for historians are eye-witness accounts of historical events. Gesta and Raymond both participated in the first crusade and wrote separate accounts of their experiences.

As a team, read the selections from Gesta and Raymond's accounts of the siege, attack, and capture of Jerusalem. Discuss the questions below.

1. When did the siege take place? How did geographic conditions (e.g., climate and terrain) play a role in the outcome of the siege?

2. Given that Jerusalem is surrounded by a wall, what might the "siege machines" have looked like? Where did they find materials for them?

3. If you were a Saracen, what would you have done to defend your city?

4. The Crusaders were outnumbered 5 to 1. How do you account for their ultimate victory against such odds?

**Design a mural which depicts the main events of the siege, assault, and capture of Jerusalem. You might consult the reproduction of a mural in this package.**

**Share your mural with the class.**

© *Program for Complex Instruction/Stanford University School of Education*

---

**ECI:** You're right. That only prevents you from having to run from group to group telling people what to do. We use two other important methods of classroom management in CI to control behavior. Last year, we prepared students for groupwork before we started with regular curricular materials. Students learned how to help each other, how to explain to each other, and how to talk to each other about their ideas. They understood that no one is done until everybody is done. We used skill-building activities in small groups to develop the behaviors that students

need for working well in groups. The students came to feel that this was the way they ought to behave and they criticized each other if someone refused to help or explain.

Another important way a teacher can delegate authority to groups is through the use of roles. Every student plays a different role and the roles rotate. For example, one student is a facilitator whose job it is to see that all group members understand what to do and get the help they need. When someone wanders away from a group, for example, it is the facilitator's job to find out what is wrong and to get the student to rejoin the group. Another role might be the recorder who keeps notes of the group's discussion and checks to see whether individual reports have been completed. In other words, you get the students to mind each other's business and to do many of the supervising jobs that teachers usually do.

**SIT:** Oh, I do that. I use roles in groupwork. I usually set up activities so that one student is the artist, another is the writer, and a third looks up all the questions in the resource books.

**ECI:** Those are the roles, too, but they're not the same kind of roles we use in Complex Instruction. The roles you use are a way to divide the labor, while the roles we use are designed to help the group interact and work together. We call CI's roles procedural roles. Dividing up the work may seem efficient, but it doesn't encourage students to interact and talk to each other. According to the research on Complex Instruction, it's the process of talking and working together that produces the learning gains.[1]

After you get the hang of these procedural roles, you can see how to make the activity cards, the cooperative norms, and the roles work for you. You don't have to solve all the groups' problems yourself. Say, for example, ten minutes after launching groupwork, you find a group floundering. In first approaching the group, you might ask them if they have read the activity card and discussed what they are supposed to do. If they haven't, you could suggest that they do so and that you will be back in a few minutes to hear the results of their discussion. Or, if some students have questions, you might ask them to find out whether anyone in the group has the answer. Only when no one has the answer can the facilitator call you over to ask the questions. These norms and roles really keep the "Teacher! Teacher!" calls at a minimum.

## Curricular Materials for Group Work

**SIT:** My groups work pretty well when I have them reviewing for a test or working on mapping activities. But I have trouble when I'm trying to focus on real thinking, on getting the hard-to-understand concepts. I don't have good activities for groupwork; the ones at the end of the chapters don't work.

**ECI:** The challenge is getting the right curriculum for that kind of groupwork. You have to begin by redesigning the curriculum. When we focus on developing higher-order thinking and on teaching central concepts, we use groupwork and the CI activities designed specifically for groupwork. Don't panic! We don't use groupwork all the time. We will still use the textbook and the good resources we've collected in this department over the years. To tell you the truth, what really sold me on participat-

ing in the program were the units, developed at Stanford, they showed us. I was willing to sign up just to get those materials.

**SIT:** What makes those materials so special?

**ECI:** The unit activities are organized thematically around a main idea or central concept. For example, in one unit, students explore a basic question in our discipline: "How do historians know?" Students learn how historians examine texts, eyewitness accounts, artifacts, music, and art of a period to make sense of historical events. In the unit, "Taking Your Proper Station: Feudal Life in Tokugawa Japan," students learn about social stratification and social barriers. They examine these central concepts in a variety of contexts: the physical layout of a castle town, clothing and external symbols of rank, legal codes, and central social activities, such as pilgrimages to religious sites. Integrated with this social studies unit is "Voices in Japanese Poetry," a literature unit. In it, students' understanding of social stratification is reinforced through reading poetry written by ladies of the courts, women who toil in the fields, merchants, and the social elite. A final example: the unit on the Maya examines the importance of time in the Maya culture and the various ways the Mayans organized their society to worship time. While working through each unit, students rotate through a number of activities; this gives them a chance to examine the central concepts in various contexts. Even if they do not understand the main idea in their first encounter, the light will go on eventually.

**SIT:** Some of my students couldn't care less about the Crusades, feudal Japan or the Maya. If something isn't directly relevant or applicable to them, they just don't want to spend the energy.

**ECI:** It seems hard to believe, but even feudalism can be made interesting to adolescents. Using the CI model, students have a chance to be active, to discuss, to figure things out by themselves—so they are more motivated. What's more, in most activities there is a built-in project that allows them to generalize about the concept and make it more relevant to them, here and now. For instance, after looking at and listening to a medieval song about a knight's dilemma between his duty to his king and his love for a beautiful woman, students write a song about a current event. I dreaded this activity, but the students loved it—music always wins them over.

**SIT:** When I did groupwork, I found that a few students usually did the work and the others just copied the answers. My students didn't really work together. They did what they usually do, except that their tables were pushed together and they could socialize more easily.

**ECI:** That's what happens when the tasks are too simple and the answers too easy to get. Now if tasks are complex and open-ended and if students depend on one another to solve problems, they will work together more and stay on task. At first, these new responsibilities and new ways of learning took my students by surprise. As soon as they realized that I meant business, they enjoyed being taken seriously, thinking for themselves, and learning how to communicate their thoughts, opinions, and feelings. Because no single answer was good enough, students found good solutions by following different paths. Open-ended, uncertain tasks make the students interact more, which, as I explained, leads to learning.

When I tried to adapt activities that I could use with CI, I found that this open-endedness was the hardest thing for me to create. We teachers tend to tell the students exactly what we want a group task to produce, to make the instructions too detailed, and to assign problems that have one right answer. We are terrified that our students will make mistakes or won't "get it."

## Multiple Abilities

**SIT:** These activities sound terrific for my high-achieving kids. But other students just don't know what to do—they really have nothing to contribute. Some of them even have trouble reading the instructions and never get anything done.

**ECI:** You've touched upon one of the main challenges of groupwork. We really need to change the way we look at the tasks and what some kids can and can't contribute. After using CI activities, I was able to see that my students had strengths, and that they could be successful in ways I never noticed before. I now know that if students are not the best readers or the best writers, they *can* make important intellectual contributions when a task is a rich multiple ability task.

CI activities are called multiple ability activities because many intellectual abilities are necessary for their successful completion. Traditionally, students don't have much of a chance to show how competent they really are. With multiple ability activities, students can demonstrate intelligence in many different ways. And I don't mean different learning styles; I really mean showing us what kinds of intellectual skills and abilities they have. Nowadays, psychologists like Gardner[2] and Sternberg[3] talk about multiple intelligences; they don't believe you can reduce intelligence to a single IQ score. You really need to think of academic competence as more than one or two domains such as linguistic and logical intelligence.

When students work in CI activities, they can use many intellectual abilities in addition to the regular academic abilities of reading, writing, and quick computation. Let me get back to the unit I mentioned earlier, "How Do Historians Know about the Crusades?" During this unit, students rotate among three types of group tasks. In the first type, students examine visual representations of historical artifacts: photos and a floor plan of the ruins of a castle built by the Crusaders in Syria. Students use visual-spatial abilities to analyze pictures, to hypothesize about the architectural strengths and weaknesses of the castle, and to speculate why the Crusaders chose that particular location. Next, students design and build a three-dimensional model of a castle or a fortress that will protect their group from enemy invaders. Designing this model requires careful planning, mechanical ingenuity, and translating a two-dimensional sketch into a three-dimensional model—all intellectual abilities.

In the second type of task, students use musical abilities as they listen to medieval ballads, identify the musical instruments, and describe the mood and the message of the songs. Some of the intellectual abilities students use in these tasks are hearing or creating melodies, hearing and creating rhythmic patterns, understanding musical expressions, and understanding how a song's melody and lyrics play off one another.

The third type of task requires understanding textual sources such as excerpts from Pope Urban II's speech calling the masses to join the Crusades and eyewitness accounts of the siege of Jerusalem. After thorough analysis of the text, students translate these verbal messages into different media. They create a mural, design an ad campaign for Pope Urban II, or dramatize the siege of Jerusalem from an Arab point of view. These activities require many intellectual abilities: understanding sophisticated texts, detecting sources of bias in a text, being empathic, relating a single textual passage to the larger scheme of events, and translating a text's message into nonverbal forms. If the students don't understand the main point of the unit with one task, they can get it with another task. When they have a chance to do all these activities, they can develop a deep and flexible understanding of different ways that historians learn, the big idea behind the unit.

I remember one particularly powerful example of the importance of multiple ability tasks for heterogeneous classrooms. Doug, a resource student mainstreamed from the special day class, became the star of his group because he was the one who best understood the schematic diagram of the castle. Doug happens to be a "Dungeon and Dragons" fan. His spatial perception ability in drawing and his visual reasoning had never been tapped in class before. When his classmates recognized Doug's contribution, they asked him to help them interpret the visual materials, to build their castle, and to present their product. It was an unforgettable day for Doug, for me, and for his classmates.

When preparing to teach a unit, I analyze the activities carefully and make up a list of the intellectual abilities necessary to complete tasks. In class, I name these abilities and show the students how each one is relevant. Gradually, they learn to recognize and to name the intellectual abilities for themselves. Most important is that they are able to recognize these abilities in themselves and in their classmates. For example, during the second rotation of the "African Dilemma Tales" unit, students told me which specific intellectual abilities they used to complete the activities.

## Treatment of Status Problems

**SIT:** This all very interesting, but I still have a problem when I use cooperative learning. I can see how you would fix the task so that everyone could make a contribution, but that doesn't mean that all students *will*. Some students are always left out and others take over the group. Let me tell you about Dusty, a student I had last year. An A-student, Dusty was used to being successful. No matter what group I put her in, she took over. It had to be her way or no way. She was so frustrated, she had her mother come in and talk to me. Meanwhile, another student, Ernesto, never got to say a word. I tried every way to encourage him, but he just seemed shy.

**ECI:** You're describing a problem we all face; it's called a status problem. The problem with Dusty is that she expects to be the most competent person in every group, no matter what the task; everyone else expects her to be the most competent at the task as well. That combination leads her to talk the most and to have the most influence in just about every group in the classroom. Ernesto has the opposite problem. He expects to be incompetent in the group on every new task, and the other students expect so little of him that they don't pay any attention, even when he tries to join in.

These different expectations for competence come from different status characteristics that work in a classroom. For instance, Dusty may have high academic status. We rarely stop to think about this, but our students create a ranking in the classroom based on how good they think everyone is in social studies. Those they think are the best students in social studies will tend to dominate cooperative groups in the classroom; those they see as poor students, perhaps because they don't speak English well, are shut out of small group discussions. Then there are those who have very few friends or maybe none at all. They have low peer status and the kids treat them as if they were incompetent, whereas they listen to those who are popular, even when they have poor ideas.

**SIT:** What about differences between African-American, Anglo and Latino students?

**ECI:** Race and ethnicity are status characteristics, too. When you have a mixed-race or mixed-ethnic group, you may see the African-American student or Latino student withdraw or be ignored. But the most important thing in a classroom is really how smart a student is perceived to be in schoolwork and how popular they are with the other students. These characteristics have more weight than race and ethnicity in the school situation. In many integrated classrooms, some of these minority students are very popular. Since popular students can dominate groups just as much as good students, you can't tell ahead of time if minority students will be low-status in your classroom. You have to observe the groups and see who is acting like a low-status member of the group. Mentioning race reminds me that we shouldn't forget about gender. By the time girls get to middle school, they are sometimes treated as low-status members of the group, unless they are strong academically or very popular.

**SIT:** This is interesting. I have seen this problem in my groups too, but I've never been able to figure out what to do. How do you handle it?

**ECI:** There are a couple of strategies for treating this problem that come from sociological theory about status. Research has shown that they work in the classroom.[4] Using the multiple ability treatment, a teacher's job is to convince students that many different intellectual abilities will be necessary for the new group task. Of course, it won't work unless you have real multiple ability tasks like those we talked about earlier. I take time before we get into groups to discuss how imagining, hypothesizing, dramatizing, reasoning, and visualizing will be necessary for the tasks they are going to do. Then I always take time to say: "No one will be good at all these abilities. Everyone will be good on at least one." This is the most important part of the multiple ability treatment because it makes all students recognize that they will be good on some of the abilities and not so good on others. They realize that the group's success depends on listening to others and on taking advantage of what everybody has to offer.

**SIT:** Don't you feel uncomfortable saying something like that?

**ECI:** I did at first, but I came to see that it was true. When you have good multiple ability tasks, kids surprise you. My resource student, Doug, astounded us all, and my A-students came to realize that they are not necessarily the best at everything—that they really can learn from others.

**SIT**: You mentioned two strategies. What is the other?

**ECI**: The other treatment we use is called assigning competence to low-status students. When the students are in their group working on tasks, I go around carefully watching the groups and taking notes. I pay special attention to those students who are usually left out of their groups. I watch for those moments when they show how competent they are on one of the multiple abilities. For example, last year when we were doing the unit on feudal Japan, I overheard that Claudine had a good idea about how to build a castle town, but her group wasn't paying attention to her. I stepped in and said, "I see that Claudine has a good plan for laying out the castle town. She can visualize exactly how it ought to go together. I think she's a good resource for this group because she has that ability to visualize things spatially." That is a powerful treatment because I am assigning competence to her on an ability that the group needs to complete the task. I have done it *publicly* so that other students know that I expect her to be competent. I have made it *specific* so that she will know exactly what she has done well. I have also made it *relevant* to the work of the group. These three things make this treatment work. Research has shown that teachers who use both the multiple ability and assigning competence treatments have fewer problems with some students dominating the groups and others not participating.[5]

**SIT**: Won't the students be embarrassed if you single them out that way? I know that some of my students are afraid to look like "schoolchildren."

**ECI**: Your power in this case comes from the fact that students are likely to believe the evaluations teachers make of them. You are being completely honest—you never do this unless the student has exhibited an important intellectual ability. You don't gush about it either. You just state it in a low-key, factual way. Sometimes I take notes on intellectual contributions low-status students make, and the next day, when I'm orienting the class for cooperative learning, I share my observations from the day before. I may talk about how roles were played, how effectively some groups worked together, and then I slip in some assignments of competence to low-status students. This approach seems to work well.

## Breadth versus Depth

**SIT**: If I do everything you say, I'll never get to the end of the curriculum.

**ECI**: You bring up an old dilemma in teaching social studies—breadth versus depth. Doing Complex Instruction takes more time than reading textbooks and doing seatwork, but the higher-order thinking that takes place justifies the time and effort. At the center of every CI unit is a conceptual theme. Take the Reformation Unit—it's organized around the question: "How do you challenge the authority of an institution?" It's only by taking the time to rotate through the various group activities that students learn how a combination of factors reshape people's ideas and lead them to seek reform. One activity focuses on how art and political cartoons form and reform public opinion; one on the role individuals, like Martin Luther, play in bringing about change; and one on the role the printing press or the media play in spreading ideas. This is a powerful concept, one that I can use in later units, one that 8th grade teachers can tap into when they teach about the American Revolution or about the Civil Rights Movement. What my students learn goes well beyond the facts and dates of the Reformation.

After watching my students in CI last year, I became convinced that all kinds of learning were taking place. They came to see major historical events as complex situations with multiple causes and consequences. To complete activities, they also had to practice making subtle judgments about the influence of these causes and the extent of the consequences—that's higher-order thinking in my book. Most important for us as social studies teachers, they came to see that big ideas or concepts in history apply to other situations. When we were studying the Reformation unit, they connected challenges to the authority of the church to their own behavior, challenging the authority of institutions like the school. Best of all, some actually said, "History can be fun." I wish I had my video on these kids dramatizing Luther's challenge of the Pope—it was fabulous. I'd rather spend a few extra days on the Reformation to give my students that rich experience.

What impressed me last year was that my students remembered the Crusades in June—and we studied them in January! You know that practically never happens. With benefits like these, I'm willing to give the time it takes to do these activities.

## Evaluation

**SIT**: I like what you're saying, and I'd like to hang my hat on this groupwork model. What holds me back is evaluation. What do you do about grades and testing when you have groups? What do you do if students don't put out equal effort?

**ECI**: I've also struggled with that question. Complex Instruction helped me rethink issues of evaluation in groupwork. Evaluation has two faces: motivation and accountability. When I had students in groups before, I graded individuals because I was afraid that if I didn't, no one would work. I used my grade book as a form of extrinsic motivation. I learned that this practice is really unfair to the low-status student—i.e., students who look as if they aren't participating may not be involved because the others in the group don't feel that they have something to contribute and, as a result, do not let them in, will not listen to them, or do not share materials with them. Students who seem to be shy or off-task may actually be shut out by the others. It isn't fair for me to give a student a low grade for participation when that participation may be beyond the student's control.

**SIT**: So how do you handle the nuts and bolts of evaluating groupwork?

**ECI**: First, I stopped seeing grades as a source of motivation. Instead, I know that because the activities are intrinsically interesting, the students will stay on task. Second, I still have to hold the students accountable. I hold the group accountable by the presentations they make to the class. Because each activity involves a group presentation, and because most students do not want to look bad in front of their peers, they will work quite hard to have a polished product.

It is important to provide groups with evaluation criteria. These criteria tell the group exactly what makes an exemplary product and presentation, and the criteria do this without telling the students how to do things or just what is the desired answer. There are also evaluation criteria specific to each individual report. In the workshop, we heard about the latest research at Stanford that shows that when you use these evaluation criteria, students turn out much better products and presentations. And when you ask the students to write essays about some of their activities in the unit, those who have worked with criteria have much more correct academic content in their essays as well as a better grasp of the big idea.[6]

The best part of using these evaluation criteria is that when the groups make their presentations, you can use the criteria to figure out how to give specific feedback to each group. You can tell them what they did well and where the next group who gets this task really needs to concentrate to meet one of the criteria. Without the criteria, it is often very hard to know what to say when a group gets up and makes a presentation that you don't expect. The Stanford researchers found out that when teachers have these criteria, their feedback to students is much richer and more specific.[7]

You don't have to be afraid to give a chapter test at the end of the unit based on the textbook plus what they have learned in the group activities. Because they have had to write individual reports and because they have talked about the academic content to prepare their product, they are ready to take a test. Students who participate in the groupwork will have a deep understanding of the content as well as a grasp of the facts, and therefore perform quite well on these tests. We learned that social studies students who had complex instruction units scored higher on multiple-choice items that required higher-order thinking than those who didn't have these curricula and group experiences.[8]

## What's Next?

**SIT**: This sounds terrific, but I'm feeling overwhelmed. I have so much to learn, and I don't think I can make up those multiple ability tasks without a lot of help. Suppose I want to learn more about this stuff. What can I do?

**ECI**: You can go several ways. It all depends on how much change you are willing to make in your curriculum and the way you run your classroom. Before we even attempted CI, we went for a two-week institute at the university in the summer; and then, during the year, CI staff developers observed us in our classrooms and sat down with us for three feedback sessions. Each session was based on three classroom visits. At the institute, we learned about the theory and research behind CI and we had practical experience with students. If you were willing to commit that much time, and if we could find the funds for it, I could help you with observations and feedback because I will go for special training this year and will be a certified CI trainer.

**SIT**: I'd love to do that, but I'm expecting a baby in June, so I couldn't commit to something that ambitious. Is there anything else I can do?

**ECI**: A good way to get started is to read Elizabeth Cohen's book, *Designing Groupwork Strategies for Heterogeneous Classrooms*.[9] If you and another teacher team up, you can each design a multiple ability task, try it out, observe each other, and decide how to improve it for the next year. That way, you will create at least two tasks you can share. Slowly, you can build a file of groupwork activities. In her book, Cohen tells how to manage the classroom and how to do status treatments.

## Conclusion

In the conversation we overheard, the teacher focuses on four essential components of small-group instruction: classroom organization, the nature of the curriculum, assessment (called "evaluation criteria"), and, most importantly, treatment of status problems in heterogeneous small groups.

## Organization of the Classroom for Groupwork

Groupwork is an effective strategy when the goal of instruction is the development of higher-order thinking and conceptual understanding. In groupwork, teachers give up their traditional role. Direct supervision of students' activities in the group becomes impractical, so the teacher delegates to students the authority to manage their groups and to complete their tasks. When teachers are advised to delegate authority to their students, they often fear losing control of the classroom. Complex Instruction, however, uses a system of cooperative norms and student roles to prevent chaos, and the teacher can hold both groups and individuals accountable for their learning. Groups are held accountable by the presentations they make to the class; individuals are held accountable by writing individual reports. Delegation of authority by the teacher and the installation of the management system enhance the rate of interaction in the groups. Interaction on rich, challenging tasks furthers learning.[10]

## Nature of the Curriculum

To get the most out of groupwork, teachers must design or adapt learning tasks specifically for that purpose. Teachers can and do design multiple ability tasks in which they have all groups doing the same task. In the case of Complex Instruction, activities are organized into conceptually coherent, thematic units. By completing the various activities of a unit, students encounter the central concept in various contexts, thus gaining a better and deeper understanding. Good groupwork tasks are open-ended and complex because more than one legitimate outcome and more than one way to approach and to complete the task are available to learners. Such healthy uncertainty enhances student interdependence and increases interaction. And interaction on tasks like these furthers learning.

Most importantly, these activities require many intellectual abilities for their successful completion. By incorporating musical, dramatic, kinesthetic, spatial, visual and linguistic abilities, we expand opportunities for students both to show competence and to gain access to understanding the tasks. Multidimensional, multi-ability tasks broaden the range of opportunities for more students to be seen as smart.

## Assessment

In a classroom where the teachers delegate authority to groups of students to complete their task on their own, it is essential to hold groups and individuals accountable for their performance. This is best done if the students have a clear understanding of the criteria the teacher is using to evaluate their group and individual products. The evaluation criteria provide this clarity and give the students a chance to evaluate their own work using the same criteria as the teacher. The evaluation criteria also provide the

teacher with a strong basis for providing feedback to groups and individuals. The more the students evaluate their group product in the course of their discussions, the better is their group performance in the wrap-up and the better is the quality of the individual essays that they write at the end of the unit.[11] Thus, there is no contradiction between well-designed groupwork and individual assessments such as an end-of-unit test or essay. If that test or essay uses the same criteria that students and teachers have worked with during the unit, the teacher will find that almost all the students show strong learning gains.

## Treatment of Status Problems

Groupwork and the multiple ability curriculum that supports it set the stage for creating equitable classrooms with heterogeneous student populations. To create truly equitable classrooms, teachers must learn how to recognize and treat status problems. Unless they treat these status problems, high-status students will continue to dominate the interaction and to learn more than low-status students, who will be shut out from the group and will learn less. The gap will widen—the rich will get richer and the poor will get poorer.[12]

In treating status problems, teachers convince students that many abilities are necessary and that although everyone is good on at least one ability, no one is good at all of them. Furthermore, teachers assign competence to low-status students by making their successes public and relevant to their groupmates. Status treatments narrow the gap between the rates of interaction of high- and low-status students by raising the rates of participation of low-status students. More balanced interaction furthers much higher learning outcomes.

Complex Instruction permits teaching at a high level in linguistically and academically heterogeneous classrooms. Although the instructional strategies described take time and effort to implement, the potential for bringing about significant intellectual growth in all students makes the effort worthwhile. Truly equitable classrooms provide equal access to the interaction in cooperative groups as well as the chance for low-achieving students to perform at a much higher level. ▨

## NOTES

1.  Elizabeth G. Cohen, *Designing Groupwork: Strategies for Heterogeneous Classrooms*, 2nd edition (New York: Teachers College Press, 1994); Elizabeth G. Cohen, Rachel A. Lotan and Chaub Leechor, "Can Classrooms Learn?" *Sociology of Education* 62 (1989): 75-94.
2.  See Howard Gardner, *Frames of Mind* (New York: Basic Books, 1983) and *Intelligence Reframed: Multiple Intelligences for the 21st Century* (New York: Basic Books, 1999).

3. Robert J. Sternberg, *Beyond IQ: A Triarchic Theory of Human Intelligence* (Cambridge, England: Cambridge University Press, 1985).

4. Elizabeth G. Cohen and Rachel A. Lotan, "Producing Equal-Status Interaction in the Heterogeneous Classroom," *American Educational Research Journal* 32 (1995): 99-120.

5. *Ibid.*

6. Percy L. Abram, Beth A. Scarloss, Elizabeth G. Cohen, Nicole I. Holthuis and Rachel A. Lotan, "The Use of Evaluation Criteria to Improve Student Talk in Cooperative Groups," paper presented at the annual meeting of the American Educational Research Association, New Orleans, April 2000.

7. Susan E. Schultz, Beth A. Scarloss, Rachel A. Lotan, Percy L. Abram, Elizabeth G. Cohen and Nicole I. Holthuis, "Let's Give 'Em Somethin' to Talk About: Teacher's Talk to Students in Open-Ended Group Tasks," paper presented at the annual meeting of the American Educational Research Association, New Orleans, April 2000.

8. Elizabeth G. Cohen, Julie A. Bianchini, Ruth Cossey, Nicole I. Holthuis, Christopher Morphew and Jennifer Whitcomb, "What Did Students Learn? 1982-1994," in Elizabeth G. Cohen and Rachel A. Lotan, eds., *Working for Equity in Heterogeneous Classrooms: Sociological Theory in Practice* (New York: Teachers College Press, 1997).

9. Cohen, *Designing Groupwork, op. cit.*

10. Rachel A. Lotan, "Principles of a Principled Curriculum," in Cohen and Lotan (eds.), *Working for Equity in Heterogeneous Classrooms, op. cit.*

11. Abram et al., "The Use of Evaluation Criteria to Improve Student Talk in Cooperative Groups," *op. cit.*

12. Cohen, Lotan and Leechor, "Can Classrooms Learn?," *op. cit.*; Elizabeth G. Cohen, "Understanding Status Problems: Causes and Consequences," in Elizabeth G. Cohen and Rachel A. Lotan, eds., *Working for Equity in Heterogeneous Classrooms, op. cit.*: 137-165.

# INDEX